I0816023

Let Me Be Frank

Let Me Be Frank

The Extraordinary Life and Music of Frank Sinatra, Jr.

Bruce H. Klauber and Andrea Kauffman

University Press of Mississippi / Jackson

The University Press of Mississippi is the scholarly publishing agency of the Mississippi Institutions of Higher Learning: Alcorn State University, Delta State University, Jackson State University, Mississippi State University, Mississippi University for Women, Mississippi Valley State University, University of Mississippi, and University of Southern Mississippi.

www.upress.state.ms.us

The University Press of Mississippi is a member of the Association of University Presses.

Manufactured in the United States of America

∞

Publisher: University Press of Mississippi, Jackson, USA
Authorised GPSR Safety Representative: Easy Access System Europe - Mustamäe tee 50, 10621 Tallinn, Estonia, gpsr.requests@easproject.com

Library of Congress Control Number: 2025942763

Hardback ISBN 978-1-4968-5865-8
Epub single ISBN 978-1-4968-5877-1
Epub institutional ISBN 978-1-4968-5878-8
PDF single ISBN 978-1-4968-5879-5
PDF institutional ISBN 978-1-4968-5880-1

British Library Cataloging-in-Publication Data available

To Joan, who has made all my dreams possible, and to Sid Mark, my lifelong friend and mentor, who taught me about all things Frank Sr. and Frank Jr.

—Bruce H. Klauber

To my family: my dad, Herman Kauffman, who shared his passion for music with me; my mom, Dorothy Kauffman, who showed me the joy of dance; and my sister, Marta Kauffman, a writer who inspired me to try.

—Andrea Kauffman

Contents

Preface

Let Me Be Frank is a collaboration between two entertainment-industry professionals, Bruce Klauber and Andrea Kauffman. Klauber is a long-time music journalist, author, and musician. Kauffman is a respected and influential entertainment-industry executive, concert producer, and agent and was the personal manager of Frank Sinatra, Jr., for thirty-one years. A substantial part of this book's narrative and timeline is based on more than forty hours of Kauffman's recollections that address virtually every aspect of Frank's life. Given this substantial role, she is quoted extensively throughout the narrative. The interviews with more than thirty of Frank's friends, musicians, and other industry professionals were conducted by Klauber at Kauffman's direction. Several magazine and newspaper pieces and reviews are presented in their entirety. It is the authors' hope that all these sources, representing five decades of the life and music of Frank Sinatra , Jr., combine to present a complete picture of his extraordinary life and music.

Introduction

Bruce H. Klauber

On Thursday, July 13, 1967, I was taken by my brother to the now-defunct Convention Hall in Philadelphia to see Frank Sinatra. Having just turned fifteen years of age, I knew that Frank Sinatra was in the movies, and I was slightly aware of him musically, as my brother played Sinatra records nightly. But Frank Sinatra really meant little or nothing to me at that time. As a young drum student, my interest in the concert focused on drummer Buddy Rich and his band, part of the Sinatra show that night, along with Sérgio Mendes and Brasil '66 and the comic Pat Henry. Just before we left for the concert, my brother made me change clothes and put on a coat and tie.

Convention Hall, an arena that was then home to the Philadelphia Seventy-Sixers basketball team, seated about twelve thousand. It was packed to capacity. Sérgio Mendes was great, and Buddy Rich and the band killed, even though I preferred Gene Krupa back then. Pat Henry was hilarious. I loved comics. Still do. After an intermission, and after everyone took their seats, a man came out on stage, unannounced, wearing a black tuxedo and bow tie.

I figured that man must be Sinatra. What I do know is that when he took center stage, to a tremendous ovation, bolts of electricity went through me. The feeling, which I've never experienced again, is difficult to explain. I had grown up in a show-business-loving family. I'd seen Bobby Darin; I'd seen Sammy Davis, Jr. But this? This was bigger than big. It was gigantic. It was beyond celebrity. To an impressionable fifteen-year-old, it seemed to me that this man could part the Red Sea, if he hadn't already.

Then he started to sing. He opened with "The Summer Wind," which he had recently recorded. By the time he got to "This Is All I Ask," I was convinced that he was singing to me and to me only. I cried during that song and couldn't explain why. "Old Man River" came at the halfway point. He must have held that low note for a minute. By then, I was a basket case. The closer was a rollicking, bluesy "That's Life." I hardly noticed that Buddy Rich played drums for the entire show, something I later learned didn't happen often, as Frank Sinatra had his own drummer.

I was hooked. I was on the team. No, I didn't become a Frank Sinatra fanatic, but I was interested in the music and interested in finding out what happened to me and why. In all honesty, as a fledgling jazz performer, with the accent on the word *performer*, I thought I could figure out how to get some of that indefinable electricity for myself.

Not long after, I learned that Frank Sinatra's son, Frank Sinatra, Jr., was also a singer and that he would be appearing at Atlantic City's Steel Pier sometime in August. All I knew about Junior was something about a kidnapping that happened around the time President Kennedy was assassinated. But I had to hear this guy. Not only was he Frank Sinatra's son, and not only was he a singer, but I could get into the Steel Pier to hear him for two bucks! Can you imagine? A cheaper Frank Sinatra. Such was the way my mind worked.

I called a childhood friend of mine who was also a Sinatra fan, told him of my experience at Convention Hall, and of my "discovery" of a Frank Sinatra, Jr., He agreed that we had to go. We were not yet of driving age, but we were fearless. One of us, I forget who, took the family car, and we were off to Virginia Avenue and the Boardwalk, location of the Steel Pier, the "showplace of the nation," as it was called then.

In those days, two dollars got you into the Steel Pier for a whole day. The admission price included listening to whatever big band was playing in the Marine Ballroom, the famed Diving Horse show, Tony Grant's *Stars of Tomorrow* talent show, three films that were played continuously throughout the day and evening, the General Motors exhibit, and seats for the headliner appearing in the upstairs theater.

The theater was packed for Frank, Jr.'s show, and I remember distinctly that he was backed by an octet, led by trombonist Larry O'Brien. Frank got a lot of applause. He looked like a young version of his father, and I think he may have started with the lightly swinging song he wrote, "Spice." He had a good voice, an amiable presence, assured phrasing, and a confident sense of swing. My friend and I were waiting for the payoff—the Sinatra tunes.

The payoff was a long time coming, as his set list, as I recall, consisted of a bunch of songs I had never heard of and, in truth, weren't very good. Finally, we heard something familiar, which was the instrumental lead-in to "Don'cha Go 'Way Mad," Neal Hefti's orchestration that was recorded in 1962 for the *Sinatra and Swingin' Brass* album. It was an obscure entry in the Sinatra discography, but at least it was a Sinatra tune. We figured this was going to be it. The Sinatra set. Finally. It wasn't. There was no payoff. The show was over.

My friend and I were confused and bewildered. What the hell had we just seen? What the hell was this guy doing? He was Frank Sinatra's son, for God's sake.

My friend, as was his wont, let it go. I didn't. I was fascinated by the experience, by the man, by his music, and by the reasoning behind his performance. Why was he singing those songs? Didn't he know what people wanted to hear?

As the years went on, I kept up with developments in his career, even though news was hard to come by. He played Vegas, mainly, and when he came east, he played some certifiable joints, including Dick Lee's in Bellmawr, New Jersey, then best known for booking lounge acts like Cook E. Jarr and the Crumbs.

I caught up with him again after gambling was legalized in Atlantic City, and Frank was performing afternoon shows for bussed-in tourists at the Atlantis Hotel and Casino, formerly the Playboy Hotel and Casino. His repertoire was still peculiar. At one point, he donned a cape and a mask and sang "The Music of the Night" from *Phantom of the Opera*. Coincidently, Andrea Kauffman later revealed that she hemmed the cape for that outfit. He also sang something called "A Horse with No Name" and "I'm Afraid the Masquerade Is Over," which remained in his book for years. It was the Steel Pier all over again. What the hell was he singing?

Later on, I learned that Frank Sinatra, Jr., was being managed by Andrea Kauffman, already something of a legend in Atlantic City as she was almost solely responsible for bringing first-rate jazz to the casino lounges, among her many other early accomplishments. In that I was very much a part of the Atlantic City scene back then, as a drummer, a columnist, and a member of the press, I got to know Andrea and to some extent, got to know Frank, Jr.

What I discovered, on the surface, anyway, was that Frank Sinatra, Jr., was all about music, quality music. He could—and did—talk endlessly about the orchestrations of Nelson Riddle and Billy May, among others: what they brought to the table as arrangers, why the charts were timeless, what the reed section was playing, what the 'bone section was playing, and what he learned from all of it.

On a personal basis, I just couldn't figure the guy out, other than the fact that he seemed to know a lot about a lot of things and that he seemed to be a loner. One time, a bunch of PR people from the Atlantis casino, as well as yours truly, gathered to have a bite in the casino coffee shop after one of Frank's shows. We were expecting him to join us. When he came in, he walked right by all of us and took a seat, alone, at the back of the restaurant. I went up to him and asked, "What's wrong, man? Why don't you come over and sit with us?"

"Can't you see I'm trying to promote something back here?" he answered. I later understood that to mean that he had his sights set on one of the waitresses.

I continued to follow his career, saw him in person whenever I could, and observed his musical growth. The songs he continued to perform from his old book had a depth and wisdom to them that they did not have before, though he still insisted on singing "The Curly Shuffle." But not long after his father died in 1998, he was much more open to celebrating the music of Frank Sinatra, and with *Sinatra Sings Sinatra*, he was doing more and more of the songs the audiences wanted, and the venues and the money were better and better. In 2015, the year before he died, he was at the Sands Hotel and Casino in Atlantic City. His father's pianist, Bill Miller, was with him. It was an all-Sinatra show, and it was pandemonium in the showroom. People were going crazy over Frank, Jr., who was as cool and as collected on stage as he always had been. By that point, however, there was something new going on with his music: Wisdom. It was as if he finally knew.

His passing on March 16, 2016, was a shock. He was only seventy-two, and those who knew him and cared about him were happy in knowing he had finally hit his stride as a revered and very well-paid concert attraction. He had become the family standard bearer, and it seemed as though he had finally become comfortable with that role.

In the years following his death, Andrea Kauffman and I spoke often about Frank's personal and professional growth, the contributions he made to American popular song that were never acknowledged, how he ultimately triumphed over working in the shadow of one of the most famous performers in show business history, and how, during her thirty-one years as his personal manager, she single-handedly made a place for him in this industry. Indeed, when Andrea Kauffman first happened upon Frank Sinatra, Jr., he was making $1,000 per week, working afternoon shows in Atlantic City in front of an audience of bussed-in senior citizens. By the time of his passing, he was making upwards of $50,000 per night.

Though he may have been regarded as a minor figure in the business through the years, by 2016, he was no longer a footnote in the entertainment industry. He was a force to be reckoned with.

The writing of *Let Me Be Frank: The Extraordinary Life and Music of Frank Sinatra, Jr.* has been an endlessly fascinating journey. The Frank Sinatra, Jr., I discovered along the way was brilliant, eccentric, talented, complex, troubled, sometimes pedantic, and sometimes funny as hell, generous and loyal to a fault, stubborn, dedicated, inflexible, and when he wanted to be, a real charmer. He loved music and everything about it. Music was in his bones, and music was his life. His passing left a major void in the lives of those who knew him. The vast majority of those who were kind enough to speak with us on the record for this book ended up in tears by the end of the interview.

I know of no other figure in entertainment history that could inspire something like that, except one: Frank Sinatra, Sr.

Hopefully, the answer to why this was so, if there is one, lies somewhere within these pages.

Introduction

Andrea Kauffman

People have asked me where I'd be today in terms of my career if I hadn't met Frank Sinatra, Jr. I know that I would have been booking jazz and Top 40 acts in the Atlantic City casinos. I know I would have made a good living. But I also know that my experience with music would never have been as gratifying and fulfilling. I got to work with brilliant musicians and had the chance to hear music that someone who adores jazz and the American songbook only dreams about. The people I met, the places I traveled, and the buyers, producers, and businesspeople I worked with far surpassed anything I would accomplish had I stayed local. Most importantly, I never would have met one of my best friends and gained a brother.

After Mr. Sinatra asked me to work with Frank, I flew to Las Vegas to see his shows at the Four Queens. It was just prior to my thirty-fifth birthday. His then manager, Vince Carbone, and his wife, Smitty, took me to dinner at Hugo's in the Four Queens. I was disappointed that Frank wasn't with us. About halfway through dinner, Vinnie, as I called him from that night on, handed me a big box. In it was a birthday gift from Frank. It was a Four Queens jacket with a Frank Sinatra, Jr., logo on it. I was thrilled, and I would have the opportunity to thank him after the show when I would officially meet him.

Through dinner, I got to know more about Vinnie, who was a veteran of the entertainment industry, having managed the very successful

Bobby Vinton. Vinnie was also VP at Gerard "Jerry" Purcell's legendary management and production agency in New York for many years before moving to California and working with Frank.

Mr. Sinatra was trying to get Frank booked in Atlantic City, so Vinnie was looking to get Frank into Atlantic City. You obviously try your best not to disappoint Mr. Sinatra, but even though Vinnie loved "the kid," he had trepidations. I certainly understood Vinnie's concerns when Frank walked out onto the stage with no introduction and a clipboard and stopwatch in his hands. He was wearing a knitted "tux" jacket that can only be described as "uniquely uncool" (there's a story about this garment within these pages). He conducted his seventeen-piece big band on such a small stage that his movement was limited to about a four-foot-square area. He opened with what he called a "four ganger," meaning that songs are performed one after another: "It's All Right with Me," which was his idea of an up-tempo opener; Rupert Holmes's "Lunch Hour"; "Name It and It's Yours" or "Until the Real Thing Comes Along"; and "Softly as in a Morning Sunrise." They weren't songs anyone would want to hear during a show in Las Vegas. About halfway through the show, as I was thinking that I had wasted my time, he sang America's "Horse with No Name." Was this hip? Kinky? Brilliant? A big-band version of this song? What was he doing? Why was he doing this song? The songs that followed "Horse" were maybe three Sinatra "B" sides. Why wasn't he playing to the audience that wants him to be Sinatra? I think, "I want him to be Sinatra. He looks like his father; he sounds like his father. He's sitting on a gold mine and won't dig."

But I believed he had great potential. The band was one of the best I ever heard. Frank's pitch was spot on, and his tone and timber were mellow and rich. My thought was that I could work with this and that maybe he just needed someone to believe in him and get him into the right venues. The residency at the Four Queens may have seemed like a feather in his cap, but it was downtown, not on the strip. So I said, "Let's work together."

He had no interest in being his father or anything like his father. He just wanted to be Frank. It took many months of working together and many conversations with him to even begin to understand his thinking. My first booking for him was in the casino lounge within Trump Castle in Atlantic City. He played with his quintet. Frank and

Vinnie flew into Philadelphia and limoed to Atlantic City. I met Frank at the front door and escorted him to the front desk. The hotel manager came from the back with a big flower arrangement and handed it to me. I assumed the flowers were for Frank. When I looked at him, he said, "Read the card." They were from Frank to me. At that point, he handed me his credit card. I'm juggling the flowers and the credit card while checking them into the hotel. He asked me to join him in his suite so we could talk. I was walking through the casino, lobby, on the elevator and down the hallway to his suite with these flowers. He never once asked if he could carry them for me or hold them while I opened the door to his room. When we finally got into the living room, I dropped them onto a table with a loud bang. There was no expression on his face when he looked at me and said, "Don't you like flowers?" (By the way, I don't like fresh-cut flowers at all except for gardenias and cala lilies.)

"Frank, I've been schlepping these damn flowers around for thirty minutes, through a hotel lobby, a casino, in elevators and down halls. They weigh fifteen pounds. You're holding the other key card to your room."

He stared at me, still with no expression I could read, and said, "Next time I'll buy you something smaller." He turned and walked into the bedroom while laughing loud. That's the moment we became friends.

I wasn't at all certain about what kind of financial jeopardy I was putting my family in by leaving my agency and my partner and solely working with Frank Sinatra, Jr. The uncertainty was daunting. The uphill climb to get buyers, promoters, and venue operators to believe in him, when I wasn't sure what it was I believed in, was a crap shoot. I knew that Vinnie was getting a monthly salary, so that made him complacent. And I heard from Frankie that his family was less than supportive. So I felt compelled.

I was with him in 1986 when the Kitty Kelley book on Sinatra, *His Way: The Unauthorized Biography of Frank Sinatra*, came out in paperback. I sat with him on his bed at the Trump Castle, night after night, while he highlighted paragraphs of untruths and complained about how unfair it was to be judged by someone who didn't know you. He spoke about the lies and the stories that were twisted beyond recognition, if they ever happened at all. There were times I felt he was defending his father, and there were times I thought he was saying, "You see how I'm the victim?"

That's when he really opened up about his family, and we started a deep friendship that lasted until his death. He talked about how "big" his father was and how insignificant he was in comparison. It was during that time that I started to get a glimmer of understanding about him. He was saying that no matter what he sang or how well he sang or how fabulous his band was, he couldn't equal his father.

I was hell bent on proving him wrong. I had to move cautiously and very, very slowly. I did just that. I had to let him be himself while I was infusing him with the ingredients that would make him more marketable. He knew what I was doing. The results became obvious. He was getting more dates and more money for those dates. The interest in Frank Sinatra, Jr., was growing. So was our friendship.

I was charmed and drawn in by this potential of the Sinatra magic. At first, when I asked him to do something differently or suggested it be changed, he never stopped flaunting the possibility that there would be something better down the line. We eventually learned how to placate each other. I knew if I suggested "A," he'd do "B." So I would strongly suggest "B," and he would do "A." The funny thing was that he knew that I knew what he was doing, and I knew that he knew what I was doing. It was a contest of wills. He wanted to be Frank, and I needed him to be more marketable.

By this time, we spoke every day. Sometimes it was about the show and dates but most times it was about his personal problems and concerns. We listened to each other, and more importantly, we heard each other. I realized he was the brother I never had, and I was the sister he wished he had. I loved my best friend fiercely. I came to understand that working with him, advising him, and listening to his problems were best dealt with face-to-face. I traveled back and forth to Los Angeles to be there for him. I was the constant reminder that he was worthy of so much more than he asked for. And I felt unbelievably lucky and special that he was always there for me.

As the years went on, the personal aspect of our relationship became as important as our business relationship. Along the way, I learned that there were dark sides to him that I never had experienced before. He was always fighting some inner demons that caused him to be angry and bitter, which made him incredibly caustic and hurtful. Frank and I traveled together with the guys in the core band and crew members, and the guys and I recognized the "moods." The musicians and crew who started with Frank before me knew how to steer clear. The newer ones learned quickly how to walk on eggshells or how to be invisible.

I had a very different relationship with him. I wasn't intimidated, and I've never been a pushover. In my mind, from a business standpoint, the biggest difference between the crew, musicians, and me was that they got paid by Frank. They had to suffer their employer's moods. I was paid by way of the commissions for work that I created; so in essence, I generated my pay and didn't have to be subjected to his arrogance or his moods. I was able to treat him in a manner unlike anyone else he ever knew and handled him differently.

I wasn't trying to change him. I was just trying to change the show. But in my attempts to do that, he felt I was trying to change him and his very essence. We had many a deep dive as to why he wouldn't sing a particular song or why he would not say "my father" on stage and instead referred to his dad as "Sinatra." The more I got to know his family, the better I understood his complete resistance. He had to prove he was his own man and not to be loved for who he almost was. He was a superb singer. His knowledge of music, arranging, and conducting exceeded his father's. Why did he think he had to compete with the man perceived as the best in the world ever? The answer, I hope, is within these pages.

Could I influence him to make subtle changes? Yes. But up until the death of his father, I could only get him to stop doing so many ballads and add more up-tempo tunes and generally pace the show differently by introducing mood lighting, eliminating some of the real "sleeper tunes," and including at least a couple of Sinatra Sr. songs that the audience and the buyers would enjoy.

At some point during our association, I hoped for a magic bullet that would hit Frankie and infuse confidence in his bloodstream and remove the self-doubt. I use the word *magic* because that is what I thought it would take. He was a sad soul who had been damaged by lovers, his family, and the public repeatedly.

In 1988, we found that the poison was also the cure. Sinatra asked Frank Jr. to conduct for him. At that time, I was just beginning to build interest in his act, and he was starting to get decent dates. How much would his father's schedule interfere with our schedule? Then I started thinking about it from a different perspective. This is what Frankie needed. Working with the very shadow he'd been concealed by might be the cure for much of his emotional damage. This could be the beginning of the process diminishing his self-doubt. He would take his place on stage with his father as an equal part of the show. The audience would see the confidence his father had in him as a musician. As his friend, I knew he needed this. As his manager, I felt it could certainly help his image.

The change in Frank was subtle, although obvious to me. During the time he conducted for his father, some of the hard-core Sinatra musicians, the ones who traveled with Frank Sr., gave Frank a hard time. He plowed right through that and earned respect from many who didn't realize what an accomplished musician he was. Because he was a singer, he knew the music differently than Bill Miller or Vincent Falcone, Sinatra's other conductors. Frank Sr. was very comfortable with his son's conducting. A perfect example of his father's comfort was the story Frank tells in this book, about conducting the incredibly complex "Soliloquy" without rehearsal.

We came into each other's lives in the last thirty-five years of his. It wasn't all highs or lows, but my God, the highs were amazing. Watching him walk on stage after having throat cancer and after being fed by a feeding tube for months was the highest it gets.

When I think about the lowest point in our career together, I think of a contract he signed with a promoter in Las Vegas. He promised and led me to promise that he'd perform a Sinatra-song-filled show. Frank understood exactly what the promoter was looking for. He even brought Hank Cattaneo, Sinatra's tour/production manager with us. Hank, who was kind enough to share his thoughts about Frank Jr. for this book, was a calming presence for Frank. He was the voice of experience and reason. Hank handled one of the most temperamental and difficult stars in the world, and watching him handle Frank Jr. was an art form and master class for me.

Promotional artwork was done to include a shadow of Sinatra Sr. behind Frank Jr.'s likeness. This promo implied that the show was going to be a Sinatra music performance. As we got into rehearsal, I was hearing the "B" sides of the "B" sides. What was he doing? We had this conversation. He spoke with the promoter. Everyone knew what was expected of us. I questioned him halfway through rehearsal, and he gave me a loud, nasty response. I argued, and he yelled at me in front of the entire orchestra and crew. I was humiliated and embarrassed. I walked out of rehearsal and was preparing to leave Vegas to go home. Hank talked me out of it. He calmed "JR" (as he referred to Frank) down. My new assignment was to assure Kayne that the show would be wonderful. We worked at the hotel for three weeks out of that year. The first week was okay, and we got lukewarm reviews. The second time in, he changed some of the music because he knew that sticking to the present program would harm his reputation and mine with Kayne and future promoters, especially in a town he desperately wanted to have a presence in, Las Vegas.

The years went by quickly, and each new year brought more success, personal complications, illness, and grief. His life was profoundly changed when his father died. His sadness was obvious, but so were the mixed emotions he felt for his father. However, the shadow had become light, and the rock and the weight were lifted. There was a new freedom. He could sing his father's music in homage, not for the sake of marketability. His career changed quickly.

Between 2000 and 2001, we created a wonderful promotional photo for his new show, *As I Remember It*, using both his father's image and his. He was doing the saloon songs, and two-thirds of the music was Sinatra songs. Once that proved successful, we created *Sinatra Sings Sinatra*, with 90 percent Sinatra music and accompanying video of his father on the song "It Was a Very Good Year." This show was an immediate hit with buyers and every audience that saw it.

I saw a new happiness in Frank. We were working hard and often. We were touring the world, and he was thrilled to keep his musicians and crew, who were his real family, working and with him most of the time. Finally, he was at peace with singing his father's music, and he was successful doing it. In 2014, we started planning the Sinatra *Centennial Celebration* show, celebrating what would be the one hundredth birthday of his father. The show was, quite simply, brilliant. From the beginning sounds of his father's favorite singers of the 1930s to the "My Way" finale, audiences met the *real* Sinatra through his son's eyes, voice, and heart.

Frankie's laughter in the dressing rooms, his upbeat manner at rehearsals, and his relaxed attitude on stage were all a joy to watch. My friend—my *brother*—was finally enjoying his career and his life. The musicians, the crew, Frank, and I had finally achieved exactly what took us decades to attain. All of us traveled this emotional journey together, as a family and as one entity. And we made it.

On March 16, 2016, at 2:30 p.m., I was talking to Frank on the phone. The conversation lasted thirty-five minutes. We were discussing what flight I should take to Florida the next day. He was happy with the way the show was running. He said the guys were happy, and I told him the promoters were thrilled. All was well in our world. Until it wasn't. About an hour later, I got a call saying Frankie had been taken to the hospital and was unresponsive. He was dead.

He was a tortured soul who helped others heal. He was an enigma, yet he was crystal clear. He was my hero, my brother, and my best friend. I'd never hear his voice or talk to him about our triumphs or problems again. We'd never get to laugh about the funny stuff on the road or the sad stuff in our lives. The void left by his passing would never be filled. He could be tough to please. You almost never knew where you stood with him on any given day, but we accepted that as the norm. His norm. But he could be sweet with us. His generosity was epic.

We will never be cared for like he cared for us again. We will never hear music like we produced again. We will never hear his laughter or bark again. He was an underdog, our underdog.

Because he was so special to me, it's important to me, for the readers of this book to understand who Frank Sinatra, Jr., really was. This book is a chance for people to see him. And that's what he always wanted.

My Father

Michael Francis Sinatra

> Frank Sinatra, Jr., is his own man, and while he's proud to be "the keeper of the flame" at this point in time, there is absolutely no doubt that he will be creating his own standards as a singer and writer in the not too distant future.
>
> —*ROD MCKUEN*

> I was the bearded lady in the sideshow. I was the freak show. That was how I was presented.
>
> —*FRANK SINATRA, JR.*, 2016

No one could tell a story quite like my father. Whether it was on stage recounting stories of my grandfather and his legendary career or in his home sharing his favorite memories of notable names and famous friends he was fortunate enough to meet during his life. Every time we went to dinner, sat in his home office, or spoke on the phone, I often felt privileged to hear his austere, baritone voice paint a picture that was always so vivid you could swear that you were experiencing the actual event yourself.

He never asserted himself as a parent but rather took pride in reminding me that I was my own man, the "head of the table" as he often alluded to with a story featuring Gene Roddenberry and his philosophy. I couldn't help but wonder if some of the anecdotes and experiences he shared with me had been products of careful practice. Perhaps he hoped one day he would be able to pass them on to me and help contribute to a life more meaningful and successful than his own, as he often confided in me. Perhaps it was his natural ability to be an entertainer, or maybe it was simply that he was looking back on his life to find meaning and peace as he believed he was approaching his final days. I also tend to believe that his time living in Japan, as I would later experience firsthand in my own time living there, imbued in him a sense of self-discipline at his craft of storytelling and sharing wisdom. In my professional life, I often think of how he would tell a story, looking forward to the chance of telling it once more in an even better way. To borrow a term from Walt Disney, my father may have constantly wanted to "plus" his stories and experiences; in other words, enhance them in ways people would never expect.

One of the stories that always struck a chord with me was about his relationship with my grandfather. It may be easy to imagine that with my grandfather's world renown, he may not have always had time to be there for his son. The stories of how my grandfather was forever affected by my father's kidnapping and ransom are well recorded. However, much to my surprise, my father would often lament that he recalled having a private dinner with his father only once in his life. On that occasion, he was called by my grandfather to his compound in Rancho Mirage to consult on some particular matter. My father went with the assumption that it would be a meeting between trusted friends. He was shocked to arrive to a table arranged just for the two of them, where they spent the evening dining together. Although he tried his best to hide it, there was a particular sorrow in my father's voice. It seemed as if from that night in the desert on, he swore to make sure that if he had a son, those kinds of intimate meetings would not be such a rare occasion. My father was fully intent on making sure that I would benefit from the fatherly advice and guidance that he had almost completely been denied. And for that, I was always grateful.

Before he passed, my father shared his vulnerable side with me as I felt he had never shared with anyone before. I always respected him as a professional in every sense of the word, a kind of invincible symbol of stoicism. But when I realized he was trying to show me his human side, I sensed that we had finally reached a true father-son bond that I had longed for over the years. My father was no longer the distant figure of almost mythic greatness. He was simply a father trying to be a positive force in his son's life.

I will never forget the night my father made a request that I never thought he would. He spoke with a faint sense of anxiety, a kind of uncertainty I felt he was incapable of showing. He spoke as a man very conscious of his age, a father put in an awkward position to ask a favor of his son. He delegated me to be his defender, to protect his reputation and ensure that he would be remembered for the good man that he was. Those who knew my father might find this surprising because he was often his own most consistent and harshest critic. I knew this was something he would not entrust to anyone in whom he didn't have complete faith and confidence. From that moment on, I have devoted myself to serve as his protector, something he deserved all his life but even more so since his death.

One such example would be exposing lies about my father's traumatic kidnapping experience. I don't believe anyone can imagine the kind of pain and emotional torment my father endured following the disgusting rumor that was spread by his kidnappers that he had helped orchestrate his own abduction for the sake of advancing his career. When my father returned to his bedroom, I would always hear the distinctive locking sound of the dual-sided deadbolt he had on his bedroom door. In my younger years, I was confused as to why he would need such measures on top of his sophisticated alarm system and other deterrents. To me, this is all the evidence one needs to understand that my father was forever changed by that traumatic ordeal. And I have been quick to remind skeptics and dispel any possible rumors to the contrary.

Around six months before he passed, my father confessed to me that he should have been a better father, that he should have been there for me. Despite all my regrets of not calling him enough or not feeling confident enough to trust in him, I will always be happy that I could assure him in that moment that he did the best he could with what he knew how to do. And I told him that was enough for me. Perhaps I took it for granted, constantly thinking of my incomparable grandmother and her vitality. I believed my father would live to be one hundred just like her. I only wish I had shown the same initiative that he did in his later years before he was taken from us so suddenly.

Sara Karloff, daughter of the incomparable Boris Karloff and a dear friend of both my father and me, said it best. As we struggle to live in the shadows of those who came before us, whether they are simple parents or world-famous icons, she would always say, "Cast your own shadow." I've often pondered how my father may have viewed living in my grandfather's shadow. I imagine he would say that telling the stories of "Sinatra" was a responsibility only he could assume, a responsibility rooted in honor and respect. I remind myself each and every day that I must carry on my father's legacy as much as he carried on his father's.

My grandfather's name and voice will always persevere, I hope, through the ages. But more than Frank Sinatra's grandson, I have preferred to embrace the role of Frank Sinatra, Jr.'s son. People often ask if I knew my grandfather well and if I spent much time with him. I always answer that I preferred spending time with my father, a man just as talented and genuine, but often underappreciated and overlooked.

Baseball legend and American hero Jackie Robinson said, "A life is not important except in the impact it has on other lives." No matter what flaws my father had—and he was never shy about admitting them—he succeeded in making a difference in many people's lives. He was a man who loved, who cared, who struggled and fought for others while often never seeming to do so for himself.

It is my sincere hope that the stories here provide much needed insight into a man who touched the hearts of many yet almost never took any credit for himself. He was a man who dedicated himself to music, his family legacy, a passion for learning and storytelling, and his own sense of decency and dignity.

Let Me Be Frank

The Early Years

Franklin Wayne Emanuel Sinatra was born on January 10, 1944, at the Margaret Hague Hospital in Jersey City. His parents were Nancy Sinatra and Frank Sinatra. When news of the birth came over the news wire, the hospital was mobbed by the press, even though his world-famous father was not present. In lieu of the physical presence of "The Voice," as he was then known, crack press agent George Evans, the same George Evans who paid young bobbysoxers to scream at Sinatra's first solo appearances, set up a photo-op, with Nancy sitting up in bed, holding her newborn with her left hand and a framed eight-by-ten photograph of the new daddy in her right. Two nights later, on his CBS radio program for Vimms Vitamins, the proud poppa sang "This Love of Mine" and dedicated it to his son, saying, "I really want him to hear this." History will show that Baby Frankie may actually have been listening.

While not occupied with his radio show, Frank Sinatra was in Hollywood, no doubt celebrating the January 1 release of his second film, the RKO musical *Higher and Higher*, where he was billed third under Michele Morgan and Jack Haley. The film grossed more than three quarters of a million dollars, big money in those days, and it was clear that the elder Sinatra was headed for a long and lucrative career in pictures. Indeed, the month after the birth of Frank Jr., Frank Sr. signed a $1.5 million deal with MGM. Hasbrouck Heights, New Jersey, the borough where Mr. and Mrs. Sinatra and young Nancy had lived since 1941, was no longer good enough. In the early spring of 1944, Frank

Sr. moved the Sinatra brood to California. Before the move, however, there was the matter of Frank Jr.'s christening. Emanuel "Manie" Sacks, a dear friend of the Sinatras and then a VP at Columbia Records, was named Frankie's godfather. The choice of Sacks, a Jew, as godfather was not entirely welcomed by several members of the clergy in attendance. Frank Sinatra couldn't have cared less.

The new Sinatra family address was 1051 Valley Spring Lane in Toluca Lake, the former estate of film actress Mary Astor, and located ten miles from Hollywood. There were fun times to be had at the Toluca Lake house, and years later, Nancy remembered that the family hosted a July 4th celebration for the community, with Frank Sinatra himself handling the fireworks. Evidently, he was home that day.

Tina Sinatra was born three years later, in 1948, which was close to the time the Sinatras moved again. Their residence at 320 North Carolwood Drive in Holmby Hills was just a few blocks away from the home of Humphrey Bogart and Betty Bacall. Tina described life at the new house as relatively normal. "My siblings and I were comfortable, but not pampered," she wrote in her book, *My Father's Daughter*. "We were obliged to look after our own rooms and tidy our beds on the maid's day off. We left our plates in the kitchen sink and our dirty laundry in the bathroom hampers. My mother believed in order and discipline, and we complied."

Nancy Jr. loved it and remembered that "the house sat on about three acres. We had a pool, a badminton court, a big fishpond, a separate play yard, a beautiful rose garden and an orchard."

Not surprisingly then or now, there was no comment about the homes or "fun times" from Frank Jr. And those who were around the family during Frankie's youth noted that he simply didn't have much to say about anything, peppering their descriptions with phrases like "He was silent"; "He had little to say"; "He gazed at his father"; or "He just occupied himself playing with his little cars and trains." He also had less to say when his father left his mother for Ava Gardner in 1949. "My brother understood just enough to draw the loss inside," said Tina in her book. "He felt bewildered and abandoned and quietly traumatized. I think that his world just fell apart."

Though he may have been traumatized by the split at the time, and Ava Gardner may not have gone out of her way to be particularly nice to the Sinatra kids, the truth is, Gardner would step forward more than a decade later to play an important part in the life of Frank Jr. For the moment, though, the boy seemed to have been internalizing everything, and he kept it there. Summing up his childhood on a Toronto talk show a few years before his passing, Frank was characteristically matter of fact about those years.

"I had normal parents who had normal attitudes about raising children, who they hoped one day would be normal," he said. "My father was very sparse in the advice department, primarily because he was not the most intelligent person to be giving advice. He would say, 'Listen to so-and-so if you're curious about it.' I believe the message was: Listen to somebody smarter than I am which, to me, is eloquently intelligent."

It seems that Frank began to come out of his shell, to an extent, when he discovered music and learned just who his father was. Dressed in a dark suit and bowtie, the ten-year-old boy accompanied his father, along with sister Nancy, to the Academy Awards gala at the Pantages Theatre in Hollywood on March 25, 1954. We don't know what Frankie thought when his father won the Oscar for Best Supporting Actor for his work in *From Here to Eternity*, but we can surmise that Frank Sinatra, Jr., was duly impressed by much of the glitz and the glamour he witnessed and wanted some of it for himself someday.

In his later years, Frank Sinatra, Jr., didn't talk a lot about his early musical education, but he did speak extensively about it on one occasion to radio host Paul Leslie. Leslie's 2015 interview with Frank was published, verbatim and in its entirety, in, of all places, *LaRevista Ro*, a Romanian/English lifestyle publication .

"I began to receive, personally, training at the age of three or four," Frank told Leslie.

> This goes back to the 1940s, and because of my father's work in those days, he always had guests in our home, who were great composers, lyricists, songwriters, orchestrators, and as it happened, they, by degrees, began to tutor me. I can remember when I was three or four, one of my uncles who was the head of the music department at Columbia Pictures in those days, back when each studio had a music department, and he gave me a book about the instruments in the symphony orchestra. I could look at the pictures that he would point to and identify each one of the symphonic instruments. At the age of five, I was started on piano

> lessons, and in that situation, I continued on all the way through college. I had once had the desire to be a composer and a pianist.
>
> I had been writing melodies, much to the chagrin of my piano teacher, when I was a boy, rather than practicing the lessons that she had given to me. I would be spending my time at the piano composing little melodies and little things for myself, and after a time, something else happened, which was really quite remarkable. I could hear a piece of orchestral music on a recording, hopefully not too complicated a piece of orchestral music, and by listening to it, I could then play it with the correct harmonic changes on the piano. This, as they say, was by ear, and at that point in time it occurred to me maybe this was what I was meant to be, which is why after high school, when I went into college, I began to study composing and things like that.

Lisa Coffey played harp in the orchestras of both Frank Sr. and Frank Jr. and became a close friend of Frank Jr. She remembered a story that he told her about his young days at the piano. "His parents had a party," Coffey said, recalling the story. "This would have been when he was six or seven years old. He was given the assignment of playing the piano when the guests were arriving. He told me that he was playing the 'Minuet in G' from his piano book. Nat King Cole came over to the piano and was standing there listening to him. When he finished his 'Minuet in G,' Nat King Cole said to him, 'Well, that was very nice, young man.' Frank replied, 'Oh. Do you play?'"

He also credited his father's pianist and sometimes conductor, Bill Miller, as one of his main influences and teachers.

"Bill Miller, who was the greatest accompanist that any singer has ever had, came on board in Frank Sinatra's career way back in 1951," Frank said to *The Washington Post* upon Miller's death in 2006.

> Frank Sinatra at that time was still as a young man, still in his 30s and in the worst period in his career, had been hired to play in Las Vegas. He was there working and late at night he would go into the show lounge and here he would see this little jazz group playing. They still had jazz groups in Las Vegas in those days, and here was this pianist from Brooklyn who had played with Charlie Barnet's big band during the big band era. He liked the way this man played in such a minimalistic fashion, and they got together, and they put their heads together, and they found out that

they liked each other. Bill Miller came on board with Sinatra at that point and stayed with him until Sinatra's final public performance in 1995.

I first met him when I was seven years old. I was in knee pants and I can remember him at the record dates. I was already at that point in my life taking piano lessons and I was absolutely in awe of the man. He was so beautiful, in terms of the beautiful things that he would play on the piano. Another quality he had was that he could read an anthill and make music out of it. He could read anything that was put in front of him, and it was absolutely incredible, and I grew up with him. I used to watch him. I used to stand by him during the Sinatra record dates year after year. I brought him out of retirement six months after my father had died and he never stopped playing for me until his death in July of 2006 at the age of ninety-one.

While Frank might not have had a great deal to say as a young kid, he was ready to use music as a form of self-expression before he hit his teens. "When he was ten or eleven, he'd perform for anyone who'd listen and mimic Dad's television appearance word for word," said sister Tina. Two years later, he was ready for the public spotlight. He performed at a dinner party that his mother threw for some notables, and one of those notables was famed, syndicated gossip columnist, Louella Parsons. Parsons wrote this in her May 12, 1957, column that appeared in the *Los Angeles Examiner* and hundreds of other newspapers worldwide:

I don't like to call a child a prodigy, but a thirteen-year-old Frank Sinatra, Jr., comes close to qualifying in that class. He played the piano for us at a buffet dinner Nancy Sinatra gave in honor of Lorayne Brock Busse and Joseph Hall, who will be married February 14.

Young Frankie doesn't care for rock 'n' roll and says he's never seen Elvis Presley. But he feels that Elvis came up too suddenly and that he should work as hard as Frank Sr., Bing Crosby, and Perry Como did for their success.

We played Frank Sr.'s new record, *Close to You*, and Frank Jr. congratulated Jimmy McHugh on "I Didn't Sleep a Wink Last Night," included on the album. Believe me, coming from Frankie that was a compliment.

Joseph Schenck, Dorothy Manners, the William Perlbergs, the George Seatons, the Harry Brands, and the Ed Leshins gathered around the piano to hear this talented boy play.

Six years later, Frank told *Life* magazine's Gail Cameron about another one of his teachers. "I've studied with Frank Sinatra, although he doesn't know I've studied with him," he told Cameron, "but I've been following him around all my life." The reporter added, "He can also quote whole scenes from his father's films, verbatim."

His Place in the Sun

Like many adolescents, privileged or not, Frank Jr. could be a mischievous lad who caused his fair share of mayhem from time to time. Somewhere around 1958, he fell in with a rough crowd whose idea of a good time was to shoot out streetlights with a BB gun. Shipping him off to Desert Sun School was his mother's decision. Perhaps she didn't know how to handle a son, or maybe the feeling was that he needed male role models other than a father who was barely at home or the neighborhood troublemakers. She may have also followed the lead of the Crosby family. Three of Crosby's kids—Dennis, Phillip, and Gary—were shipped off to a Jesuit-run school in San Francisco.

In September of 1958, Frank Sinatra, Jr., became a student and a resident at Desert Sun, a boarding school located west of Palm Springs in the San Jacinto Mountains. In an article written for the *Los Angeles Times* in 1990, the year of the school's closing, writer Jennifer Warren described the institution. "The school educated children of the famous and wealthy," she wrote, "turning often unmotivated teenagers into college-bound graduates with its formula of rigorous academics, live-in faculty and wilderness study programs. Nestled beneath a canopy of pines and oaks outside Idyllwild, the school cultivated the children of Frank Sinatra and Art Linkletter, as well as the offspring of many American corporate captains and foreign magnates."

In 1965, Dr. Richard Elliott, one of the school's founders, specifically detailed Desert Sun's mission. It doesn't sound like a load of fun. Elliott wrote,

> Desert Sun School attempts to restore to normalcy the large family atmosphere and to raise children with their teachers and house parents in a constant association. The same people who guard their morals in the dormitory, their etiquette at the table, and their sportsmanship on the playground, also guide their intellects in the schoolroom and their ethics in family living. Desert Sun feels that the adjustments made between students and between students and their counselors are the same as those made between grown people and their family and business associates. We feel these associations, properly made, will eliminate many of the sources of friction in domestic and public life. In short, we would develop self-reliant individuals whose self-reliance recognizes the individual's place in and responsibility to what Lincoln called "the great family of man."

Depending upon who you talk to and when you talk to them, Frank was either the life of the party at the school, or his time spent there was the beginning of a life of misery and bitterness that he held against his parents until his passing. What did happen as a result of his four-year stay was that, by his own admission, he lost his position within the family. Whether or not he ever reestablished that position, or whether or not he really wanted to, remains a question.

At Desert Sun, Frank Jr. met Ronna Brodsley, who became a lifelong friend and confidant. Brodsley recalled,

> I came from an abusive home. Both of my parents were really messed up. In the eleventh grade, I was in special classes, called "enriched classes." That was too much pressure, and I just needed to get out of my house. I went for a polio shot, and the doctor took one look at me and said, "What can I do to help you?"
>
> I said, "Get me out of the house."
>
> That started it, and I ended up at Desert Sun midyear.
>
> To me, Frank was wonderful. He was a year younger than I. We had some of the same classes. At first, he was kind of cold. He wasn't always able to let down his guard when he didn't know somebody or wasn't sure of somebody. But about a week or two after I got there, we were having lunch together. There were two people inside of Frank. One was the person who emulated his father. The other was his true self, and with me, he didn't have a lot of trouble showing that side. With most

people, he did. I didn't care who the hell he was. That didn't impress me. But the more I was with him, I saw how kind he would be. He was very sensitive, and that scared him. Coming from where he came from, he needed to be tough guy, or he felt that he did. That didn't work for me. I knew better from the start. He was so caring and so sensitive, and so easily hurt.

Frank didn't want to go away to school. He was just negative about it all. He wanted to stay home, but his mother didn't want it. He hated Edie Elliott, the owner and principal of Desert Sun, and he hated the school. He hated it because he wanted desperately to be home.

I went to his house in Beverly Hills a number of times. I hated it in there. Frank's mom was one of the coldest people I ever met. But only to him. She had these two girls, and they could do anything. Frank was totally left out. Her attitude toward him was just cold. I don't know how he could stand living in that house. He was desperate for her attention, but she never gave it to him. Ever. Up until the time he died. But he adored her. That's been his problem. He was so wanting to be accepted. It was his mother. He carried that over to women. Let's just say that he deserved better.

He was different with me. Not to say he wasn't moody because he was. He was overly dramatic sometimes. At Desert Sun, the parents would visit on the weekend. His father, while I was there, would say, "I'll be up Sunday." And he did come once. The three of us went out to a little cafe in Idlewild, and we sat at the counter. But that's the only time I know of that his father visited him. On the other days that his father promised to visit him, Frankie would stand in front of the front gates. He would get up in the morning and stand there until late afternoon. He dressed like his father, he acted like his father, and he slung his jacket over his shoulder. He slumped, and minute by minute, he was more concave. I just hated to see him like that. His mother rejected him, and his father just didn't get it.

Even though he hated the school, he could let it go. He could get up on the stage and be a lot of fun. The summer after graduation, we had a summer together that started when he took me to Disneyland. There was nothing intimate about our relationship. I didn't want it. He might have, but he was so sensitive that he knew I didn't want it. I just couldn't handle that then, but I loved him, and we pretty much spent the summer together, starting with that night at Disneyland.

> He had always talked about singing and wanting to do what his dad did. I really thought it was going to be the wrong thing for him. I said, you have so many talents. You're so musical. You don't want to do what your dad is doing. Do something that you know you can do well, like conducting or writing music. I just didn't want him to try to be his father, because there's only one of them. I didn't want him to be hurt. So we went to Disneyland that night, and there was a band there.

Andrea Kauffman is crystal clear when it came to Frank's feelings about Desert Sun:

> He was bitter about being in boarding school. He did a couple of things as a kid that angered his mother. He was working in the mailroom at William Morris. He was sixteen years old, and they gave him a bicycle to drop things off and pick things up. A couple of times, he put the bike up against a building and smoked a cigarette. Once or twice, he got caught. Even at the boarding school, there was a bakery that the kids used to steal into. The one time that he went for a hot loaf of bread, he got caught. They called the parents.
>
> His father wasn't around, and there was no real father figure. His mother, I think, was afraid that he'd become the pseudo swinger that his father was. He was going there, and I think this is the only way the mother could handle it, even though it was wrong. It took all the piss and vinegar out of him, and he ended up a pretty bland personality.

The Start at Disneyland

Stories about Frank's first professional stage appearance vary, though we do know that it happened at Disneyland. Ronna Brodsley, who was there, recalled that the band playing at Disneyland that fateful evening was the Tommy Dorsey "ghost band," that Frank went backstage to ask the leader if he could sing, and that he ultimately took the stage for a couple of numbers. Entertainment writer James Bacon said that the band playing at the park that night was one led by Disneyland favorites, the Elliott Brothers; that the evening in question was July 30, 1962; that Frank asked if he could perform with them; and that he actually did sing Cole Porter's "At Long Last Love." That was an interesting choice. Frank Sr. had first recorded it in 1956 for Capitol Records. By the time Junior was on the Disneyland stage, Senior had rerecorded it for the Reprise (Frank Sr.'s record company) album, *Sinatra and Swingin' Brass.*

Frank Jr.'s recollection, as detailed in an unfinished memoir given to Andrea Kauffman, is entirely different. On a visit to Disneyland, Frank and his young "screw-up" friends, as he described them in his memoir, stopped to hear a dance band that was performing in one of the outdoor pavilions. The band was, in fact, the Elliott Brothers, and one of Frank's nervy friends went up to the bandleader in an attempt to get Frank to sit in. The bandleader agreed, and Frank performed a passable version of "It Happened in Monterey," another of the old man's records for Capitol. Again, he thought he was lousy, though he did admit that he "could never have imagined how wrong I was, or what door had just opened in my life."

Elliott was impressed, saying, "We could use you," and he invited Frank to join the band for the summer. Ronna Brodsley was with him. "We went every night," she said, "and I got to hate Disneyland. But he was so happy, and I wanted him to be happy."

However it happened, Frank Sinatra, Jr.'s professional career as a singer had begun.

His performances with the Elliott Brothers led to an appearance on a locally televised show, *Meet Me at Disneyland*, where he sang his father's Tommy Dorsey hit, "I'll Never Smile Again." Frank's mother tuned in. "I was thoroughly convinced that she was underwhelmed," Frank wrote.

Despite her "disinterest," to use Frank's words, the train had left the station. Jack Benny's people had seen Frank on the Disneyland broadcast, which led to a well-received appearance on Benny's popular television show. In addition to doing bits with Benny, Frank sang "My Kind of Girl." Of the appearance, Frank said, "It was evident that I was a complete amateur." Still, he was pleased when he discovered that his father had watched the telecast while on a break from recording the first Frank Sinatra–Count Basie collaboration. "You were very good, my boy," his father told him.

In October of 1962, Frank Jr. moved to his own apartment and was given a job in the promotion department of his father's record company, Reprise. In the evenings, he took night-school classes at UCLA.

Also in October of 1962, Frank Jr. sent a fan letter to the popular young actress Hayley Mills. The two went on a date, photos were taken, and the couple made the cover of several fan magazines. The Sinatra-Mills pairing didn't work out. Frank maintained that he made a complete fool of himself on the evening they got together, which happened to be the opening of Sammy Davis, Jr.'s two-week stand at the Coconut Grove.

Teen Idol in the Making

Word was out about Frank Jr. and his fledgling singing career. *Photoplay* magazine, one of the first and biggest fan magazines, heard about the noise he was making and knocked out a story, possibly the first of its kind on Frank Jr. The precursor to today's supermarket tabloids, *Photoplay* featured tantalizing headlines, supposedly candid photos of the stars, and "reporting" from Hollywood's biggest columnists, including Hedda Hopper. The stories themselves were often fabricated by press agents or based on unfounded gossip and rumor. Fine journalism, it wasn't. When this piece on Frank was published in April 1963, the reporting certainly seemed authentic. But that was the whole point of magazines like this.

Most *Photoplay* stories had no byline, but whoever did write this placed him- or herself smack in the middle of Frank's life. The writer was somehow at the wedding reception for Nancy Jr. and Tommy Sands in September 1960 and at Disneyland in the summer of 1962 on the night Frank first sang in public. The writer's main sources were Eddie, a close friend of Frank, and Frank himself. The direct quotes from Frank were in his voice, though likely the work of a press agent, perhaps Tino Barzie. But some parts of the story, like the early tendency toward self-pity, ring true. Andrea Kauffman confirmed that Frank did have a stuttering issue, and a slight lisp as well, which she believes were the reason for his slow, mannered way of speaking. Though Frank didn't yet rate a cover story—Elizabeth Taylor graced this issue's cover—it was still an important feature in a major fan magazine that clearly portrayed, at least in the opinion of *Photoplay*'s editors, a teen idol in the making.

How Would You Like It if Frank Sinatra Were Your Father?

Photoplay Magazine, April 1963

Not long ago, Frankie visited Disneyland where the Elliott Brothers were entertaining. He listened to them for a while, and then the urge became irresistible. "I said to myself," Frankie explained, "I was going to have to take my chances alongside every other guy my age who wanted to become a singer. I sauntered over to one of the bandleaders and told him I'd like to try a song or two with the group. He hesitated, but he finally said okay."

Frankie did well and got a tremendous hand when he finished. The leader said, "Hey, what's your name?" Frankie laughed and started to say it, but he didn't have to. One of the musicians hollered out, "That's Frank Sinatra, Jr., and it was great."

"I didn't care that they knew who I was. The important thing was, they didn't know until I finished."

The bandleader later called Frankie back for an all-Dorsey show a week later. Young Sinatra couldn't have been more pleased. He had his professional baptism. Then he appeared on a couple of Los Angeles television shows, and finally a star spot with Jack Benny, who assured all concerned that he was using junior for his talent, and not for his name. Sinatra Sr. upon learning of the turn of events, grinned like a kid. "I always said that son of mine was full of surprises."

"I'm proud of my name. I'm proud of my father. People will never know what a wonderful parent he's been to us. I'm proud to be Frank Sinatra, Jr. My father gave me my name, and the best way I know to show off my gratitude is to earn the right to use it. It's something every son should do for his father. I like it that way."

Getting Sentimental

The Dorsey Years

This was about the time that the promotional wheels and promotional minds, in the form of Bobby Burns and Tino Barzie, began turning. Both men were swing-era veterans involved in the management of Tommy Dorsey's big band, whose legendary swing-era orchestra was home to Frank Sinatra, Sr., from 1940 to 1942. Burns had been one of Frank Sr.'s managers after he left Dorsey to pursue a solo career, and by 1962, he had become a respected booking agent with MCA.

Tommy Dorsey died in 1956. The following year, his widow, Janie New, licensed the Dorsey name and library to veteran big-band booker Willard Alexander, who promptly installed trombonist Warren Covington as the leader of the Tommy Dorsey "ghost band." No one knew bands better than Alexander, and he was certain there was some life left in the Dorsey name by going the ghost-band route, ala Tex Beneke's and Ray McKinley's success with the leadership of the Glenn Miller band in the 1950s, years after Miller's death. Covington even had a hit in 1958 with "Tea for Two Cha Cha," but by 1961, he realized he could do better on his own as a studio player.

When Tino Barzie, who was still involved in some Dorsey-estate matters, heard that Covington was leaving the band, he stepped up and convinced Janie New that the Dorsey band could continue as a successful enterprise under the leadership of saxophonist Sam Donahue. And Barzie, who always had his ear to the ground for something to promote, and never fully believed that the swing era was over, was also likely hearing the buzz about the son of Frank Sinatra singing at Disneyland and on *The Jack Benny Program*.

It was a press agent's dream: Put the youngster in front of the band where his father became a star two decades ago, add some veterans of the original Dorsey band who were still working, and take the whole package on the road. Barzie called Bobby Burns at MCA (no one knew the Dorsey band better than Burns) and told him of the idea. Burns was as excited as Barzie. He was sure he could book the package, but he immediately got on the phone to Frank Jr.

Burns told Frank in no uncertain terms that if he had any interest in singing with the Dorsey band, he needed to call Tino Barzie in New York as soon as possible.

On paper, it was a can't-miss package. In October 1961, Sam Donahue was installed as the leader. Donahue was a superb saxophonist who had not only worked with the swing era's biggest names, including Dorsey, but had led several of his own ensembles. Groups under his leadership, especially Artie Shaw's navy band, which he led when Shaw left the service, were critically acclaimed but never caught on with the public. Still, Donahue was always chomping at the bit to be a leader, even if the band operated under the Tommy Dorsey name.

Hard-swinging and hard-living Dorsey trumpet veteran Ziggy Elman, who was still blowing credibly, was the first swing-era star to be hired. Trombonist Larry O'Brien, a veteran of several postwar name bands, including Buddy Morrow's, joined in January 1961 and would play with Frank Sinatra, Jr., into the 1970s. The original singers were Billy Raymond, who worked with Dorsey, and Jeannie Thomas, who would go on to sing with Harry James in the 1970s. Vocalist Helen Forrest, one of the most popular singers of the swing era by way of her work with Benny Goodman and Artie Shaw, would also be added to the touring nostalgia package, though she never worked with Tommy Dorsey. Who cared? Forrest to Barzie personified what the swing era was all about.

For the moment, however, Frank Sinatra, Jr., had a decision to make. Did he have any interest in singing with the Dorsey band?

Frank made the call to Barzie, and the two agreed to wait until Frank's school year was finished in May before any move was made. "Through all of the early weeks of the New Year," Frank said in his unpublished memoir, "I pondered the offer that Tino Barzie had proposed. I wondered what it would be like to play jobs from which you didn't get to go home at night."

While he was pondering, he got a call from singer Russ Arno, who had made a slight impact with Liberty Records in the mid-1950s. They were not strangers. Frank had actually cut his teeth as an arranger by making a chart for Arno the previous year. Arno secured a job at the Hampton House in Kansas City, Missouri, and told the owner about his friend Frank's recent activities as a singer. The owner asked Arno if he could get Frank out to Kansas City to join the band for a short stint. Frank took the plunge.

"I came away from my weekend at the Hampton House believing that the road was not a bad life," Frank wrote of the Kansas City experience. "I heard all the stories about the travel, the fatigue, the inconvenience, and the undisputed drudgery of it all. But my experience in Kansas City influenced me in making the decision about joining the Tommy Dorsey Orchestra. The date for my joining the Dorsey Band was set for the first weekend of May, in Dallas."

Frank went on to say,

> Sam Donahue was leading the Tommy Dorsey Orchestra the way he had also fronted the Billy May band and several bands of his own. I had heard about Sam for years but never thought I would actually get to work with him. Many other people who I had worked with thus far had gone out of their way to make me feel welcomed, but Sam seemed to be disinterested in my joining his organization. After our first meeting, I worried if he could accept me into his company of musicians, who were all veterans. I never did find out if they were at all aware of how much I learned from them during our years together.

Years later, Frank would rave about Donahue. "When I started with Sam, I was a clean sheet of paper," he said to writer Toni Ruberto of *The Buffalo News* in 2004. "He taught me how to interpret phrases in music. He was my first real teacher. He was a working teacher, and we were working musicians. I was delighted."

During a stop at Disneyland, booked at Frank's suggestion, another jazz icon joined up. Trumpeter Charlie Shavers, who spent years in and out of the original Dorsey band and was best known as the composer of the jazz classic "Undecided" replaced the sometimes-unreliable Ziggy Elman, whose love for the sauce often got the better of him. Of Shavers, Frank said, "When he died two days after Louis Armstrong in 1971, I lost one of the greatest teachers I had ever known. His contribution to understanding and interpreting jazz has never failed me."

It wasn't all big-band bliss on the road, as Frank Jr. learned after getting a scathing newspaper review from Vegas columnist Ralph Pearl. Pearl's commentary made Frank Jr.'s self-esteem issues and periods of depression and self-doubt worse. "More and more of the time, I was now hiding in my hotel room and only coming out to do the shows," he wrote in his memoir. "The only thing I could think of was to try to do better each night, but it takes real flair to make an ass out of yourself as consistently as I did."

This was not the time for self-doubt as after Labor Day, the Barzie ballyhoo machine went into overdrive. The band was booked at the Royal Box of the Americana Hotel in New York City. Barzie had Frank running all over the place, doing advance interviews and appearances, including one on the *Ed Sullivan Show*. "Everything that I could tell these interviewers about Frank Sinatra was the sum total of their interest," Frank said of that period. "Soon I realized that this was the reason for my presence. The fact that I was in New York for my first nightclub appearance was, to them, a matter of complete indifference and of no interest whatsoever."

Though the Americana job was to start on September 8, 1963, the publicity drumbeating for it began in the August 23, 1963, issue of *Life* magazine.

Frank Sinatra's Son Comes On Singing Like His Old Man

Gail Cameron, *Life* magazine, August 23, 1963

He is only nineteen years old, and he has never made a record, but he sets off an uproar in the audience simply by walking on stage. "The living image of his father," people say. In a civic arena in Nebraska, a nightclub in Atlantic City, a dance in Vermont, the scene keeps repeating itself as a newcomer named Frank Sinatra, Jr., comes on to sing with the Tommy Dorsey Orchestra—a job that twenty-five years ago launched his pop to fame. Frank Jr. steps up to the microphone, takes the mike

> in both hands, bends his knees, leans way back and begins: "You make me feel so young . . ." A wave of surprise sweeps the audience, and the room erupts with sighs. "I'm so nervous—this is killing me," muttered Frank Sr., listening to his son in Las Vegas last week. The new Sinatra sound is an eerie, incredibly exact echo of Frank Sr.'s singing. Frank Jr., a music major at the University of Southern California, tried out his voice in public for the first time last summer at Disneyland, sang on the Jack Benny show, and then came the offer from the Tommy Dorsey band.
>
> Frankie feels he has already had the best singing training he could get. He lugs a stereo tape recorder with him on tour and every night while he is getting dressed, and he warms up his voice for an hour by singing along with Sinatra recordings.
>
> "I think the kid has a future," his pop predicts, "but he needs experience." And then, reports Frank Jr., "He added as only the boss can, 'that by experience I mean he's got to learn to drink, carouse, and stay up all night.'"

The remainder of the *Life* article consisted of "advice to the boy from the master," probably written by one of Pop's publicity people, on the fine art of singing, as well as crucial topics such as handling the jitters, handling girls, and handling the press.

On the evening of September 8, 1963, the Royal Box of Americana Hotel in Manhattan reopened for the fall season. Other hotels featured such established performers as Sheila and Gordon MacRae at the Waldorf, Peter Duchin's orchestra at the St. Regis, and Xavier Cugat with his "discovery" Abbe Lane at the Plaza. The Royal Box presented the Dorsey band, conducted by Sam Donahue and featuring Frank Sinatra, Jr. Press reports listed Frank's age as twenty-one. He was actually nineteen.

Among those in attendance were comics Jackie Gleason, Joe E. Lewis, and Jack E. Leonard. Leonard made it up to the stage, insulting one and all. Conspicuous by his absence on opening night was Frank Sinatra, whose rationale was that he didn't want to steal the kid's thunder.

Abel Green, editor of *Variety* at the time, gave the youngster a good write-up, saying that he "packed his twenty-minute stint with commendable professionalism." The piece went on to quote Frank, who told Green that he learned about band singing from Sam Donahue and the others in the band. "The best way to learn about something is to be around the experts," he said. "Pilots hang around with other pilots; mechanics hang around other mechanics. I stayed around musicians. Formal education is important, of course, but you have to go out there and do it."

Not surprisingly, Sam Donahue's ego was bruised by all the attention Frank was getting. He was, after all, the leader. "This show is a team," Donahue barked at Frank. "Every time you talk, it's me, me, I, I." Frank learned his lesson, and in his memoir, he wrote the following: "Beginning that day, I never again spoke of my work as 'me,' but always as 'us.'"

Trombonist Larry O'Brien, now retired and living in Hawaii, was there. He remembered,

> I joined the Dorsey band around January of 1961. I became manager of the band a couple of years later, as well as trombone soloist. Sam Donahue was a hell of a player and a role model for me as a bandleader. He never got the credit he deserved. He came in at the tail end of the big band era. If he would have been around earlier in his life, he would have been a giant. We were already performing all over the world when Frank joined us. Tino Barzie put all that together. He ran the Dorsey band and ran things for Junior. When Junior came on the band, he definitely had talent; there was no question about it. He played piano, he wrote songs, and he sang. He could sing well. Unfortunately, he came up the hard way. Instead of doing his due diligence as a singer, he learned on the job. And sometimes it wasn't too good, but it got better and improved every night. He finally got to the point where he was really a good singer. And he was really a good piano player.

The very fact that Frank Sinatra's son was now working as a professional singer in the "same" band where his father started made headlines all over the world. The cover of *Life* was pretty big stuff, especially when the biggest records in pop music that year were the Angels' *My Boyfriend's Back*, Martha and the Vandellas' *Heat Wave*, Bobby Vinton's *Blue Velvet*, and Allan Sherman's novelty record, *Hello Muddah, Hello Fadduh!* But Vinton and Sherman didn't make the cover of *Life*. Frank Sinatra, Jr., and his father did. Such was the power of the Sinatra name.

The record industry took note of the excitement. The Dorsey band was tied to RCA Victor and thought it possible to capitalize on the Sinatra, Jr., publicity. Victor recorded the band and Sinatra live and titled the session *Live at the Royal Band Box, Hotel Americana* (RCS Victor LSP-2830). The taping, on September 22, 1963, did include a vocal by Frank Jr. with the Pied Pipers, "I'll Never Smile Again." Frank, evidently, wasn't ready for recording prime time at that early stage. The take was rejected, and the completed album contained nothing by Sinatra.

The road continued, and the reviews, and Frank's singing, were improving. By the time the caravan reached Harrah's at Lake Tahoe on December 2, 1963, things were going pretty well.

Frank took stock at this juncture and recalled in his memoir,

> Seven months had passed since I had joined the band, and I still wondered what the people I was working with really thought about my being there. Each of them had been very nice to me, and I was always very nice to them, but during the hours I was alone, worrying about their true feelings where I was concerned, haunted me each and every day. I had always realized I was nowhere near the same league with them professionally, and I feared that I was only being tolerated. And if that were true, I had to admit that my coworkers were being generous to go that far with the amateur that I was. But now, as the newness of my being part of the company was wearing off, I asked myself another question. Would any of the guys in the band regard me as a friend?

The answer to that question, Frank said, came unexpectedly on the first Sunday night of the engagement, December 8, when he had a heart-to-heart conversation with trumpeter and roommate John Foss. Foss expressed a desire to leave the band to be at home with his family during Christmas. Frank volunteered to intervene with Tino Barzie to make the parting easier. "He said that he felt better about everything because he had needed someone to share his hurt with," Frank wrote. "In that moment, a long-standing question I had held inside was answered. Yes. Maybe the guys in the band would regard me as a friend."

Then there was a knock at the door.

The Kidnapping

The kidnapping of Frank Sinatra, Jr., on December 8, 1963, was one of the biggest news events of the century in terms of press coverage, public interest, and sheer sensationalism. Almost without question, it was one of the pivotal events in his life.

The facts have been told and retold. The story has been made into a second-rate movie and most recently was the subject of a smarmy, bordering-on-the-absurd, podcast hosted by John Stamos, who played host to the "mastermind" of the scheme, a misguided youth named Barry Kennan.

This account of the kidnapping comes from the famous cases and criminal files of the FBI:

> On December 8, 1963, a group of amateur criminals hoping to strike it rich engineered one of the most infamous kidnappings in American history.
>
> For several weeks, two twenty-three-year-old former high school classmates from Los Angeles—Barry Keenan and Joe Amsler—had been following a nineteen-year-old singer from city to city, waiting to make their move. Their target: none other than Frank Sinatra, Jr., son of one of the most famous singers in the world, "Old Blue Eyes" himself. Their plan was bold but simple: snatch the young Sinatra and demand a hefty ransom from his wealthy father.
>
> The pair decided to strike on the evening of December 8, 1963—just days after the assassination of President John F. Kennedy. Sinatra, Jr., just

beginning his career in music, was performing at Harrah's Club Lodge in Lake Tahoe on the border of California and Nevada. Around 9:00 p.m. he was resting in his dressing room with a friend when Keenan knocked on the door, pretending to be delivering a package. Keenan and Amsler entered, tied up Sinatra's friend with tape, and blindfolded their victim. They took him out a side door to their waiting car

The singer's friend quickly freed himself and notified authorities. Roadblocks were set up, and the kidnappers were actually stopped by police . . . but they bluffed their way through and drove on to their hideout in a suburb of Los Angeles.

By 9:40, the FBI office in Reno was brought in on the case. Agents met with young Sinatra's father in Reno and his mother in Bel Air, California. The motive was presumed to be money. The FBI recommended that Sinatra wait for a ransom demand, pay it, and then allow the bureau to track the money and find the kidnappers.

The following evening, Keenan called a third conspirator, John Irwin, who was to be the ransom contact. Irwin called the elder Sinatra and told him to await the kidnappers' instructions. On December 10, he passed along the demand for $240,000 in ransom. Sinatra Sr. gathered the money and gave it to the FBI, which photographed it all and made the drop per Keenan's instructions between two school buses in Sepulveda, California, during the early morning hours of December 11.

While Keenan and Amsler picked up the money, Irwin had gotten nervous and decided to free the victim. Sinatra, Jr., was found in Bel Air after walking a few miles and alerting a security guard. To avoid the press, he was put in the trunk of the guard's patrol car and taken to his mother Nancy's home.

Young Sinatra described what he knew to FBI agents, but he had barely seen two of the kidnappers and only heard the voice of the third conspirator. Still, the bureau tracked the clues back to the house where Sinatra had been held in Canoga Park and gathered even more evidence there.

Meanwhile, with the FBI's progress being recounted in the press, the criminals felt the noose tightening. Irwin broke first, spilling the beans to his brother, who called the FBI office in San Diego. Hours later, Keenan and Amsler were captured, and nearly all of the ransom was recovered.

Although the defense tried to argue that Frank Sinatra, Jr., had engineered the kidnapping as a publicity stunt, the FBI had strong evidence

> to the contrary. The clincher was a confession letter written earlier by Keenan and left in a safe-deposit box. In the end, Keenan, Amsler, and Irwin were all convicted.

It was the defense's position that Frank had engineered the kidnapping himself to boost his fledgling career and/or simply to get the attention of his father that some say would cast a shadow over his credibility for the rest of his life. Newspapers all over the world were screaming headlines, like the one in the *Los Angeles Times* that read, "Sinatra, Jr., Desperately Fights Charge of Hoax." A late December piece in *Time* magazine was among the first to comment on the hoax defense and added a bit of nonsense about Frank Sr. as well. According to *Time*, "As the drama continued to unfold, there were rumors that it was all a publicity stunt or some other sort of hoax, and indeed that was one of the first avenues of investigation probed by the FBI. Then, too, there was the matter of Frank Sr.'s genial flirtation with a kind of shadow clan of his own, consisting of high-echelon hoods. No one figured out the connection, if any, but many were prepared to view the kidnapping as something less than the real thing. They were wrong."

Trying to shift or at least share the blame, at one point, Keenan claimed that the whole mess had been financed in part by none other than Dean Torrence of Jan and Dean recording fame, a Keenan friend. This turned out, in part, to be true, and when Keenan eventually sold his story, Torrence was in for a percentage.

In the end, Amsler and Irwin were in prison for three and one-half years. Keenan, sentenced to life plus seventy-five years, was released from jail in 1968, after four and one-half years, on the grounds that he was legally insane. In the Stamos podcast, Keenan spoke of his insanity at the time, saying he often spoke to angels and that while listening to the radio, God had told him to kidnap Frank Jr. Amsler, who died in 2006, worked for several years as Ryan O'Neil's stunt double. At the time of his death, his occupation was that of handyman. Irwin seems to have dropped off the grid, his whereabouts unknown.

Attorney Gladys Root, who represented Irwin at the trial, concocted the hoax defense. In 1964, Root was indicted for fabricating the story, which included charges of conspiracy, suborning perjury, and obstruction of justice. The charges were dropped in 1968. Not too many years later, the IRS got on her case, claiming she owed nearly a quarter of a million dollars in back taxes. She took the case to the Supreme Court. The court wasn't interested in Root or her appeal and refused to hear the case.

The kidnapping was front-page news all over the world. Media coverage often included the word *hoax* and did not die down with the verdict. As Frank said at the trial, "With or without my consent or with or without my personal information, sooner or later, the, shall we say, lower crust of publication would make something out of that, which is what they do with anything."

By and large, Frank Sinatra, Jr., then nineteen years of age and still in the Dorsey band, was left to handle this unmanageable situation by himself. Support and understanding did come, and it came from an unlikely source: the second wife of his father, Ava Gardner.

In remarks at the Ava Gardner Historic Marker dedication ceremony in Durham, North Carolina, delivered on November 18, 2015, Frank told the story of the kidnapping, the hoax defense, and how Gardner rescued him from the international media frenzy.

The publicity following Frank Jr.'s kidnapping was enormous, especially given the kidnapper's defense that the whole thing was a hoax designed to garner publicity for his singing career. The media hounded him wherever he went, including Europe and Great Britain, where he was a part of a Dorsey tour in February and March of 1964.

Prior to his departure, his father's office compiled a list of people who pledged to be in touch with Frank during the tour, which included visits to England, Scotland, Denmark, Wales, Belgium, the Netherlands, Germany, Spain, and Portugal.

No one on the list stepped forward to offer Frank some solace on the tour by way of helping him get a few minutes' peace from the European media circus. The last stop was Madrid. "I spent my time hiding," Frank remembered, "a charming thing for a kid who just turned twenty."

He checked in at the Roma Hilton in Madrid and found a message by his phone that read, "Call Miss Ava Gardner." Though his father was married to Ava Gardner from 1951 to 1957, Frank Jr. really didn't know her. He said, "She was someone who did not know me except that many years ago she met a little boy in knee pants, probably somebody that she would never see again."

He got Gardner on the phone. She said she wanted to pick Frank up at his hotel and bring him to her house. He was, as he said, "pretty damn startled" by this turn of events. Gardner, wearing "no makeup and looking gorgeous," as Frank recalled, was driving. They drove to her house, and he was informed that dinner would be an hour later. There were a few friends there, and she introduced her guest by saying, "Everyone, this is Frank Sinatra, Jr., the son of my former husband."

After dinner, when Frank announced that it was time to return to his hotel, she insisted that he stay the night—on the couch—in her home. "I want you to stay here," she said. "I would be remiss because you traveled so far." They discussed, among other things, her marriage to Frank's father. He went to his hotel the next morning, and at his show that night, she and several of her friends were in the audience. He suggested that she leave when the show was half over in order to avoid the press.

Frank was touched. "Here's a woman who was married to a man who was married before, and I was one of his children," said Frank. "She owed me nothing. But she went out of her way to bring me to her home. That happened to me when I had just become twenty, and I've never forgotten her gesture to me, and I never will." He did not see her again for years.

Frank Sinatra, Sr.'s thoughts on the kidnapping were never made public until a letter written by him came to light in 2018. The elder Sinatra's missive, or one drafted by one of the family's lawyers in his name, was in response to a letter written to him in the summer of 1964 by Father Roger Schmit, then prison chaplain at the Medical Center for Federal Prisoners in Springfield, Missouri, where convicted kidnappers Keenan and Amsler were being held. Schmit was asking Sinatra to go easy on the kidnappers. Sinatra had absolutely no intention of doing so.

In the letter, Sinatra said it was "presumptuous" for Father Schmit to ask that the Sinatra family forgive the kidnappers. "The very request presumes that we harbor some antagonism towards Keenan and Amsler," Sinatra said. He went on to say that the family believed strongly in the law and that the trial was "fair" and "impartial," adding that "the crime is not just against the Sinatras, but a crime committed against society."

After praising the efforts of the courts and the FBI, his anger about Father Schmit's plea to "go easy" on the kidnappers became evident. Sinatra wrote that he resented Schmit's reasoning that the kidnappers' actions, as well as the hoax defense, caused the Sinatra family "some embarrassment" and that the kidnappers have "often expressed their sorrow and regret the suffering caused by the kidnapping."

Sinatra especially took issue with Schmit's phrase that the kidnappers caused the family "some embarrassment." He said that the conduct of the kidnappers and their attorneys, and the manner in which the press reported the case, caused the Sinatra family "great anguish and suffering," that "suspicion was created in the minds of many people as to the honesty and truthfulness of our son," and that "nothing has been done by the defendants subsequent to the trial to help remove that suspicion."

Sinatra said that the defendants lied on the stand about the kidnapping being a hoax and that the situation required "more than expressions of regret to a Chaplain to atone for their sins." Sinatra concluded the letter by writing, "In my opinion, my son has either gotten over the effects of being kidnapped or will easily get over any adverse effects of the kidnapping since I think he is a strong person; however, unless something affirmative is done by the defendants, the cloud of suspicion which hangs over his head will continue to affect adversely his life and his career." He signed the letter, "Very truly yours, FRANK SINATRA."

The Aftermath

Through the years, the word *kidnapping* almost became synonymous with the words *Frank Sinatra, Jr.* Interviewers always seemed to ask about it, even if they were asked not to. Mary Hart of *Entertainment Tonight* could not resist bringing it up, even twenty-six years after it happened, during a rare Junior/Senior interview that took place at Bally's Grand Hotel and Casino in Atlantic City.

Hart: When you look back on that kidnapping experience, what does that mean to you?

FS Sr.: My feeling about that period was very confusing. I mean, between anger and anxiety and wanting to hang someone by the neck if I could find him, it was a very difficult situation to try to hold onto and be calm.

Hart: I remember that time. It was such a horrible thing to have happened.

FS Jr.: It was a painful reminder of reality for a nineteen-year-old. When someone, under the pretense of delivering a Christmas present, screws a thirty-eight in your ear, it gets your undivided attention. You become conscious of many things. The first thing that struck me was that I had to change my shorts.

Hart: That whole issue of being a part of a famous family; that was the cause of it. How did you feel, and how long did that stay with you?

FS Jr.: Being part of a famous family is the reality. It would not have happened were it not for that. The people who pulled that crime were originally going to kidnap Bob Hope's son. That came out in

> the investigation because it turned out that Bob Hope was wealthier than Frank Sinatra. Then they decided that Bob Hope, being the great humanitarian, wouldn't be good for their public image, so instead, they took me.

Sinatra's sisters' opinions differed as to how the incident affected his career. Nancy believed that "this incident soured his life and ultimately hurt his career." Tina believed that his career issues had to do with changing times. She described her brother's career as "swimming upstream in the music world. By the mid-1960s, tuxedo singers with big bands were an endangered species. Frankie might have been a victim of bad timing and his own stubbornness as much as anything."

William Rinehart, a Los Angeles Police Department lieutenant in the early 1960s, became friendly with Frank at that time. "I didn't see a big change in him after the kidnapping," he said. "But he did have protection while we stayed at the Americana Hotel when I went with him to the New York World's Fair in 1964. When the protection detail took a break, I'd cover for them."

Years later, during a visit to Frank's house, childhood chum Ronna Brodsley observed that the experience was still very much on his mind. "I went upstairs," she said. "It was a bright and sunny day outside, and I asked him to open the drapes. He said, 'No. I never open the drapes. I don't want people looking in.' I could see the look of terror on his face when he said that. I think he was still terrorized by the experience with the kidnapping."

In the mid-1980s, Andrea Kauffman was helping Frank and this then manager, Vinnie Carbone, check into their hotel suite in Atlantic City. "The first thing we had to do was to check the room for cameras and a phone that might be tapped," Kauffman recalled. "Frankie was still a little shell-shocked from the kidnapping, and Vinnie, who was busy unscrewing the receiver from the phone to check for bugs, said, 'Don't worry, you'll learn the drill.'"

Legally insane or not at the time of the crime, in the years to follow, Barry Keenan made a mint in the real estate business and wouldn't let the kidnapping incident die down. He saw big money and yet another chance in the spotlight when, in January of 1998, five months before the death of Frank Sinatra, Sr., Keenan allowed himself to be interviewed about the kidnapping by a writer named Peter Gilstrap, then working for an "alternative weekly" newspaper called *New Times Los Angeles*. The article appeared in the January 15 issue, and suddenly, the kidnapping was big news again. Columbia Pictures read the article, thought it might make for good cinema, and bought the rights from Keenan, the writer, and the magazine. Dean Torrence was also in for a piece of the pie.

Frank Sinatra, Jr., was not happy and took the matter to court, suing Keenan, Gilstrap, Columbia Pictures, and the magazine. He invoked the Son of Sam law, which forbids convicted felons from making money from their crimes. Keenan and his lawyers, not surprisingly, trotted out the free-speech statute.

From the start, Keenan repeatedly and publicly stated that the only reason why he gave the interview and later cooperated with Columbia Pictures was, in his words, "to set the record straight." He also believed, according to his lawyer, Stephen Rohde, "that the government has no business deciding whether or not a man can write a book (in this case, a newspaper article) and make money from it," adding that Keenan has "paid his debt to society." Keenan also had the nerve to send a somewhat remorseful note to Frank Jr. dated July 14, 1998, in which he wrote, "My sole purpose in cooperating (with Columbia Pictures) is an attempt to set the record straight." He added that the money he was to receive had been earmarked for charity from the start.

In the meantime, the headlines were blaring again, twenty-five years after the fact. "Kidnapper Targets Sinatra, Jr. Again by Selling Story," read the *Dallas Morning News*.

Frank's lawyers initially filed for a preliminary injunction, whereby Columbia Pictures would not pay Keenan anything until the suit was resolved. Keenan's team fought against this injunction and lost. Keenan and his team were not done yet. Their appeal came up in 2002, and he won.

"So we took it to the California Supreme Court, and the Supreme Court said it was a violation of freedom of speech," Keenan told John Stamos on his podcast. "And they were all Republican judges, so it was really quite a surprise when they came back, unanimously throwing the injunction out. And so, that's where I made history in that regard."

Payday aside, Keenan was consistent in his claim that all he wanted to do was set the record straight. "The publicity stunt still hung over Frank Jr. and still bothered me," he said on the Stamos podcast. "I wanted to emphasize the facts. Emphasize how the publicity stunt story got started, about Junior being very brave, and about all the other things. I wanted to set the record straight on."

The result from Columbia, a 2003 made-for-cable movie for the Showtime channel, was hardly factual and barely entertaining. *Stealing Sinatra*, described as a "semi-dark comedy," starred David Arquette as Keenan, Thomas Ian Nicholas as Sinatra, Jr., William H. Macy as Irwin, and Ryan Browning as Amsler. It was barely watched and barely reviewed, save a few lines in *New York* magazine that read, "This project just sort of ambles along between the ears, behind the eyes, to nowhere much."

The Swinging 1960s

Frank was tremendously busy after the kidnapping and throughout the 1960s, with the Dorsey band and with solo projects. Some of those activities included the 1965 recording of *Young Love for Sale*, released on his father's Reprise label; appearances on television's *Password* the same year; a supporting role in the 1966 film *A Man Called Adam*; a 1967 guest shot with sister Nancy on *The Smothers Brothers Comedy Hour*; a 1969 television special for Monsanto called *Frank Sinatra, Jr., with Family and Friends* (friends included sister Nancy, Sammy Davis, Jr., Jack E. Leonard, Jack Benny, and a surprise visit from Pop); and a couple of other interesting film projects. And on January 12, 1967, the worldwide press announced the engagement of Frank to a Pamela Peterson, a one-time airline stewardess from Trenton, New Jersey. According to the photo caption that went out over the Associated Press wire, Frank met Peterson while flying to a nightclub job. The engagement lasted about a year, and Peterson's name and the engagement never came up again.

It was important to let the media and the public at large know that Frank's career was not affected by the kidnapping mess, that life was good and was going on as usual. In fact, as a part of his latter-day press kit, his hectic 1964 schedule was highlighted. In part, it read, "In 1964, Frank worked 345 days in the US and overseas, interrupting his schedule of personal appearances only for courtroom appearances at which he served as a witness for both the prosecution and the defense. 1965 was even busier. He worked 358 days out of 365." As Frank Jr. commented in that press kit, "A famous father means that in order to prove yourself, you have to work three times harder than the guy who comes in off the street with a song to sing."

There's no doubt that Tino Barzie was working overtime on behalf of his prized client. He was a hustler, that's for sure.

Tino Barzie, born Caesar Zottini, was an old-time showman whose roots in the swing era predated his connection with the "new" Dorsey band and Frank Sinatra, Jr. Originally, he played clarinet in some grade "B" swing bands like Johnny Long's and Tex Beneke's, before getting involved in the business affairs of the Dorsey band.

He was instrumental in reuniting the always-feuding brothers, Tommy and Jimmy Dorsey, who came together in 1950 after some fifteen years apart as leaders of their own bands. Barzie was also managing the Tommy Dorsey "ghost band" that continued under the leadership of others since Dorsey's 1956 passing. He was also instrumental in bringing Frank to that band, so it was natural that he would latch onto Frank as his manager.

Andrea Kauffman spent hours with him during the time she was representing Steve Lippia and talked to him about the years he managed Frank. "Barzie would probably do the right thing for Frank, though it may have been illegal," she said with a chuckle. She went on to say,

> A straight commission from Frank's jobs wouldn't have been enough to keep Tino going in the manner he wanted to become accustomed to. Tino would collect the performance fee from the buyer, take his "cut," which far exceeded a 10 percent or 15 percent commission, pay all the musicians, and then pay Frank. Very often, his "cut" was more than Frank made for the date. For example, he would give Frank $250 and then put $500 in his own pocket. And there wasn't that much money coming in. When Tino had to explain himself to Frank's accountant, Sonny Golden, Sonny said, "This isn't adding up." Frank was walking home with $250 a week while he was on the road, and Tino was putting $500 in his pocket every week, whether he was on the road or not. So, Frank had to go into his personal money to live on the road from day to day. Something was wrong there. What was wrong was that Tino was taking care of Tino.
>
> Tino operated on the fringes of what was reputable, and after they broke up, Frankie was known to say more than once, referring to Barzie's heavy aftershave, that he could "smell him before he saw him."

In 1970, Barzie and two others were indicted by a federal jury on the charge of conspiracy to use stolen credit cards to purchase thousands of dollars worth of airline tickets. The tickets, Barzie said, were used to fly Sinatra's troupe to various engagements. Barzie would purchase the tickets for half off from Jimmy Poppo (a.k.a. Vincent Tortora), a convicted receiver of stolen goods. Barzie would then reimburse himself, from his own Tin-Bar Amusement Corporation, for the full amount of the tickets.

He could have been sentenced to years in prison, but his sentence was suspended. He continued managing Frank and, in the years to come, became one of the first of the big-time sports agents. At one point, he claimed to have managed eighty major- and minor-league baseball players. Barzie's last client of note was Pia Zadora, whom he put into a couple of films he produced, notably a real dog titled *Voyage of the Rock Aliens*. The best review of the film came from a customer called "Adam E," who bought the movie on DVD and could only comment, "Frikking mental! That's what this film is!"

When Frank and the Dorsey band returned from the 1964 international tour, Barzie and Frank thought it was finally time to go into the recording studio. Frank's first recorded effort, *Young Love for Sale*, was produced by Sonny Burke and released in 1965 on the Reprise label. Sam Donahue led the orchestra in a dozen standards. Four of the songs, "I Only Have Eyes for You," "In the Still of the Night," "From This Moment On," and "Too Close for Comfort," were recorded commercially by the senior Sinatra.

It was a good first effort. Vocally, his style was not yet fully formed, and it's clear that Frank's range was limited. His rhythmically jazz-tinged phrasing was in place, though the reading of the lyrics doesn't go much below the surface. All in all, it was good fun, and Reprise even tried to go the "teen idol" route by promoting the LP in tandem with a Scopitone film short that featured Frank singing and cavorting around a swimming pool with a bunch of bikini-clad young lovelies. These Scopitone shorts, much like the 1940s Soundies film shorts, were early versions of the MTV music video, though the Scopitones were played mainly on specially built juke boxes placed in taverns, restaurants, and other public locations. *Young Love for Sale* was the first and last Frank Jr. album ever released on Reprise.

Two years later, RCA took a chance on Frank and released three pop-oriented singles aimed at the teen market. Titles of the 45 rpm recordings were "Shadows on a Foggy Day," "Building with a Steeple," and Gordon Lightfoot's "I Want to Hear It From You." None were memorable, and none sold well. In his latter-day shows, Frank would joke about some of these ridiculous song titles, as well as the quality of the material he was given to sing back then, particularly "Shadows on a Foggy Day."

On the motion-picture front, Frank's early involvement in films ranged from the ultraridiculous to the almost sublime.

The release of the first and last movie he scored was in 1965, though he wished that people would have forgotten it. *The Beach Girl and the Monster*, also known as *Monster from the Surf*, was as lousy as the titles suggest, but given that one of Frank's earliest ambitions was to compose film soundtracks, he at least managed to get that out of his system.

In 2015, Fiona Shepherd, a reporter working for the Scottish newspaper the *Scotsman*, dug up the film, which had Frank's name on it, on video. Frank told Shepherd,

> It's the movie you wouldn't want to watch. It was hackneyed, about this terrible sea monster that comes out of the ocean and molests all the young girls in their bikini bathing suits. Then the hero comes along, kills the sea monster, and then he molests all the young girls in their bikini bathing suits. Some video company found this terrible low-budgeted teenage movie about ten or fifteen years ago. I went to a store that was selling it and said, "You'd better be nice to me or I'm going to chain you all to chairs and force you to watch this movie, which is cruel and unjust punishment."

A Man Called Adam, from 1966, was something else entirely. While not a great film by any means, it was innovative for the time and did break some new ground. Directed by Leo Penn and starring Sammy Davis, Jr., as a self-destructive jazz trumpeter, Frank was featured in a supporting role as the trumpet student of none other than Louis Armstrong, in a rare and effective dramatic role. Bosley Crowther bent over backward to be kind to the film in his 1966 *New York Times* review. "The picture fails," wrote Crowther, "although it tries hard and, in some ways, admirably. Almost as provocative as the theme—a king trumpeter's decline—is the heartening fact that the movie not only stars a Negro artist but also has both Negro and white players in key roles, another rarity. Produced by the star's new movie company, with Ike Jones and Jim Waters as co-producers, this Embassy Pictures presentation rates credit for pluck." The soundtrack, composed by Benny Carter and featuring trumpeter Nat Adderley (who ghosted Sammy Davis, Jr.'s trumpet playing) was superb, and the acting by Cicely Tyson and Ossie Davis was impressive. Frank's notices were fair to good. As an actor, he improved with age.

Frank and his sister Nancy appeared on *The Smothers Brothers Comedy Hour* in 1967. They sang "Something Stupid" together. Their performance of it was charming, but they never did it again. The original, 1967, recording featured Nancy singing with her father and managed to break out as a worldwide hit. It miraculously topped the *Billboard* "Top 100" chart and stayed there for four weeks. It spent nine weeks on *Billboard*'s "Easy Listening" charts and reached number 1 on the *Cashbox* "Top 100" chart. Though nominated for a Grammy that year, it lost to "Up, Up and Away" by the Fifth Dimension.

Years later, in 2003, as Andrea Kauffman remembered, Frank Jr. and Nancy had a date in Budapest for Reinhart Trucking. Kauffman said,

> It was for a lot of money, and it's the only time we ever did a "Frank and Nancy" show. Frank Reinhart, who booked us, wanted to get together with me. "I want them to do 'Something Stupid' together," he said to me.
>
> I said, "Please review our contract. That will not happen. You're paying for Frank Sinatra, Jr., and you're paying for Nancy Sinatra. It's like paying for any opening act, meaning Nancy, and nowhere does it say in the contract that the star has to sing with the opening act?"
>
> He said, "Will you at least ask Frank?" I told him I'd be happy to. Frank came down to the hotel coffee shop but just stood there at the table. He saw the contracts spread out and asked, "What are all these papers?" I told him I just needed to pull out the contract to go over something.
>
> I asked him, "Is there any song that the two of you would sing together?"
>
> Frank said, "No." Not anything sarcastic or mean. He just looked at Frank Reinhart and said, "No." Then he turned around and left. From

> my point of view, if that were ever going to happen, do you think that the first time that would happen would be in Budapest? I can assure you, it would have happened on every Las Vegas and Atlantic City stage that there is. Then, the following night, we went to a Hungarian restaurant together. We're all sitting around, and whoever was sitting next to Nancy got up. Frank Reinhart sat next to her and tried to talk her into singing with Frankie. She told him, "Whatever you want." He said that Frankie doesn't want to do it. She asked, "Oh, you've already spoken to him? Well, then what he says goes." Afterwards, she asked me, "What does he have against doing a song with me?" I told her he wouldn't do it because he didn't want to be his father. They did nothing together on stage. When he came on stage, he could have said, "I hope you enjoyed Nancy, my sister." But he said nothing. Remember that Frankie was the big attraction there. The Budapest audience only remembered Nancy from "Boots."

Throughout the 1960s, Barzie booked Frank on just about every variety show on the air, including those hosted by Jackie Gleason, Red Skelton, and Mike Douglas, and even on an early *Hullabaloo* telecast with Gary Crosby and the Dorsey band. On *Hullabaloo*, Frank sang "Everybody's Twistin'," a forgotten opus his father recorded in response to the twist dance craze.

He also appeared on the popular *Hollywood Palace* variety hour, and for the 1968 and 1969 summer seasons, Joey Heatherton and Frank cohosted what was called *Dean Martin Presents the Golddiggers.* This summer replacement program was important to Frank personally and professionally, and the fresh-faced Frankie and Joey even landed on the cover of the July 27, 1968, *TV Guide.*

The general format of the show was a celebration of the 1930s, which allowed the cohosts to sing, individually and together, pop songs from the decade, including "Ain't We Got Fun," "I Like the Likes of You," "Exactly Like You," and "Anything Goes." Comedy was provided by Paul Lynde, Stanley Myron Handleman, and the comedy duoof Skiles and Henderson. Typical production numbers included a spoof of the Charlie Chan mystery movies and a musical tribute to Shirley Temple.

In the *TV Guide* article within the magazine, written by Dwight Whitney, Frank took stock of his career to date:

> I've done *Ed Sullivan* and every panel there is. But the world hasn't exactly been breaking down my door. Not until I did that Dean Martin Christmas special with my father and sister, anyway. Then it happened. Greg Garrison, Dean Martin's producer, told me, "Hey kid, we need a guy for the summer show and you're it." I guess he thought the kid might be able to do something after all. Now I've got my own show with Joey Heatherton. Joey, she's terrific! This has been such a great step for me. You can't begin to know the feeling. Me, I have to prove my worth. Nancy, she's a pretty girl. My father, he wrote the book. He's a living legend and I have to learn to live with it.

Dwight Whitney also mentioned that Frank's one-time fiancée, Pamela Peterson, was in the room but that their engagement was called off. "The road is rough," Frank commented to Whitney, "but we're still friends."

The talented and versatile Heatherton was all over television in the 1960s, and her Las Vegas shows were always well attended. Frank and Joey were very close friends—Heatherton's extensive list of lovers included James Caan, Sonny Bono, and Warren Beatty, but not Frank—and he stuck by her when her career began to tank and when she dealt with a myriad of other personal problems in the 1970s. After Frank's passing, Joey Picuri, Frank's coproduction manager, said, "He definitely resonated with people he thought were maybe downtrodden or forgotten. Like Joey Heatherton. I knew her as a young kid on television with commercials and stuff, but the beauty thing is a temporary thing. Frank was so generous and so kind to her when she was older because he knew she wasn't getting any gigs."

Meet Me in Las Vegas

The arrival of the Beatles in 1964 forever changed the landscape of the music industry. Julius LaRosa told this book's coauthor, Bruce Klauber, "We used to be thrilled if we could fill a four-hundred-seat showroom. But after the Beatles came along, if you couldn't fill a ten-thousand-seat arena, you were nothing!" By the late 1960s, the Las Vegas showrooms and lounges were becoming refuges for performers such as Tony Bennett, Steve and Eydie, Jack Jones, Peggy Lee, and the like. Many had lost or would lose major-label record contracts, and nightclubs that could afford a Bennett or Peggy Lee were closing. The *Billboard* "Top 100" chart for 1969 was filled with names such as the Rolling Stones, the Temptations, Sly and the Family Stone, Neil Diamond, and Three Dog Night. Only Sammy Davis, Jr., Henry Mancini, and a one-time giant on the comeback trail, Elvis Presley, managed to make the list that year. Even Frank Sinatra was recording soft rock covers in search of a hit.

For Middle America, Las Vegas was still cool, and there were lucrative opportunities for the old guard in the main showrooms and lounges of Las Vegas. The Mary Kaye Trio came to the lounge of the Last Frontier Hotel and Casino in Vegas in 1953, and the Louis Prima/Keely Smith group landed in the lounge of the Sahara the following year. Those two groups were responsible for the Vegas lounge concept as we know it today. The lounges were havens for performers on their way up and, in some cases, on the way down. Don Rickles and Shecky Greene started in the lounges, and Buddy Greco found a home in the lounges for decades.

Frank Sinatra, Jr., had worked Vegas from time to time with the Dorsey band. His first documented appearance there was in the Driftwood Lounge of the Flamingo Hotel in late 1962. As a solo act in the late 1960s, backed by an octet led by trombonist Larry O'Brien, he found himself working there more and more often. Frank would work with O'Brien and the eight-piece group until the late 1970s.

The 1969 CBS television special for Monsanto, formally titled *Frank Sinatra, Jr., with Family and Friends*, was important for several reasons. As it was filmed in the lounge of the Frontier in Vegas, it served as a national announcement that Frank Sinatra, Jr., was now entertaining regularly in Sin City. And it attracted a national sponsor in the Monsanto Company as well, though it certainly had to help that among Frank's "friends" in the special were Jack Benny, Sammy Davis, Jr., sister Nancy, Jack E. Leonard, Arte Johnson, and "surprise guest" Frank Sinatra. In the rare footage that exists—the entire program is in the collection of the Paley Center for Media in New York City—Frank announced that he was on the stage of the Frontier's lounge, "where anything can happen." He's quick and agile with the wisecracks as well, especially when he spies his dad in the audience. "Is he coming up here?" Frank says, as his father mounts the stage and joins his son in a swinging and sometimes funny version of "All or Nothing at All." As a whole, the program was basically an advertisement for Vegas. There are film clips of various lounge acts, as well as footage of the nearby Nellis Air Force Base, Valley Fire State Park, and Hoover Damn.

The Vegas Chamber of Commerce was well aware of how important this program was to tourism. Not long after its airing, Frank was surprised onstage with a trophy, presented by Frontier's administrative director, Keith Hanna. Then Vegas mayor pro-tem Hank Thornley stepped forward to read a proclamation of appreciation from the Vegas community, commending Frank Jr. for the television special. Not long after, he became a Las Vegas fixture. When talk-show host Merv Griffin aired a show that emanated live from Caesars Palace in Vegas at that time, Frank Jr. was on the guest list along with Zsa Zsa Gabor and comic Norm Crosby.

Wild about Harry

Bandleader Harry James, still a major name in the business and a favorite of the Vegas high rollers in the 1970s—James himself was an inveterate gambler—had been a Flamingo lounge regular since the late 1950s. The James Band and Frank Jr. alternated in the Flamingo's lounge in the late 1960s, but by 1970, the James/Frank Jr. package, with the addition of veteran comic Phil Harris, moved to the Frontier. The show, with the hilarious and hard-drinking Harris billed first and Frank billed third, was so effective in terms of bringing in the high rollers that the Frontier signed the three to a sixteen-week-per-year contract.

Frank loved Phil Harris, often said he was the funniest man he ever worked with, and even included some Harris tunes, like "Watermelon Wine," in his own shows. Harris lived in a trailer parked at the rear of the stage and cooked for Harry, Frank, and the musicians in the band.

Harry James was a big influence as well. Frank told author Peter Levinson, in Levinson's biography of James, "That Harry had the best taste. He would hire different orchestrators to write his music, and they changed with the times, decade by decade."

A highlight of the Vegas show was "Autumn Serenade," a song written by Frank's friend Vic Foquet at Frank's request, as a Sinatra/James feature. "For once he had something to play that was lovely," Frank told Levinson. "Harry just broke my heart with it. The first time we performed it, people stood up in the audience. For the rest of the engagement, we did the tune. Harry smiled at me just a little bit paternally because of the fact that he remembered once before when he had another young singer . . . well actually many young singers."

Drummer Les DeMerle at twenty-four years old was already a jazz veteran when he joined the James band at the beginning of the Frontier engagement.

"By the time I got with Harry, he was pretty much playing his hits," said DeMerle, who still works frequently with his own big band and small groups in the Amelia Island area. He went on to say,

> When I joined, he had a sixteen-week contract at the Frontier. It was broken up to, like, three or four weeks at a time. The package was with us, Phil Harris, and Frank Jr., and we did that up until about 1976. The way the show ran was, Phil Harris got top billing, with Harry James Orchestra second, and special guest, Frank Sinatra, Jr. We would open with Harry's band and play a few instrumentals, maybe with "Cherokee" as a drum feature. Then we'd bring on Phil Harris with his tune "Old Man Time," which he wrote. Then he would do all his famous tunes like "The Dark Town Poker Club," and "Smoke! Smoke! Smoke! (That Cigarette)." Phil was a ball. Then we'd bring on Frank, and he would do some of his dad's hits.
>
> To be honest with you, Junior was a little bit stiff in those days. He was very serious when you got to know him. He wasn't like his dad, with a Rat Pack vibe. He was young, but so was I. I was young and cocky. He was young and confident. Harry and Phil, because they knew the old man so well, would pull that Vegas humor with him. For instance, Frank would be doing a ballad, singing "I love you," and Phil, off stage would say, "Does a snake have hips?," and that would take him out. He loved to mess with Junior. But he was a gentleman. He always dressed meticulously. And he always liked to watch movies. He'd invite the band up to his suite—the whole band—and then show a movie.
>
> This package was tremendously popular. First of all, you had all the different generations. Harry James and Phil Harris were best friends, so they had the same kind of chemistry that Frank Sinatra and Dean Martin had. Every show was completely different, and the people knew that. Harry was loose. He would do comedy with Phil, and these guys drank constantly. They would have four or five drinks during the show! They would take a full glass of vodka and down it on the stage. Then

Frank Jr. would come on, straight as an arrow, with a Coca-Cola. They pounced on it, man! It ended around 1976, mainly because Phil didn't want to work anymore. That really bugged Harry. Phil wanted to only do benefits. That's when the James band hit the road.

Film and Television Miscellany

In 1970, Frank spent several months in Beppu, Japan, filming *The Walking Major*, a Japanese production that received little stateside distribution. Starring Dale Robertson, Dina Merrill, Linda Purl (in her first screen appearance), and several well-known Japanese actors, including Toshiro Mifune, "The Walking Major" received a Golden Globe nomination for Best English Language Foreign Film. Frank, third billed, plays Jimmy Dixon, a private in a US Army platoon led by army captain Dale Robertson. The platoon walks the length of Japan, back and forth, in order to raise funds to rebuild an orphanage. Suspicious of Robertson's motives, a Japanese newsman traces the captain's background until he discovers the motive behind this long walk. Leisurely paced with beautifully photographed scenery, Frank does very well as the wise-cracking private and even gets to sing two very credible blues choruses .

During the Vegas residencies, Frank also participated in two interesting television projects. The impressive one, an early 1970s pilot for CBS titled *Swing*, never aired. The oddity, something titled *Once upon a Tour*, did. *Swing* featured Frank, the Harry James big band, and the dance troupe Swing. Mainly a stroll down memory lane, with James performing his hits and Frank singing songs such as "(I've Got a Gal in) Kalamazoo," it was nonetheless an entertaining half hour that never made it to the air.

Once Upon a Tour, filmed in 1972, starred Dora Hall, something of a footnote in show-business history. Hall, who had a modicum of singing and dancing talent, married Leo Hulseman, CEO of the Solo Cup Company. Aware that his wife had show-business aspirations, Hulseman bankrolled a number of her recordings, which he included as giveaways with Solo Cup purchases. But Hall wanted more. She wanted to be on television as the center of an all-star variety show. Hulseman, who also owned a television studio in Culver City, California, made it a reality. As guests, he hired Rosie Greer, folk/rocker Oliver, impressionist Rich Little, and direct from Las Vegas, Phil Harris and Frank Jr. The thread of the thing was Hall's bus trip to Hollywood from the boondocks in search of stardom. Frank's rendition of the Turtles' "Happy Together" was okay. He wasn't in top form. Hulseman syndicated the project to television stations that had time slots to fill. The commercials were mostly pitches for various types of Solo Cups.

On the Road Again

Opportunities for Frank in Vegas and elsewhere were drying up, as they were for most middle-of-the-road acts. He wanted to work, and given the Sinatra name, there were always opportunities. It helped to have something to promote, especially a new recording, and throughout the 1970s, he went into the recording studio several times. *Spice*, released in 1971 on Daybreak Records, was highlighted by the title tune, a Frank Jr. original that he would perform throughout his career. The following year and on the same label was *His Way*, arranged and conducted by Nelson Riddle. *It's Alright*, a Churchill release, came along in 1977.

Spice, produced by Sonny Burke and with several charts by Nelson Riddle played by an augmented Larry O'Brien Octet, is peppered with some Frank Jr. originals such as "Black Night," various covers that include "Everybody's Talkin'" and "We've Only Just Begun," and a few standards. Only "Love Is Here to Stay" was recorded by his father. "Black Night" was a Riddle chart for this haunting song, later used as the title number to Rick Alverson's film of the same name. Frank told Bruce Klauber that his father walked into the recording studio while this was being recorded and was startled not only by the chart but also by the fact that his son had written the song. Overall, *Spice* was an ambitious project, and shows a technically and emotionally evolving singer, capable of conveying any mood. But it was evident that the twenty-seven-year-old Frank was still searching for musical direction.

The *His Way* project from the following year contains only one Frank original, "What Were You Thinking?," with the remainder made up of semi-obscure compositions by Johnny Mercer and Anthony Newley and Leslie Bricusse. The covers were Carole King's "It's Too Late" and the Marilyn Bergman/Michel Legrand theme from *Summer of '42*. It's possible that the material for *His Way* was recorded at the same time as the songs on *Spice*.

It's Alright was quite a departure. This was Frank's foray into country music, with pared-down instrumental accompaniment that included pedal steel guitar and harmonica and vocal backing from the Lea Jane Singers. This may have been Tino Barzie's idea, as he is listed as executive producer. It was a good try, and Frank certainly sounds sincere, particularly when strings are added on "The Best I Ever Had." It's just not his genre, though he did keep some of these songs in his repertoire for years to come.

In Vegas with James and Harris, he had to sing songs made famous by his father lest he risk the wrath of hecklers who came to hear a man whose last name was Sinatra. On the road, however, his shows were anything but "Frank Sinatra's greatest hits."

Alto saxophonist Terry Anthony joined Frank's accompanying group in 1975 and would become one of Frank's few close friends. He stayed until Frank's passing. Anthony recalled,

> A few weeks after I got off the Glenn Miller band, I started with Frank Jr. and the octet. Not long after that, Bob Chmel joined on drums and stayed with Frank until the end. When I came on, Frank would do "All or Nothing at All," and that was the one tune by his dad that he would play in the show. And if we had to do two shows in a night, sometimes he wouldn't even do a Sinatra tune. If he did, it would be some number you never heard of before. We were working a lot. A lot. Because of his name alone, people wanted to see him. We had good houses. They knew it was going to be a Sinatra. He would tell the audience, "My name is Frank Sinatra, Jr. I'm not *the* Frank Sinatra. That music is done by him and he's out there working. If you really want to hear that, I'll tell you that he's the best one to do it, and he sounds great. I love him, but you should hear him do it. I'm not going to do it." And the whole time his father was alive, he wouldn't.

Paul Rostock, a strong, reliable and inventive bassist, was also there at that time. He said,

> I came on in 1978 when I was twenty-one. I was in the house band at the Mount Airy Lodge in the Pocono Mountains. The bandleader at Mount Airy was friends with Larry O'Brien, who was leading the octet. Frank wasn't doing the Vegas lounges anymore. His manager was Tino Barzie, who was a whirlwind of activity when it came to booking. My first itinerary was four months of one nighters. He didn't have the Vegas thing anymore, so he was just booking dates all over the country. We were everywhere. Around the fall of 1978, they just shut down the octet. He just went back to Los Angeles and would do an occasional date here and there.
>
> He wasn't doing a lot of his father's material then, maybe just "All or Nothing at All." If we did two Sinatra songs in a show, that would be it. By the fall, I think Frank was burned out. He was used to doing the Vegas thing, and the road thing was tough, and there were some things on the band he wasn't happy with. He just decided he needed a change.

It may have been at Tino Barzie's urging or just Frank's need for a change, but in the late 1970s, Frank was again on television, this time as an actor.

Jack Webb, creator of *Dragnet* on radio and television, was a major jazz fan and big-band aficionado. He was married to the sultry, jazz-oriented singer Julie London, and he would use jazz singers and players in his projects whenever he could, such as the 1955 film he directed and starred in, *Pete Kelly's Blues*, which costarred Peggy Lee and Ella Fitzgerald. And you never knew who would show up on Webb's television revival of *Dragnet*, which ran from 1967 to 1970. Bobby Troup, the singer and composer who later married Julie London after she divorced Webb, was a regular, as was Bing Crosby's son, Gary. Trumpeter Jack Sheldon showed up often, and even big-band singer Dick Haymes was booked for a guest spot.

Webb and Frank Jr. were made for each other. They both loved jazz, hated hippies and the drug culture, and were devotees of law enforcement and the military. The military became something of an obsession with Frank, and he sometimes fancied himself to be a military veteran. Andrea Kauffman said,

> I think he was fixated on the discipline and power of the military. But Frank was not physically strong. He never hunted; he never fished. His hands were soft. He once told me a story very early on about a time when he was in the Marines—and he was never in the Marines—and they gave every Marine a bucket of sand. The story was that you had to let your fingernails grow, and you had to continually put your hands in and out of the bucket of sand to sharpen your fingernails so they could be used as a weapon. It was really a tall tale. He was never in the Marines or any branch of the service. But he'd try to impress women with that. He'd never try to pull it on a guy, only women.

Still, Webb saw something in Frank, and when the *Dragnet* spinoff, *Adam-12* took off, he called both Frank and sister Tina to guest in small roles in an episode called "The Late Baby" that aired in the fall of 1972. Webb was impressed and saw star quality in Frank. In 1974, Frank filmed a two-part series for *Adam-12*, titled "A Clinic on Eighteenth Street." Frank starred as detective Gino Bardi, obviously a nod to manager Tino Barzie, who was investigating a quack doctor responsible for the death of a patient due to diabetic shock. Webb envisioned the two parter as a television pilot for an *Adam-12* spinoff. After all, the successful *Adam-12* was a *Dragnet* spinoff. Perhaps, Webb thought lightning would strike twice, especially with a young, sincere, and good-looking chap as the star. For Frank, it would have been a much-needed respite from the road, as well as the possible start of a new, second career. Sadly, the pilot did not sell as a series.

Kent McCord co-starred as Officer Jim Reed in the series, which ran from 1968 to 1975 and is still popular in syndication today. McCord looked back on the whole experience fondly. "The premise of *Adam-12* was simple," McCord explained.

> It was two guys in a black and white in the streets of Los Angeles, doing what two guys in a black and white in the streets of Los Angeles would do. Period. We weren't trying to solve the social ills of the world. I can't tell you how much fun it was to have people like Frankie and Gary Crosby on it. People loved coming on it. Jack Webb loved big-band music. He loved Frank Sr., he loved Frankie, and he loved the family. I think he identified with them.

> Frankie did a two-part series, *Clinic on Eighteenth Street*, that Jack Webb was going to use as a pilot. Ed Nelson and Sharon Gless were also in it. It didn't take off. The problem with his career, I think, was Frankie was too much of a chip off the old block. But what else could he be? But he wasn't given credit for using his own talent to achieve what he wanted to do. His father didn't push Frankie into doing that. Or Nancy. They decided they wanted to do that. Tina went a different way.
>
> He was fun to be around and a hell of an entertainer. My wife and I were in New York City for something, and we went up to the Rainbow Room to see him perform. That was the first time I'd ever seen him perform. What a performance! I've never forgotten it.

Frank came away from the experience with a great deal of respect for Jack Webb. Andrea Kauffman and several others in the Sinatra retinue said that Webb was Frank's idol. Indeed, Frank told Kauffman that he wanted to be buried next to Jack Webb.

The next year, Frank Jr. guest starred on the ultrapopular *The Love Boat* series. The episode broadcast on October 27, 1979, had a Halloween theme, with Melissa Sue Anderson, of *Little House on the Prairie* fame, dressed up as Cinderella. Prince Charming, who serenaded Cinderella with a version of "Witchcraft," was Frank Sinatra, Jr. He also sang "Once Upon a Time," which moved Anderson to say, "Boy can he sing."

The two became close platonic friends, wrote Anderson in her 2010 book, *The Way I See It: A Look Back at My Life on Little House*. The relationship eventually turned romantic. Frank was thirty-three, and at the time of their meeting, Anderson was seventeen. Anderson was quick to say that they didn't start dating until two years later.

The relationship was serious, and as a measure of that seriousness, she was able get Frank to open his ears to contemporary rock, a genre he had pooh-poohed for years. Guitarist Dan McIntyre, who was with Frank in the 1970s and for a time in the 1980s, said that Anderson actually "got him to listen to rock. He got into Rupert Holmes, and that's when we started doing stuff like 'The People That You Never Get to Love' and that type of stuff. She was a big part of him stretching out musically. I was really shocked when he started doing that stuff. I stayed at his house for several weeks at that time, and we rehearsed that music. They were a couple, and they were definitely having a good time."

Frank took her home to meet the family, which included a few dinners with his mother, Tina, and Nancy. The initial attraction, Anderson said, was that Frank "was willing to listen to me instead of treating me like a kid." By 1981, they were seeing each other exclusively. The relationship eventually cooled. In 1990, Anderson married producer/writer Michael Sloan.

Given that the television pilot and acting in general didn't work out in a big way, there was no other choice than to go back on the road. Maybe new management could make a difference, so Frank made a change. He hired a Tino Barzie colleague, Vincent Carbone, to handle him. Carbone was a Julliard graduate who played saxophone in Glenn Miller's army air force band in the 1940s and later gravitated toward the business end of big-band management. In the 1950s, he joined Barzie as one of the managers of the reconstituted Tommy and Jimmy Dorsey big band.

Carbone was not as aggressive as Barzie. Andrea Kauffman got close to Carbone when she became involved in Frank's management in 1985. "Carbone was on retainer," she said. "And," she added, "when you're on retainer, you don't have to work hard." Carbone did scare up dates, some good, some lousy. He had a long and good run at the Fairmont Hotel in Dallas in June 1984. After Dallas, it was on to Washington, DC. The DC visit was memorable for several reasons.

Carbone teamed up with Tony Renaud, a Washington, DC-based radio executive who later became an actor and producer, to present Frank at the Capitol Hill Hyatt House in DC. The hotel had no showroom, but instead, the Hyatt staff converted a large banquet room into what looked remarkably like a large nightclub. During the run, Frank got a phone call from the White House. Nancy Reagan wanted to have a meeting with him.

Andrea Kauffman vividly recalled the conversation she had with Frank about this get-together. Frank told Kauffman that the First Family was worried about his father. "She said my father was giving away everything he had to his wife, Barbara, and that this lavishness, which included a gift of a Learjet, could only lead to my father's ruin," Frank told Kauffman. Frank had a hard time at first believing this, though he did come to believe that, in his words, "the trouble was very real." Not only was he worried about his father, but, as he said, "I was more worried about what the future might hold for him."

The Washington shows went well and were well attended, but the following week, Frank was stuck performing at the Seipsville Hotel in Easton, Pennsylvania.

Frank's set list from Seipsville on the night of July 29, 1984, was a good example of the type of show he was putting on in those days and shows why he was working joints like the Seipsville Hotel. The ten-song set list, not counting an overture and encores, featured songs such as "One Mint Julep," "Until the Real Thing Comes Along," "Pete Kelly's Blues" (a bow to the Jack Webb film of the same name), something called "Too Old, Too Mean," and "The Curly Shuffle," which he continued to perform, much to the band's and management's chagrin, for years to come. Only two songs—"That's Life" and "Luck Be a Lady"—had anything to do with his father.

I'll Never Smile Again

When he came off the road in the late 1970s, he just wasn't the same. He wasn't working a lot. He had aged, put on some weight, and was no longer the wise-cracking junior swinger with the pompadour and the pinkie ring. There were fewer and fewer places out there booking the type of music sung by Frank Sinatra, Jr. Now that he didn't have his road family at the ready, perhaps he saw this break as a chance to reconnect with his real family and/or try to finally get their acceptance and approval.

That didn't seem to be working, either.

Michele Martin, who is the daughter of the famed agent Hershey Martin of the William Morris Agency, knew Frank from the time she was four years old. She was privy to a lot of the family goings-on through the years, and not all of them were pleasant. Martin explained.

> He really had a rough time with his father and with his family. It hurt him. There was a situation where his mother was so rude to him and diminished him in front of me and in front of Steve Bailey, who was his contractor, I turned around and said to Steve, "Okay, we're walking away." I just couldn't stand to see what she was doing to him, and what both of his parents did to him. I mean, his father was not a nice person. He wasn't nice to him. And all Frank wanted was to make his dad happy, to make him love him. And he didn't feel loved. I think that maybe as time went by and he started to grow up and get to know himself better,

> he realized that he wasn't loved the way he needed to be. He reached out to a lot of people for love.

Andrea Kauffman recalled that Frank didn't talk to his father very often: "I know that Sinatra put his son down publicly several times. I asked him whether he asked his father about some of the negative things he was saying. He said, 'No. You're the only one who can get away with that.' The old man would just say that he had to get a thicker skin. I asked Frankie if he wished things were different. He said, 'I wouldn't be who I am if they were.' That was his way of saying, 'I can't change it.' Were they close? Not like Nancy and Tina were."

Kauffman said, "His mother wasn't much help." Nancy Sr. told me, "Frankie was born a hundred years too late." I said, "The person he's become is because of you and his father, not because of when he was born. No! You two did this. You guys screwed him up."

Still, Kauffman characterized his mother as

> the most underrated woman I have ever met. Her strength was admirable. I'm not saying she was right because I don't like the way she handled Frank. She was very hard on him. Big Frank was rarely around. According to Frankie, she wasn't the kind of mother who would say, if he did something wrong, "Wait till your father comes home." She handled it.
>
> Neither parent wanted Frankie to go into show business. They didn't want it for him because they knew what a struggle it would be. They knew he was going to be compared to his father constantly and would be living under a huge shadow and a rock that was too heavy to lift. To me, it felt like they were truly protecting him. Unfortunately, they didn't know how to express that without it feeling cruel to him. How that translated to him, was that he didn't have the talent. So he lived with self-doubt his entire life and never once was truly uplifted or celebrated by his parents in any way.
>
> Big Nancy never approved of his choice of women. Frank's one and only marriage to Cynthia was met with complete contempt. Nancy Jr. was civil, but Nancy Sr. didn't talk to Frankie for two years. I come from a very close-knit family, so this broke my heart. And Frank always sought his mother's love and approval, so I'm sure it broke his. Big Nancy was so tough on him; unreasonably so. I don't think that his

mother and father understood that by not supporting his personal life or career, he interpreted it believing he wasn't good enough to be loved or talented enough to be successful. He certainly wasn't loved enough.

As for support from his sisters, said Kauffman,

Nobody has a good relationship with Tina unless she lets you. She thought her big brother was a big lump of nothing important. I want to say that I never saw any kindness from Tina to Frankie. No affection, kindness, admiration, or support. Though he had many relationships that went nowhere, there was never a shortage of female companionship on the road. This is how he tried to find closeness and love but failed.

Even though he was close with Nancy Jr., she was always criticizing his singing. We were in the recording studio, and she said to me, "He's got to round off that hard *R* sound when he sings." She started to hound him about it. And the more she hounded him, the more he shut down. End of session. The next day, she brought her mother. Nancy Sr. started on him about how he was singing. "Frankie, you shouldn't sing like that," she would say. "You sound like you're singing through your nose. Listen to your sister." Really? What did they know? The album was *That Face!*, and it was wonderful!

Karen Carbone Anthony, wife of Frank's saxophonist, Terry Anthony, believed that Frank

had a great disdain for women. The more they liked him, the less he liked them. What I saw was a guy who was no longer young and beautiful, but he was an older, good-looking guy who dressed well, had a well-spoken manner, a lovely vocabulary, which he used impressively, and was honestly and truly in love with his art. When Frank sang, he became a different person. His interpretations were so meaningful to him that it was hard for a female—or anybody—not to get a little soft-hearted.

It was, "Oh . . . that's just so real. Look at him; he's crying." He was so in touch with his heart, and I think that women in general thought that the caring, the softness, and that gentleness that he could appear to have with his art would carry over to them. I've seen him cry in the middle of a song because the music moved him. That was part of his charm. He

> could be haughty, but underneath that was a man who could be saved. That's hard for a lot of women to pass up. When he had a relationship, they were never the ones who wanted to go away. I never saw anyone leave him.

"When Frankie first started touring with us, he had never married, and people would ask me if he was gay," recalled Tom Dreesen, the comedian who opened for Frank Sr. for fourteen years. "I said, 'Is he *gay*?' This guy would have three broads on the road. He'd have a girl on the second floor, a girl on the fifth floor, and a girl on the twelfth floor."

It's clear that out of all the women who didn't seem special, apparently one of them was, and it's quite possible that she was the reason Frank Jr. changed and soured so drastically. She evidently arrived on the scene sometime in the late 1970s, shortly before Frank left for Vegas.

Kauffman remembered,

> If you look at photos of Frank prior to the mid-1970s, most of them show him with a big smile that reached his eyes. If you look at photos after the incident that I'm about to describe, you'll see a difference in his entire persona. I'll even go as far as to say that on Facebook today, in the Sinatra groups, people will often comment and ask what happened that changed Frank Sinatra, Jr. Some speculate that it was the kidnapping. It was not. It was his father.
>
> I have no proof that the incident I'm about to tell you really happened. I only know the story Frankie told me many years ago. I've discussed this with a couple of close friends, but they won't corroborate the story for the book, even though Frankie told them the story too. Did it happen the way he told me it did? I have no way of knowing that. I do believe something dreadful happened to cause such a drastic change in his demeanor and personality. Do I know for certain that this was the very incident that did it? I do not. But it sure rings all the alarm bells and whistles as the incident that traumatized him even if he didn't understand what it would do to him in time.
>
> There was a woman Frankie was engaged to who was a showgirl in Las Vegas. I think her name was Vicki. At that point in his life, he was still that pompadoured guy with the cigarette and the pinky ring. To be very clear here, the kidnapping didn't seem to affect him in any other way than he was more cautious when he was traveling. He even had

swagger back then. I'm not sure of the year, but he was about twenty-six or twenty-seven, so this would have been around 1970 or 1971.

He told me he was very much in love with this girl and bought her a very expensive engagement ring even though his parents were adamantly against the engagement. Despite the fact Frankie was in love with this woman and seemed very happy, his father flat out didn't like the girl, and his mother didn't want him to marry a "showgirl." Frankie was always looking for his parents' approval and was not getting it. I believe this caused him to look for love in the wrong places.

Sinatra and Frankie were both working in Vegas. Sinatra called his son and said, "Let's have a bite to eat after my show." Frank told him to let himself in when he got up to the suite. He walked in looking for his father, calling out, "Pop . . . pop?" No answer, so he walked through the suite and into the bedroom. And there's Pop with Frankie's fiancé. His father's excuse was, "You wouldn't listen, so I had to show you."

I don't know what they were doing. Frankie never said if they were under the covers, sitting on the bed, or just standing and talking, but whatever he saw, it caused him to bleed out that night. I believe, with every fiber of my being, it was from that very moment that he'd never truly know happiness again or be able to trust again . . . EVER.

Career-wise, he was at a crossroads, and it seemed like he was just taking what little work came along. In 1979, he played a small role in a long-forgotten film called *Do It in the Dirt*. The following year, Frank appeared in the television movie *Police Story: Confessions of a Lady Cop*, and in 1982, he did a bit in the popular syndicated television series *Tales of the Unexpected*. *Do It in the Dirt*, a film about dirt biking, was an example of how far Frank's star had fallen. It is nearly impossible to find details about this low-budget exploitation project, except that it was produced by Stephen C. Apostolof, who was responsible for gems such as *Orgy of the Dead*, written by Ed Wood of *Plan Nine from Outer Space* fame.

Then there was the 1978 television commercial for the New York–based Lenny's Clam Bar Italian seafood chain. Wearing a large mustache that may or may not have been fake, Frank extolled the virtues of Lenny's menu items, including his favorite, "Italian lobster tail topped with shrimps." At the end of the spot, Lenny himself walked out to remind viewers, in a heavy Italian accent, to "mention Frank Jr. and get a free glass of wine."

While the entertainment landscape had changed, and Frank was demoralized by events in his personal life, it didn't help that his new manager was anything but aggressive. Looking back at the situation with Vinnie Carbone years later, Andrea Kauffman said that "Vinnie stopped fighting for his client's dream, and remember, Vinnie was on retainer and didn't have to work hard."

Of that period, Bob Chmel, Frank's drummer for almost forty years, commented, "He didn't do much during that period, until he came back with the five-piece group with (trumpeter) Buddy Childers. Until that time, he just never worked much."

Hank Cattaneo, Sinatra Sr.'s production manager and often record producer, was with the Sinatras for decades. He believed that Frank used this time to take stock, musically. "By the late 1970s, tastes were changing," he said, "but so was he. He was changing direction."

One direction he frequently considered was the musical long form. In 1976, Frank wrote "Over the Land," a fifteen-minute patriotic suite for symphonic orchestra and narrative, with a focus on the United States flag and America's experiences with the flag since the War of 1812. "Over the Land" would be resurrected and performed from time to time on tour years later, but it was performed publicly and for the first time in 1984. The occasion was the American Showcase Inaugural Gala at the White House for President George Bush. The suite was performed by the United States Air Force Symphony Orchestra, under the direction of Major James Bankhead. At this televised gala, Frank Sinatra, Jr., was introduced by his father:

> One of the most difficult things a performer has to face comes when he's asked to introduce a member of his own family. We all love our children and clearly want the best for them. However, when they choose to make their career in a profession that is very good to *you*, you have all kinds of emotions going at the same time. I mean to say that you think to yourself and say, "Is he really good, or do I just want to believe that he's good?" Will the audience accept him, or will they bring their own kind of prejudices into their judgment? But I'm about to introduce my son and namesake, Frank Sinatra, Jr., and all of those questions go right out of the window because I think he's terrific, and I think he's written a deeply felt piece of music for this occasion. The emotion I am feeling more at this moment is one of pride. Ladies and gentlemen, his own man, Frank Sinatra.

The Start of Something Big

Philadelphia native Andrea Kauffman's parents were both entertainers. Her mother was a dancer, part of a the Modernistic Maids, and her father, who made his living in the plumbing and heating wholesale supply business, played thirty-two instruments. "I watched them both so closely," remembers Kauffman. "It was in my genes. I loved it because it was such a happy part of my family's life. My mother loved to dance. Dad would play one of his favorite instruments, clarinet, during every family function that had a band. The band leaders all knew him. It was so wonderful."

Kauffman started in the business as a singer in the Anita O'Day/June Christy vein, but by her own admission, she wasn't capable of producing that sound. She decided on booking instead, with her goal being to open an agency that booked jazz acts. "And I was going to make sure they were paid well and not be taken advantage of anymore," she said. After some local success with Stan Lawrence Productions in the early 1980s, she began producing some shows and continued, "looking for that diamond in the rough." The first diamond in the rough she discovered was singer Dane Anthony. Anthony, who later became Kauffman's husband, was her first client. One client, however, wasn't going to make Kauffman a force at the shore.

She teamed up with Tropicana Entertainment Director Jim Martin, who was ready to leave the corporate world. The agency would be called Oreo Productions—"where the cream always rises to the top"—with the plan being for Kauffman to book acts such as Billy Daniels,

Morgana King, Frank D'Rone, Bobby Scott, Chris Connor, Johnnie Ray, Keely Smith, Buddy Greco, and Johnny Hartman. Martin's focus would be on Top 40 acts.

Kauffman said,

> I booked them all at Elaine's Lounge at the Golden Nugget. I think that's why Sinatra looked for me. He knew that I was the only jazz agent in town and that I booked many of his friends. There was nobody else. This is what I wanted to do, and nothing was going to stop me. This is who I wanted to be. At Elaine's, I'd sit down with entertainment director Frankie Randall and say, "This is who I've got."
>
> He'd say, "I could get them directly."
>
> I said, "But you didn't. I got them directly." My leverage was that I was bringing stuff in that was filling up the room. I didn't play the game, and I didn't take the nonsense.

With Jim Martin back in the corporate fold, Kauffman teamed with Mike Pedicin Jr. and Dan Mulhern to expand operations. The agency was booking acts such as Mel Tormé, George Shearing, and Lainie Kazan, as well as producing revue shows and cut-down Broadway shows perfect for the Atlantic City audience. It was a heady time.

Kauffman said, "Our reputation, particularly the integrity of the agency, was spreading. People were calling and saying, 'Please manage us.' I had offers on the table from the biggest agencies, asking me to come with them. They told me I'd make a fortune. I knew I wouldn't make a fortune, and I told them I didn't want to work for them. I don't have any regrets."

The scene at Elaine's Lounge in the mid-1980s was electrifying. Frank Sinatra, who had been performing at Atlantic City's Resorts International, had been wooed by the Golden Nugget's Steve Wynn to perform at his venue, and he appeared at the Nugget frequently. Kauffman's roster of lounge stars were all jockeying for a spot within Elaine's when Sinatra was working the main room upstairs. The hope was, of course, that Mr. S. and his entourage would come into the lounge after his show to enjoy whoever was on stage. Most of the time, whoever was on stage was an Andrea Kauffman client. On one evening, singer/guitarist Frank D'Rone was on stage, and Kauffman was in the audience to enjoy the show.

Sinatra and his group, which included Don Rickles, Red Buttons, and Jilly Rizzo, came into Elaine's through the rear entrance and took a seat at a large banquette at the rear of the room. Andrea Kauffman was summoned to join the Sinatra party.

Kauffman remembers the scene vividly:

> Frank Sinatra asked me to book his son. I told him that I hadn't seen Frankie since 1967. I was happy and confident enough in my business, and in my business sense, not to be swayed just because Frank Sinatra asked. Sure, there was a part of me that said, "Oh my God, this is Frank Sinatra I'm sitting next to." On the other hand, I'd been working with some very heavy hitters. Okay, it was Frank Jr., *his* son, but I didn't know what his show was about, how he sang, or how he was to work with, so I hesitated. Rickles was looking at me and shaking his head. But I think Mr. Sinatra respected my hesitation because he respected who I had booked in that room. I told him that I needed material on Frank Jr. and that I had to hear something he recorded.
>
> He said, "Okay, call my office, and tell Dorothy to send you whatever you need." What surprised me most was the lack of confidence Mr. S. had in Frankie's longtime manager and responsible agent, Vinnie Carbone. When I asked Sinatra about that, he said, "Do you see Frankie in Atlantic City?"
>
> I think that's when Red Buttons finally said something. With his finger pointed to the ceiling, he said, "Ah ha!"
>
> I had a lot of thinking to do. I decided to get in touch with Dorothy Uhlemann and ask for a press kit. And how dare I ask for a press kit on the old man's son! I got two cassettes and two LPs, *It's Alright* and *Spice*. The tapes were live, and the sound was horrible. I thought, "What the hell is he singing? What is this?"
>
> I called Dorothy, and I asked, "What happens to my career if I send this back?" She cracked up. We had a very candid conversation, and she said, "You do whatever your heart tells you to do."
>
> I said, "I've got to see him. The records don't mean a thing. What does his live show sound and look like?"

In 1985, casino gambling in Atlantic City had been legal for seven years. Given the shore's proximity to Philadelphia and New York, Atlantic City became a year-round mecca for day trippers, many of them senior citizens, who came to the resort on buses to play the slots, enjoy a buffet lunch, and perhaps enjoy an afternoon show, presented and produced especially for them. Under Carbone's management, Frank Jr. had yet to appear in postgaming Atlantic City. He had, of course, appeared with the Dorsey ghost band at the Steel Pier years before.

Carbone came to Atlantic City, as he had set up a meeting with the bookers of the long-defunct Playboy Hotel and Casino, later named the Atlantis Hotel and Casino. He wanted Kauffman to come along because she knew the Playboy management and had booked the venue previously. Playboy wanted to present Frank Jr. with the Rick Szabo Orchestra for a bunch of afternoon shows that catered to the bus crowd, but Carbone wasn't making any headway. Kauffman decided to come along. In casual conversation along the way, Carbone spoke of Frank Jr.: "He may not sing the songs you want to hear," he told Kauffman. "And don't compare him to his father."

At the meeting, Kauffman found that Carbone was asking for something close to $25,000 per week. "Who's going to pay that much for Frank Sinatra, Jr., in 1985?" asked Kauffman.

In the end, Frank Jr. took $5,000 a week, which included a couple of rooms. "Frankie doesn't need the fuckin' money," Carbone said. Sinatra concurred, saying, "It's not about the money."

Andrea Kauffman still hadn't heard him in person, so Carbone and Frank flew her out to the Four Queens Hotel and Casino in downtown Las Vegas, where Frank worked frequently. It was right before Kauffman's thirty-fifth birthday, and in the midst of a meeting with Carbone, Frank, and Carbone's wife at a restaurant called Hugo's, Frank asked to be excused. Then out of nowhere, there was Frank and all his musicians singing "Happy Birthday" to Andrea. Frank gave her a box, which contained a Four Queens jacket, with the Four Queens logo on one side and Frank Sinatra, Jr.'s name on the other. She was impressed. She was being wooed.

She enjoyed the show, though she didn't love the idea of Frank singing and conducting a seventeen-piece band. "You look like you're making pizza up there," she said to him. Musically, she did like the show and Frank's singing, but she wondered why he wasn't doing more of his father's material and singing many unusual songs. His answer was, "I'm not my father."

"Then why would you go into the same business?" she asked. "What are you thinking? If your name was Eric Gold, would anybody book you? Because I know ten acts that I would book before him."

He said, "Let me do the Playboy dates, and I'll see what I can do. Come in, and we'll talk some more." In the end, he was booked three more times at the Playboy. The weekday afternoon shows were always mobbed, and the day trippers went away happy.

Kauffman was fine with the good business he did but was concerned about the voice itself. She went to jazz singer Morgana King, who had finished her engagement at Elaine's and was living at Kauffman's house. "I needed her opinion," said Kauffman. "She came into the Playboy with me, and her comment was, 'He's certainly not his father, is he?'" Kauffman asked her to take that out of the equation and then come up with a judgment. King said, "He's a decent singer who needs work."

Andrea Kauffman was getting drawn in. "I loved Vinnie, but I didn't like the way he was handling Frank," she said. "I saw a young man there that desperately wanted to be good and desperately needed approval. He loved the music, and he wanted this. It was the first time that my managerial instincts just stood at attention and said to me, 'If you work with him, there's a possibility that he'll go where I think he belongs.' I gave myself five years to finesse him to the point where he realized the potential that I thought he had."

Vinnie Carbone didn't give Kauffman a lot of encouragement, telling her, "There's no reasoning with this man. You're not going to get it out of him."

Kauffman pulled no punches in her reply: "Then in five years, if he can't pull it all together, I say goodbye. Then either he does it or he doesn't. It's a plan. It's a mind thing."

The issue was repertoire, and it was something that remained an issue for years to come. Though audiences paid to see a "Sinatra," Frank Jr. simply did not want to perform the songs made famous by his father. Those who saw him may have been entertained and may have walked out of the theater smiling, but some audiences were confused. You can't blame them for asking, "Where is 'My Way,' and where is 'The Summer Wind?'" Instead, audiences got one or two Sinatra obscurities at the end of the show.

Even his nonmusical friends were familiar with the situation. "He couldn't be pushed too far, that's for sure," said Michele Martin. "I remember everybody trying to push him, saying, 'Well, you've got to act this way, or you've got to do this or that.' He would not, and we would say, 'No, Hon, I can't. It's not going to happen that way.' He stretched to a degree, and that was it."

Saxophonist Mike Smith was one of Frank's closest friends and confidants. He lived with the "issue" every day. He remembered: "I know Andrea would get upset with him sometimes over his musical choices. He didn't want to do the hits of Sinatra. He just wouldn't do it until the very end. But even then, he'd find some kind of oddball tune to do. I could understand that. I can't tell how many times we went out to dinner together, and someone would come up to him for an autograph. Then they would say, 'I just love your father.' Shit, that gets old after a while."

It was something that Andrea Kauffman would have to address, but the immediate concern was to facilitate a booking that would help turn Frank's failing career around. It came in the form of an engagement in the Gypsy Lounge of Atlantic City's Trump Castle hotel/casino, with a five-piece jazz group led by crack trumpeter Buddy Childers. The engagement as a "turning point."

Kauffman hedged her bets and decided to cobill Frank, Jr. with popular Atlantic City comic Pudgy. "This was my first bonafide booking of Frank Jr.," said Kauffman.

> He did a decent job. The music was okay. He looked so much like his father at that time. It was a curiosity for the people who came in. I knew that, and I had to face that. There was so much going against him. But he wasn't a curiosity, and he wasn't like the bearded lady in the circus. People thought that because he was Sinatra's son he had to be "God Number Two."
>
> This is around the time I started talking to him about repertoire. I said, "Here's the thing. Nobody has to hear 'Indian Summer.' Do the Nat King Cole song, 'Nature Boy.'" He was okay with that because it was Nat King Cole. Then I suggested "Just One of Those Things." I couldn't say "The Summer Wind" or any of the "A" tunes because I would have gotten shot. At that time, I had (influential broadcaster) Sid Mark coming in and reviewers in the house. Sid was his friend and never gave him a bad review, but the other reviewers were a crap shoot.

Frank did good business. Donald Trump was changing the name of Trump Castle to Trump Marina, and he wanted Frank Jr. to be a part of this big changeover at a gala dinner. Trump wanted him to come to a high-rollers dinner at Patsy's restaurant in New York. That would have involved some glad handing, but Kauffman was firm about Frank's not being a social butterfly. Always the tough-but-fair negotiator, she worked out a deal where he would perform first in the Castle/Marina's main room with a twenty-piece band on a weekend, and only then would he do the high-rollers dinner and the glad handing.

Rob Heller, one of the most respected agents in the entertainment business, first heard Frank at the Castle/Marina. "That's where I met Andrea," Heller recalled.

> I thought that he sounded like his father, which probably would have been the worst thing I could have said to him. I felt that he didn't want to sound like his father, and it was almost uncomfortable for him to sing or reference the Sinatra brand. There certainly wasn't any warm and fuzzy feeling when he was performing the songs of dad. There was no "dad" in that show. Frankly, through all the time I knew Frank Jr., his primary reference to his father was "Sinatra." He did not embrace the relationship, the legacy, and I think others around him did.
>
> Booking-wise, things got better when he at least started to do the music of his father, even though he was a reluctant participant. I'm not sure he ever really embraced his father's music. He was proud that his father created that music, but as far as embracing it, he embraced the Sinatra brand. But in the latter years, not only did he embrace his father's music, but there was a show that we put out that said he was the only legitimate heir who was able to say *Sinatra Sings Sinatra*.

As Andrea Kauffman got to know her new client, she was first struck by his awkwardness. He was out of his Las Vegas element in Atlantic City and was nervous and acting strangely. He wanted a fruit basket removed from his room; he wanted to ensure that he wouldn't be "under scrutiny" in the restaurant where the two planned to have dinner; and in general, he was not particularly nice to Kauffman. "You're going to have to speak to me the way you want to be spoken to," she told him. She told Carbone, "At this point, he's not Frank Sinatra, and he's not Frank Sinatra, Jr., to me. He's another act, and he's not going to treat me poorly."

When they finally sat down and talked at length, Kauffman found Frank to be a lonely, sad, and moody man. She almost turned her back on the whole thing because she didn't know whether she wanted the emotional challenge. She asked Vinnie Carbone how he did it. He would only say, "I take the check."

During the Atlantic City sojourn, there was a pleasant interlude when Frank was visited by Paula Jane D'Amato, daughter of Sinatra Sr.'s close friend Skinny D'Amato, owner of the famed 500 Club, where the elder Sinatra had performed many times. Skinny, whose connections to organized crime were well known, was an icon in Atlantic City and was one of the very few to stand by Frank Sinatra and book him during the period when Sinatra's career tanked. Paula Jane was beautiful, and her career as a model lasted well into the 1980s. And according to Kauffman, "Paula Jane was convinced that Frank Jr. was going to marry her."

Paula Jane knew Frank Jr. for years. She fondly recalled,

> When we were both little, Frankie's mother and his father would come to Atlantic City, and I'd play on the beach with him, Nancy, and Tina. Nat King Cole would bring Natalie Cole when Nat worked at the 500 Club. Later on, I think my father did have Frank Jr. in the front room at the club, and that's when I first really heard him. He was very good. He had a beautiful voice and sounded just like his father. He didn't have the pizzazz that his father had. It was a shame. Sometimes I think he behaved in a way completely opposite from his father deliberately. He was very odd, but he was talented and very bright. We'd go out to dinner at a diner at ten o'clock at night, and he'd meet up with these former army people or navy people. They'd talk about the army and the navy. In a diner! I think he was close to being a genius, but he had no personality whatsoever. He was a real womanizer. It was unbelievable. He really was. We were an item. We dated off and on, but I put a stop to it. There were just too many women in his life. He didn't know how to have a relationship, or he didn't want one. At one point, he said he would like me to have his baby (something he said to Heidi Fleiss and other girlfriends over the years) and how happy his father would be if we got married because of my father. But I think it was just talk. I don't

think it was sincere about it. He did fly me out to Vegas once, and I had the feeling that there was another woman there. He picked me up at the airport and had somebody check me into the hotel. Hours later, he came back. I think he went and picked up another girl. One time, there was a note he left at the desk for me. It said, "I'll be back later. Have a great day." And he came back at six o'clock at night! So, what was he doing? I think he was a real cheater. Merrill Kelem, who was working security for Frank, would call me when Frank came to Atlantic City. He would say, "Frank says you never call him, and that he really wants to see you." I broke down one day and called him. I called him, and he said, "Will you come see my show?" I went and brought a friend of mine to the show.

He said, "Come back and see me after the show." He even spoke about my father during the show, and what was amazing was that when he did that, there was a tremendous round of applause for my dad and the 500 Club.

The show was over, and I think Merrill came out and told me, "He can't see you now. He's being interviewed by (*Atlantic City Press* columnist) David Spatz." Now, David Spatz and his then-wife and I were very good friends. We sort of raised our kids together. It wasn't like he was being interviewed by Barbara Walters. I knew David Spatz better than he did. I had to wait an hour. I said, "You know what? This is why I don't call the shit." Because he is that. He was just a pompous ass. And that was it. I never saw him again and never talked to him again.

Andrea Kauffman and Paula Jane D'Amato were friendly, as their daughters were the same age. They would get together and talk about the trials and tribulations of motherhood—and about the trials and tribulations of Frank Sinatra, Jr. Kauffman said,

When Frank was at the Playboy Hotel and Casino in Atlantic City, my dear friend at the time was a singer named Susan LaMusta. Not knowing Frankie well at the time, I wanted to introduce her to him. As soon as he saw her, he flipped. I didn't know he invited Paula Jane to the shows. I had no idea. At one point, I was walking into the Playboy; Vinnie Carbone was walking out to grab me. He said, "Susan LaMusta is on her way down. Grab her; make it seem like the two of you are together, and take her out to the boardwalk to get rid of her because I'm meeting Paula Jane to take her up to Frankie's!" This happened three times, but then we didn't leave it up to chance.

I finally told Susan about Paula Jane. She went to Frank and said he had to make a choice. He said, "Okay, it's you." With that, he flew her out to Las Vegas, and he wanted me to go with her. He's at the Four Queens, and Susan and I have one room. I'm assuming that means she's going to stay with him. We saw the show, had a bite to eat, and then he said good night. Susan goes, "What the heck was that?"

The next night, we saw Frank's show again, but this time, Susan didn't come back to the room. The next morning, we had breakfast together. I said, "Well?"

And she said, "I wouldn't wish him on a dead enemy of mine."

I said, "What are you talking about?"

She said, "He's just not normal. Not when it comes to sex. I can't wait to get home." When we got home, she was done with him, and Paula Jane was done with him.

By definition, a personal manager is responsible for everything and anything that enhances the development of a performing artist's career. Andrea Kauffman went back to Las Vegas knowing full well that some things in the "enhancing department" needed immediate change. Frank Jr.'s wardrobe, for one, was awful, and it had to be changed immediately.

First, there was the matter of the pants. He wore his pants too short, and everyone knew it. "He told me he buys unhemmed pants," she remembered.

His tailor was a guy named Angelo. I told Vinnie to get me over to Carroll's, the place where he bought all his clothes. I had a box of cannolis, candy, and a one-hundred-dollar bill, all wrapped in boxes. I walked into Carroll's with Vinnie. We asked for Angelo the tailor. He's sitting at the sewing machine, and Vinnie introduced me to Angelo as Frank's new agent. I tell Angelo that I specifically wanted to meet him and see what kind of work he did. I saw that he beautifully hand stitched everything. I said, "In here is candy, and in here is a thank you. I want every single pair of Frank Sinatra, Jr.'s pants hemmed an inch and a half longer than you're currently hemming them, no matter where you pinned them." I said, "Is that agreed?" He said something in Italian

> that meant, "Thank God . . . finally!" I gave him the three boxes, and that was it. Vinnie said he couldn't believe I got away with that.
>
> We're on the road with Frankie, and he's got six pairs of pants on hangers. He's getting dressed, and I'm sitting there. He's talking to himself while he's trying on all the pants. He says, "You've got to do me a favor. You've got to find me a tailor. These pants are too long."
>
> I finally told him what I did. He told me he'd never talk to me again and asked me to leave. I said, "Once you see my back, you'll never see my front. You have to stop looking like a six-year-old." His pants were never quite that short again.

There was one more wardrobe issue that needed immediate attention: the god-awful knit tuxedo jacket. Frank said he needed a jacket made of that type of fabric to make it easier for him move when he conducted. But it looked terrible, and the black tux pants he wore didn't match the jacket's shade of black. Kauffman said,

> We were checking into Atlantic City's Trump Castle, and I asked how many pieces of luggage he had. He said eight, plus the suiter that had three tuxes and the knit jacket. I knew his opening in the lounge would attract some celebrities, like Buddy Greco and popular Atlantic City comedian Sal Richards. His suiter was in the dressing rom. I got my hands on the knit tux jacket. In those days, I had acrylic fingernails. I looked at the jacket, and I was trying to figure out what the most obvious part of it would be to put a hole in it. I decided to do it right over the heart, where his white tux shirt would show through. Then I did another little one over one of the patch pockets, but you wouldn't be able to see that one. He put on the knit tux jacket and said, "A moth got to my conductor's jackets!" Thank God I had the wherewithal to get his tuxes pressed. He put on the tuxedo, and the knits were retired.

No one else was willing to do things like that.

Writer Don Heckman was a respected jazz critic who often wrote for *Down Beat* magazine. His review of Frank's show at the Flamingo in Vegas in the *Los Angeles Times* in December of 1985 was an accurate appraisal of just where Frank was, musically and career wise in that pivotal year.

Heckman wrote:

> The younger Sinatra has been plagued for most of his career by comparisons with his illustrious elder—justifiably, perhaps, since the decision, very early on in his career, was to emulate both the style and substance of his father's music. Sinatra, Jr.'s first show at the Flamingo Music Center Saturday night exposed the hazards, as well as the benefits of that decision.
>
> On the plus side, the genes are right; his voice has matured into an elegant baritone lightly touched with the buzzing edge that made the elder Sinatra's sound so appealingly new when he made his comeback in the early 1950s. In fact, Sinatra, Jr.'s vocal instrument is now the real stuff, as good—dare I say it?—as his father's ever was.
>
> What he does with it is another story. Most of his program could have been lifted bodily out of the fake book of a 1950s cocktail lounge singer: "It's a Marshmallow World," "Straighten Up and Fly Right," "The Girl Next Door," "Sunny," and "River, Stay 'Way from My Door."
>
> Dependable stuff, all of it, not quite in the war horse category, and sung with a nice lyric sense and a surprisingly strong rhythmic flow (especially "Sunny").
>
> Brief forays into, ahem, "contemporary" material such as Harry Nilsson's "Remember (Christmas)" and America's "Horse with No Name" were poorly arranged, confusingly interpreted, and doomed to predictable failure. There are topical pieces that would adapt well to Sinatra, Jr.'s style, but these were not the ones.
>
> More to the point, Sinatra, Jr.'s performance demonstrated that he has the talent and skill to reach beyond the diminishing musical territory of his paterfamilias. It's still not too late.

The challenge was what to do with a forty-one-year-old Frank Sinatra, Jr., in 1985. Television variety shows were all but gone, and the business had changed drastically. One possibility was to book him as an opening act. He did open for Don Rickles in 1986 and even appeared as a surprise guest on Rickles's 1986 television special for the Showtime network. He also opened for George Burns at Caesars and did well. Unfortunately, said Kauffman, "It didn't work out the way I wanted it to. His prices, in the beginning, were not opening-act prices, and there were not that many comedians then, other than Rickles or Red Buttons, who were getting a tremendous amount of money. It was cost prohibitive, and he wanted what he wanted."

No matter what the showbiz climate, his extracurricular activities continued unabated. One got him into trouble. A United Press International Report, written by William C. Trott and posted on December 11, 1987, told the story.

> Frank Sinatra, Jr., says he was only defending himself when he pushed away a former girlfriend in a Houston nightclub last year. Sinatra is being sued for $1 million by Charmain St. Cyr, who claims he made her fall over backward and injure her left shoulder.
>
> Sinatra testified that he met St. Cyr, forty-three, in 1985 and later "became intimate" with her once. He said the relationship soon went sour, and St. Cyr called his home and repeatedly left threatening messages on his recording machine. The real trouble came at their next meeting—before a Frank Jr. performance in Houston in July 1986. He said she was embarrassing him in front of his friends, and at one point they got "nose to nose." Since he could not see both of St. Cyr's hands, Sinatra testified he felt threatened and pushed the woman back at arm's length. St. Cyr is representing herself in the trial. In a UPI follow-up dated several days later, the headline read "Frank Jr. Cleared."
>
> It took a Houston jury only twenty minutes of deliberation to decide that Frank Sinatra, Jr., did not intend to injure a former girlfriend when he pushed her away in a nightclub last year. Sinatra, forty-three, was being sued for $1.3 million by Charmain St. Cyr, who claimed his shove injured her shoulder.
>
> Sinatra had said he was only trying to avoid trouble when he pushed St. Cyr away in the club on July 24, 1986, and his lawyer had described her as a "poor, pathetic woman" obsessed by Sinatra. He claimed that St. Cyr had threatened to kill him—a charge she denied—but evidence showed St. Cyr had phoned Sinatra's home fifty-eight times between July 11 and July 15, 1986. St. Cyr said she was not surprised by the verdict "considering the evidence the judge let into court."

By this point, Andrea Kauffman was well aware of Frank's issues and career challenges. Her decision was to embrace the challenges and meet them head on. As she explained it,

> There were many things that were happening that made me realize he had more potential than people gave him credit for. It was going to take

> somebody who believed in him as a human being. I knew that underneath this damaged man was another guy looking to get out, musically and personally. There was a point when I decided I wouldn't let him down and that I had his back. Too many people walked out on him, including his family. I wasn't going to do that.

The most important factor was repertoire. Audiences came to a Frank Sinatra, Jr., show because he was a "Sinatra," and it was "Sinatra" they wanted to hear. Potential buyers knew that as well. Kauffman had faith in Frank's potential, but the repertoire issue was frustrating and remained a sticking point for years.

Producer Hank Catteneo pulled no punches when he said, "Getting him to sing his father's songs was like pulling teeth. One time, Andrea and I pleaded with him for about an hour. He finally looked at me and said, 'I'll do it, but only because you asked me.' I guess that's because he respected my relationship with his dad. And when he did his father's songs, people went crazy."

Terry Woodson, who would conduct for Frank Jr., maintained that Frank Jr. did not want to be another Sinatra wanna-be. He wanted to be his own man. The unfortunate part of it was that he picked a music style that was his father's music style. So he was competing with him, though he'd say, "I don't want to compete with my father." A lot of times, he'd do his own thing, but the audience would say, "Hey, when are you going to do your father's songs?" He tried to be his own man, and he would say, "I don't want to wear another man's coat."

Jim Fox played guitar in the Frank Jr. orchestra from 1996 until Junior's passing. The two became close, and Fox believed he knew what his friend was feeling. "Frank never said this to me, but I thought he was tired of people wanting him to do his father's material," Fox explained.

> I believe that he didn't want to be on a long list of imitators. He didn't want to be perceived that way. That's the feeling I got. Everywhere we went, there were Sinatra impersonators. Every town we'd play in, there would be one in the lounge. There were people doing Sinatra everywhere. Some were just singing in the style, but there were all different kinds of levels of "Sinatra" out there. And I don't think that Frank wanted to just be another person doing that. I can understand that. It

> was, like, "Let them do that." And he tried many times, as you know, to do different kinds of music.

There were some who knew Frank well and appreciated what he was singing and why he was singing it. Lorraine Hunt-Bono, a one-time entertainer who later became the lieutenant governor of Nevada, knew Frank for years and appreciated where he stood. "He had great depth," she believed.

> His interpretations were his own. The way he treated a song, it became not just a song, but a Frank Sinatra, Jr., song. So many people, when they saw him, they said, "Oh, I just saw Frank Sinatra, Jr., and he doesn't have what his father had."
>
> I said, "No. He's his own man." They expected him to come out there, snap his fingers, and be real glib and be the kind of character that made Frank Sinatra who he was. But I appreciated who he was, and so many musicians appreciated it. They loved his uniqueness. He didn't try to come out and be Frank Sinatra. I really appreciated that because it was authentic. And it was beautiful.

Bobby Rydell was a contemporary of Frank and a good friend. As a result of his million-selling hits of the early 1960s that were aimed at the teenage market, he was pigeonholed as a teen act, and that sadly masked his considerable talents as a singer of American popular songs. Indeed Frank, Jr. once described Rydell as "the most underrated singer in the business." Rydell, in turn, had a sincere appreciation of Frank's talents.

Rydell recalled,

> I met him through broadcaster Sid Mark in Philadelphia. We became friends. We hit it off and became really good friends. I only wish that Bernie Lowe and Kal Mann of Cameo-Parkway Records could have recognized my talent beyond the teen stuff. I would have liked to do more things like Bobby Darin and Frank Jr. I thought Frank Jr. was marvelous. I really listened a lot to his early recordings. He sounded so good. He really sounded good. He sounded so much like his old man, and his phrasing was superb. I thought he had great chops.

The 1985 to 1988 period was transitional for Frank, Kauffman, and Vinnie Carbone. Carbone was slowly stepping aside, allowing for Kauffman to step in and manage Frank exclusively. Kauffman said,

> He did the Fairmount in San Francisco and Chicago, and he booked a cruise, which Frank hated, but he wasn't working a lot. Vinnie didn't work hard for him. He made good money with Bobby Vinton, his wife was getting a pension from the airline she had worked for, and he just didn't want to work hard. Frank would take things as they came along. When I booked Frank into the lounge at the Trump Castle, Vinnie didn't even come out to see him. At that point, my role was to see that all the dates ran smoothly because Vinnie didn't want to travel. And he was giving me a hard time about a lot of dates, and I never quite figured out why. Maybe he was afraid that I would lose interest and that, possibly, the reviews wouldn't be good. The show, at that time, was not a great show. Frank's voice would crack, and he would sing such obscure songs. The band was so great, even a dull song sounded wonderful, but it's still a dull song. He never sang a ballad with tenderness. He was still feeling his way around how to present a song, how to sing a song, how to phrase a song that his father didn't sing. If his father sang a particular song, then Frank Jr. knew how to phrase it.I presented several possible bookings to Vinnie, but he turned them down for no good reason. He wasn't motivated to do the footwork it took to get the job from the offer stage to the performance stage. This resistance from Vinnie came to light when I told Frank I was getting dates, but Vinnie was turning them down. He wanted to know what kind of resistance, and I told him about all the excuses. Frank said, "I need to call him directly." He'd take care of Vinnie. This is when he stopped Vinnie's retainer.Vinnie wanted to retire and backed off. I was dealing directly with the agent for the Four Queens, Billy Rizzo. Jeanie Hood, widow of the Queens' owner, and I renegotiated his deal. He was there three or four weeks a year with a seventeen-piece band, doing three shows a night. He was losing $5,000 every time he went in there. I got him a $21,000 increase for each year's run. At least he was going to break even.

Vinnie Carbone died in 1997. And though he was called Frank's personal manger until then, Kauffman had been doing everything since 1987. "Vinnie was doing absolutely nothing for Frank for the last ten years of his life," as Kauffman recalled. "I didn't call Vinnie directly to discuss anything. I spoke directly to Frank to discuss dates, money, everything."

Kauffman's role was made "official" when Carbone passed. "Frank asked me to become his personal manager, or the 'heir apparent,' as he called it," Kauffman said. "I'd officially be the sole person responsible for his success. I knew that we were going to sink together or that we were going to swim together. I just couldn't afford to have this position, being his manager and working for the Sinatra family, fail. I could not fail."

At some point in the early days of Kauffman's association with Frank, she was invited to see Frank's show at Tavern on the Green in New York City. Her former partner, Dan Mulhern, was also invited. On that fateful evening, she met Louis "Domes" Pacella, known as "Uncle Louie," said to be a soldier in the crew of the Genovese family under Caporegime Michael "Trigger Mike" Coppola. In other words, "Uncle Louie" was in the mob.

She remembered the evening very well.

> Frank always talked to me about Uncle Louie. I didn't know who he was, but I was told that if I ever did, that I show him as much deference as I would show the pope. We walked in, and Vinnie Carbone was waiting for us. Uncle Louie came out. I've never seen a better put together man in my life. Not one hair was out of place. I don't care how gorgeous Sinatra dressed. No one could dress like Uncle Louie. Vinnie, to give me a heads up, said, "Andrea Kauffman, meet Uncle Louie. Uncle Louie, this is Frank's new RA (responsible agent)."
>
> Uncle Louie says, "Ay . . . how yadoin'? You got here all right? Everything good? You okay?"
>
> I said, "Yes sir. Everything is fine. Thank you." Then I introduced him to my partner, Dan Mulhern. Dan said "Ay, how YOU doin'?"
>
> Uncle Louie said, "Hey, you from Brooklyn?"
>
> Dan said, "No."
>
> Uncle Louie said, "Then why yatalkin' like that?"
>
> Thank God it was okay. I said, "Who doesn't want to be Uncle Louie? Let him be Uncle Louie for a minute; the poor kid's Irish." That got us through that moment, and Uncle Louie laughed.

> Uncle Louie was the head of the mob in most of New York State. Frank had a connection to him. He did a favor for Uncle Louie. When Joey Heatherton had a problem, Frank called Uncle Louie just to make sure this problem didn't happen again. He didn't ask for anyone to be killed; he just wanted to make sure that the guy causing the problem would feel threatened and that the problem wouldn't happen again because she was endangered physically. Did Frank run with the same crowd his dad did? No. He always kept them at arm's length, but he was always respectful. If they came backstage to see him, and there were a few—quite a few in Chicago, specifically—I'd get some last-minute ticket requests, per Frank's orders.

The year 1988 was transformative. In that year, Frank Sinatra, Jr., received a telephone call that would affect his life and his career, as well as the lives and careers of those within his orbit, until his passing twenty-eight years later. Frank Sinatra, Jr., would be called to conduct for his father.

The Call to Conduct

The actual call to conduct his father's orchestra came while Frank Jr., Andrea Kauffman, and alto saxophonist Mike Smith were sitting around in Frank's suite at the Trump Marina (formerly the Trump Castle) Hotel/Casino in Atlantic City. Kauffman vividly remembered the scene.

> We had one more date in Atlantic City, and a call came in through the switchboard. I heard Frank talking to Dorothy Uhlemann in Sinatra's office, and he said, "Will you excuse me?" He went into another room, and I remember hearing him say, "Hi, Pop. Is everything okay?" Then there was silence for a while until I heard him say into the phone, "If you need me, I'm yours." Not, "Thank you." Not "I'd love to." Not "This would be great." He said, "If you need me, I'm yours." Next thing I know, he came out, and his eyes were like saucers. He said, "Guys, I have to go on the road with my old man."

Later on, she learned the whole story. Kauffman explained,

> When Frank got the call to conduct for his father, it was not a complete conversation. His father said, "I want you to do something for me. I think I'd like you to conduct. But we'll talk about it when you come home." Frank Jr. was over the moon. As far as he was concerned, his father gave him the job. That's the call I was privy to. Frank told him

> when he'd be home, and on that date, he got the call from his father, who said, "Come to dinner. I'm ready to discuss it."
>
> The old man wasn't allowed to fry onions or garlic in the house because the orange couches were made of silk, and the silk would absorb the odor. Barbara [Frank Sr.'s wife] wouldn't allow it. But at this point, it was like "Fuck you Barbara" because when Frankie walked in, his mouth started to water when he smelled the garlic cooking. The old man cooked, and they ate in the kitchen. Frankie asked his father where Barbara was. "Oh, she's not feeling well tonight," his father said, "but it's just as well because you and I have business to discuss." Then Barbara came down to get orange juice. She had bandages on both wrists.
>
> After she went back upstairs, Frankie asked, "Did she try to commit suicide? Did she try to slit her wrists?"
>
> The old man said, "I should get so lucky. But no. She had a hand lift. That's where they take the wrinkles out of her hand because the hands were giving away her age." That was the night his father said, "This is what I need you to do. Conduct for me. [Conductor and long-time pianist] Bill Miller is having a hard time."

Hank Catteno, who was working for the elder Sinatra at the time of this decision, agreed that there were problems with Bill Miller:

> Eventually, Frank wasn't content with Bill Miller conducting. Sonny Golden, Sinatra's account and financial adviser, called me up and said we were considering making a change. He asked what I thought about Junior doing it. I said I thought it was a good idea but that salt and pepper might never mix in the beginning. Sure enough, he joined up. We only spoke a couple of words for the first couple of weeks. After a while and with only two words between us to that point, he walked over to me just before rehearsal. He stood at attention and then saluted. He said, "Sergeant? Major?"
>
> I said, "Where'd you get that?"
>
> He said, "My father said you were a major or something."
>
> I said, "You're right. I was a sergeant major." From there on in, his first line was, "Sergeant major," and I couldn't get rid of the guy. Then we became the closest of friends. He loved the military. He used to quote Jack Webb.

The party line and the story that Frank would repeat to the press for years was that Frank Jr.'s father called him in 1988 to conduct because only a singer could understand what another singer needed in a conductor. While that certainly made sense musically, there was more to it than that.

Some twenty-eight years after Frank got the call to conduct, he opened up about the factors, other than musical, involved in his father's offer and his acceptance. In an interview with *Billboard* magazine some months before his passing in 2016, he explained, "From the time we're children, we're used to our parents providing for us. I always wanted personally to be able to say I put something back. When he reached out to me that time, I was absolutely delighted because I was hoping, just maybe, I would be able to put something back, so it wouldn't be the only thing I've done my whole life is take."

Those close to the Sinatras also knew that the elder Sinatra needed his son to be there for him on the road. "It must be admitted that he was by this point slowing down," Frank told *Palm Beach Post* writer Leslie Gray Streeter in September 2016. "His vision was no longer what it had been; his hearing was not what it had been. And everyone else knew it. I used to say, 'Come on, Pop. You're too old an athlete. You know you've gotta go in, and you're gonna fight.' The business of getting up in front of an audience kept him alive."

The issue with Bill Miller's conducting was never mentioned publicly.

For Andrea Kauffman, Frank's decision to conduct for his father was a troubling issue.

> When he took the conducting job, I was concerned about the financial downside for my company and what was going to happen to me personally. He was just beginning to make minor changes in his repertoire. I was finally getting him to a place where he was doing seven or eight songs of his choosing for the first portion of the program, and then he finished the show with Frank Sinatra [Sr.] music. I had him just a bit closer to where he needed to be, and I saw the momentum beginning. He was ready to work with me. He liked the applause. And he was making a profit with me for the first time ever. How would being on his father's dates interfere with his own?
>
> He wanted me to go with him to a few dates to see how his father's operation worked. I thought, "Who better to learn from?" But traveling

> while not working a paying job could become an expensive education for me. Would this pay off for all of us on the back end? I had to look at the possible upside to this arrangement. By conducting for his father, Frank would get the credibility and legitimacy that he may not have had previously. I just hoped it wouldn't interfere too much with the dates that were already booked for him.
>
> Then there was the possibility that, because Frank would now be totally immersed in the repertoire and the classic orchestrations of his father, that exposure to this timeless and iconic music would be the impetus to, once and for all, include more "Sinatra songs" in his own shows.

Kauffman took stock and realized that the elder Sinatra, then around seventy-two years of age, was slowing down and wasn't doing the number of dates that he used to. "When Frank was called to conduct for his father, we still worked, but we had to work around the old man's schedule," said bassist Paul Rostock. And that, Kauffman did. But the immediate order of business for Frank was to adjust to his new role as conductor. That wasn't always easy.

Opening Night

Frank's first night as the conductor of his father's orchestra came on April 1, 1988. The occasion was a charity concert in Palm Desert with Buddy Greco, Peter Nero, Diane Schurr, Sammy Davis, Jr., and Frank Sinatra, Sr., as the stars. The host was Roger Moore.

Frank Jr. wrote about that fateful evening in his memoir:

> The concert was sold out, and of course, Sinatra was to be the final act. As the minutes ticked by, I watched the proceedings of the show from backstage in order to see how the other conductors communicated with the orchestra. Funny, I felt more anxious than nervous. As the time for my father's appearance drew near, I suddenly became aware that he had walked into the darkened wings and was standing beside me. "This is the proudest night of my life," I said. He looked at me vaguely with a quick sideward's glance, but I could tell that something else was distracting him.
>
> "Have we got 'Soliloquy' in the book?" he asked. This of course, referred to the twelve-minute plus aria from the Rogers and Hammerstein musical *Carousel*.
>
> "Yes," I answered, dreading what I feared was coming.
>
> "Good," he said. "Let's do *that* tonight."
>
> "We haven't rehearsed it," I almost pleaded. He turned and looked full on at me.
>
> "Play it now. We'll rehearse it later," he said. I had just had my first lesson in unpredictable Sinatra spontaneity. I remembered how he had

> performed "Soliloquy" for the original recording back in 1963 when I had witnessed the making of *The Concert Sinatra* recording. I took a chance and directed the music with the same tempo I remembered from that night twenty-four years before. Imagine the relief that all of the orchestra and I felt when we reached the end of the work without a problem.

It would have been great if everything had gone as well as it did on opening night. Word travels quickly in the professional music world, and the word was out, after Frank took over the conducting reigns for his father, that there was discord to spare among several veterans in the Sinatra orchestra, specifically members of what was called "The New York Orchestra." "I wondered if there was something personal about me that they didn't like," Frank wrote. "My attempts at engaging any of them in conversation away from the stage were met with complete disinterest. More and more, I began to feel that they regarded me as some kind of enemy."

Eventually, he started hearing about specific beefs, including a ridiculous rumor that he was getting $10,000 a night for conducting the band. "It became abundantly clear that the musicians had no faith in me as a fellow musician," Frank believed. He said,

> I never hesitated to admit that I was nowhere near the caliber of talent that every member of the orchestra had, and I was only there because I knew the music better than anyone else, in spite of [longtime drummer] Irv Cottler's opinion. Cottler was unhappy with my ignorance, not only about conducting, but also about my lack of knowledge of the tempo of many of the songs. At first, he had given me pointers about directing the orchestra, but he began making subtle suggestions that I should quit. I soon learned that many of Sinatra's people felt the same. I had to remind myself that before taking this all-important post, I knew full well that the people I was to work with would not be welcoming me with flowers and speeches. I hoped that in time, they might begin to accept me.

The headstrong Cottler, who long had the reputation as a stubborn know-it-all, never did accept Frank. But it really didn't matter. Due to illness, Cottler didn't last a year under Frank's baton and was replaced, unsatisfactorily, with several big-name drummers, including veterans Sol Gubin and Alvin Stoller. Ultimately, circa 1991, the powerful Gregg Field joined up and remained to the end. As time went on, and the disgruntled veterans began to fall away, Frank finally got some respect.

In time, he would become a heck of a conductor. "He could read a score, as opposed to his father," Terry Woodson said. "He became a good conductor for his father, even when he had to fight resistance from the band. His father gave him a shot, and he stood behind him. Junior was loyal to his father, regardless of whatever their relationship over the years might have been. When he got that call, he rose to the level."

Mike Smith, who was in Frank Sr.'s orchestra when Frank Jr. came in to conduct, said,

> Irv Cottler had a problem with him in the beginning, but it all smoothed out. Frank Jr. really knew that shit. He did his homework. I think what was going on between Irv and Junior was a disagreement on tempos. Irv was always used to being the straw boss and laying it down where he wanted to. But Junior had nothing but respect for those guys. The old New York guys were giving him shit. But little by little, I ended up bringing in all my buddies, and it worked out. His relationship with his father was difficult at times. There were some hurt feelings over the years. But can you imagine if your father was Frank Sinatra, and your parents are divorced?

As the elder Sinatra's opening act for so many years, Tom Dreesen had a unique perspective on things personal and professional. In Dreesen's opinion,

> When Frankie was called to conduct, I think that his father wanted a closer relationship with Frank Jr. that he didn't have throughout the years. Also, I think he really believed that Frank Jr. really knew that music and could really do the job. And he did. I don't know how the band felt prior to his coming in, but I know that once he was there, they really respected him for doing a great job conducting. I could see that in them. He knew the music. He sang the music. And he knew how to conduct.He was a better musician than his father. Frank Sinatra, Sr., was not a musician. Frank Sinatra, Sr., could not read music. Frank Jr. could. And Frank respected that. When he first came on the tour with

us, he really worked hard at preparing that evening. I remember when he pulled out "Soliloquy" when the old man was getting older, which was some years after he pulled it on Junior on Junior's opening night. And I thought that was a long, hard song for Frank Sr. to sing by that point, but Frank Jr. sometimes insisted on putting into the evening's line up. His line was, "It'll keep the old man frosty." It was a tough song, but it would get him up. I would be in the old man's dressing room before the show. He liked to watch *Jeopardy*, which was on at 7:30. Frank Jr. would come in and lay out the songs for the night. His father could have easily said, "No, I don't want to do that tonight." But for the most part, he trusted his son.Frank Sr. would joke in the act. He would introduce him and say, "His mom called and said, 'Give my son a job.'" He would joke about that. But he was really glad that Frank Jr. was with him.In the fourteen years I toured with Frank Sr., twice he had to cancel because of his throat. Frank always called it "my reed." Both times, I had to go out to the audience and tell them that Frank Sr. would not be performing; however, Frank Jr. was going to do a show, and I told the people that they were more than welcome to stay. Both times, he knocked it out of the park. He was excellent. He could really sing. He was a good singer. And a good musician. My point is that people would say, "Yeah, but he doesn't sing like his dad."

My answer to that was, "Who the fuck did sing like his dad?" What a dumb thing to say.

Father and Son Meet Mary Hart

This Junior/Senior joint television interview was probably the only time in their careers that such a thing was done. On-screen, neither looks particularly thrilled to be there, but there was an event to promote, in this case, the "Ultimate Event" with Senior, Liza Minnelli, and Sammy Davis, Jr. The segment was taped in 1989 after a show at Bally's Grand, formerly the Golden Nugget, in Atlantic City. Hart, of course, brought up the kidnapping episode. That exchange is detailed in an earlier chapter in this book.

Hart: What brought you together, as father and son, on stage?

FS Sr.: It was about time that we did work together. He wasn't doing enough work, so I figured I'd better keep him busy. But I thought it would be lot of fun to work with Frankie because he's been around the business so long, and we never had that much chance to work together.

Hart: How was it, the first time on stage together? Was it that father-son feeling and that pride? Or was it a professional relationship, strictly?

FS Sr.: Well, it's a combination of both, actually. I know that he's an accomplished musician, pianist, and conductor. You get somebody who knows what he knows about what we're doing, then I'm straight.

Hart to FS Jr.: You were chuckling.

FS Jr.: Once again, my dad's being very kind. I've made my share of mistakes, but fortunately, he's a very patient man.

FS Sr.: I'm a patient man? That'll be the day.

FS Jr.: But I'm learning.

Hart to FS Jr.: Did you ever feel that you got robbed because your dad was so famous?

FS Jr.: I wouldn't say for any length of time, no.

FS Sr.: He just had his pocket picked a little bit.

FS Jr.: And it's all the more pleasant that I get to work with my old man today—now that I'm at this age—that it ever could have been at a younger age.

Hart: It's got to give you some pride to hear him say those words.

FS Sr.: I'm as thrilled as he is, probably more so, because I have rarely worked with anyone as a chum. You know, it gets lonely out there, doing an hour and a half by yourself.

Hart: We saw you in Australia with your arms around the reporters. Are you mellowing? Has your attitude changed?

FS Sr.: My attitude has never changed. I treat people as I find them and how they treat me. That's all. I mean if someone's going to walk up to you for five minutes and abuse you verbally, you're gonna get back at them. Or if they're nice to you, you pay it back. That's all.

Sometimes the onstage comments his father made could turn cruel. Frank Jr. would get angry after the shows where he thought his father crossed the line, and he would occasionally take it out on Andrea Kauffman. Once, she told him to "take it out on your father, not me."

He said, "I wish I could."

Kauffman tried to convince him to say something. "I just wanted him to realize that his anger was a useless reaction and that the person responsible was right there on the stage next to him."

The next night, he took her advice. He decided he wanted to have a live microphone by the piano, something that no one in the show knew about. Sinatra Sr. used the same line about Frankie's mother telling him to give Frankie a job. This time, Frank Jr. interrupted and said over the live mike, "She's gonna kick your ass anyhow. She wants me to have a raise."

The Children's Hour

According to Andrea Kauffman,

> If he [Frank, Jr.] had one, single, ultimate, horrific, fatal flaw, it was the way he thought of and treated women. And that had nothing to do with his father, because his father was very different when it came to women. As for the children he fathered, I think he liked the drama. He was just as happy to pay for an abortion as he was to ignore the child.
>
> It was a different era, and I chose, in large part, to ignore his reprehensible behavior, when it came to women. I shouldn't have, but it was my job to be critical of everything from what he wore to what he sang and how he sang it, and I thought that was quite enough. In retrospect it wasn't.

In that Frank Jr. was constantly seeking the approval of his mother and father, the news of illegitimate children through the years did nothing to strengthen his relationship with his parents. Discretion and image were important to his parents, but Frank's behavior was anything but discrete.

Isaac Tamburino is the son of Andrea Kauffman, and he has show business and music in his blood. He began working for Frank as a roadie on weekends when he was thirteen. He eventually became coroad and production manager and was there until Frank passed. Of Frank's penchant for women, Tamburino simply said, "Everyone has their vice. Women were his vice. For the most part, even if there was a steady woman in his life, there was almost a person per city. I got to know these women. It wasn't like a rock band. These were women who knew him for twenty-plus years who would see him every time he came to town. They would just hang out. They would have drinks with us. They were sweet, and most of them looked alike."

Tamburino recalled an incident in Shreveport, Louisiana, during Frank's run at a riverboat casino.

> I was tidying up the stage before the show when someone from the casino came up to me and said, "I have a woman at the box office here to see the show. She says she has Frank's daughter with her and would like to introduce them. How should I proceed?" I said to tell them to enjoy the show, and I'd take this up with Frank.
>
> Frank and the guys were sitting in the Green Room watching a college football game. I went up to Frank and asked if I could talk to him privately in the other room. He told me that I could say anything I wanted to in front of the guys. I told him about this woman—she was about twenty-one years old—who wanted to come backstage and introduce Frank to his daughter. Frank took a beat and answered, "Isaac, if every child that claimed to be mine was mine, then I'd be living in a test tube somewhere." Frank did not meet the woman and her daughter backstage.
>
> There were three children that Frank did acknowledge. Despite tabloid reports that came out and named others after Frank's passing, only Michael Francis Sinatra, Francine Anderson Sinatra, and Jocelyn Scanlon were named in the will.
>
> Born in 1972, Francine, or Francie, as Frank affectionately called her, whose mother is Mary Wallner, was "obviously a Sinatra, and she looked like Nancy Jr.," said Andrea Kauffman. "Frank didn't talk about her much. Occasionally, he would bring her to a gig and say, 'This is my daughter,' but he didn't have a lot to say about her. Though he seemed to be very fond of her, he certainly didn't have the same affection for her that his father showed for Nancy and Tina. It was nothing like that. There was nothing deeply emotional about the relationship. When Frank died, I know she gave Michael a hard time, and that broke his heart, because they had gotten close over the years. I got the impression from an attorney who was involved with the estate that she was looking for every penny that might be due her."

Frank and I were already working together when Michael, whose mother is Patricia Fisher, was born in 1987. He told me after Michael was born that he had a son. I didn't meet him right away, but Frank started showing me family photographs from the Easter and Christmas holidays, and Michael was in them. That's when I became aware of him.

Michael came with us on a job at Disney World. He was about ten years old. Cynthia was there with her two girls, and everyone was in one big suite. Michael hated it, and he ran away. Everybody was looking for him. Why wasn't Cynthia or Frank paying attention? Hours later, he finally showed up. It was the one time that I really had the opportunity to sit with Michael one on one and say, "I know you're not happy. Nobody's happy with Cynthia and the two kids. It's a horrible situation. But you can't do what you did. I understand that you're angry, but we were so worried that you might have been kidnapped. We love you. You want to get away? I have a two-bedroom suite, with a living room. You come stay with me." Cynthia would have liked him to disappear. Then we didn't see him for a while.

When he grew up and started going to college, he began coming around, and I suggested to Frank that he give Michael a job, just to bring him into Frank's life. But he wasn't interested in the business. He's a different kind of person. He has different abilities and interests. He's a baseball fanatic; he loves everything Disney and the history of Disney; he loves anime and just has a vision of life that's totally different than his father's. He didn't grow up in the limelight, so I don't think that being in the business ever attracted him. My son was treated more like a son than Michael. I know that Frank's mother adored Michael, and so did Nancy. But I sometimes felt bad because Frank put so much time into Isaac and so little time into Michael.

They eventually built up a relationship. Francine and Jocelyn were byproducts of relationships, but I think that Michael represented the continuation of the Sinatra lineage to Frank and the family. And Michael was so much like Frank in certain ways. He could be just as tough on his father as his father was on him. Michael got married and never told his father, and there were a lot of things that Michael did that said, "Hey, you weren't there for me. So either buck up so we can have a good relationship, or don't bother me."

Frank was aware of his son's brilliance, and that's also what attracted him to Michael. He had a high IQ, and I'm pretty sure Frank was

> thinking, "I did it right. This kid's bright; this kid's smart, handsome, and this kid's a Sinatra."

Michael inherited his father's intellect and sensitivity, and it's clear from the beautifully written piece he contributed to this book that he inherited his father's thoughtful and judicious use of the English language as well. Above all, as it applies to his father, he's a realist. On January 10, 2017, the occasion of what would have been his father's seventy-third birthday, Michael wrote, in part, the following:

> Looking back at his 70th birthday (2014), things seemed so optimistic. He had beaten cancer for the second time, regained his ability to eat after more than a year of using a feeding tube, and as he cut his birthday cake, he had the same never-give-in attitude of my (then) 99-years young grandmother. "Same time next year," he said.
>
> Later that year, upon hearing I had no plans for my birthday, he planned a birthday dinner at Larsen's Steakhouse with some of our dearest friends in less than thirty-six hours.
>
> Even later that year, when I was commuting to work at Disneyland, he lent me his home to help save some time and frustration. I never really told him how that saving of time and stress was nothing compared to the joy and happiness I felt now that we finally had a chance to live together under the same roof, eat meals together, and so on.
>
> I know I need to stop feeling sad that he's not here. I need to stop feeling guilt and regret for all the things I could have done but didn't. I know that I need to find closure and remember the good times as well as the bad.
>
> My father taught me many things, but more than anything else, he taught me the importance of giving to those what you may not have had yourself. "I'm going to give you what my father never gave me," he often said to me. In our case, it was time for talking just the two of us, as father and son. Even though I know he had very little idea how to do it, he would still take the time to spend with me, and I was always so grateful for it.
>
> Happy birthday, Dad. I really wish I could have given you another great new history book for your birthday this year, but instead, I'll have to tell you all the great stories when we meet again someday.

Frank made an uncharacteristically big deal about breaking the news of Jocelyn's birth to Kauffman. As Kauffman remembered,

> Frank called me and said, "I'm coming to Atlantic City. Get me a room. I have something I want to talk to you about." The night he arrived, we went to dinner. He didn't usually ask for a specific table in restaurants, but this night, he wanted a table out of earshot and away from everybody. It was just the two of us, and that was also very unusual. He said, "I have something to tell you. I don't know how you're going to feel, and your reaction is going to be very interesting to me. I have become a father again. Leslie, the woman that I was dating for quite a while, just had a little girl, and her name is Jocelyn."
>
> He called her "my little pixie." She had just been born. He was still seeing his ex-wife, Cynthia, and as far as Cynthia was concerned, they were still together. He went on to tell me a story that Cynthia was going through his jacket and found a receipt for the two dozen yellow roses that Frank sent to Leslie when she had the baby. He claimed that Cynthia was furious. But nothing made her mad enough or tweaked her self-respect enough to leave him.
>
> I asked him why he thought it was important to tell me about Jocelyn. His answer surprised me. He was hoping and needed me to be happy for him. I was very happy for him. He seemed like a real new daddy who'd give out cigars if the circumstances were different. He wasn't going to get any congratulations from his mother or sisters. He reached out to the one person that would be happy for him regardless of circumstances.
>
> He was crazy about her. He babysat. He would play with her, he would read her books, and he would tell her stories. She's probably about twelve at this writing. Her mother really went after the estate. She wanted to wring every cent there was. There was a deal he made for a song he wrote, "Black Night," that was used in a movie. He sold it for one price and allowed the song to be used in perpetuity. The contract was clear. But she wanted to get paid if the song was used again. She went over everything with a fine toothcomb and was very tough. I know that she made it hell for Michael and Francine, and it took two years to settle his estate. According to his attorney, it shouldn't have taken that long. She just made life miserable.

They're Lookin' for Me, but They're Gonna Get You

While Frank was happy to be conducting, he was still, perhaps for the first time in some years, excited about his own career. He wanted to work, and as a solo act, momentum was building, and his stock was rising. Musically, he was closer to his father's music than he had ever been, and little by little, he was getting more comfortable with that music. The proximity to his father, his father's music, and his father's musicians gave him a credibility, and a visibility, he didn't have before. Harpist Lisa Coffey said of Frank's time as conductor of his father's orchestra,

> Frank saw himself as a custodian. The instrumentation had been getting reduced and cut. I think the primary impetus was the general hacking away at everything that was going on in Las Vegas at the time. When Frank Jr. came on as musical director, he restored the instrumentation. Sinatra hadn't been using a harp for quite a while. Junior restored the instrumentation, so that harp went back in, and I happened to get the call.
>
> It very quickly became apparent to me how motivated he was by his love for that music. When we would be out with his father, Frank would go through the library and pull out charts for us to play at sound checks. We didn't need to rehearse, but when we did the sound checks, he would pull out charts that were not in the show. I think that he did that because he just wanted to play those charts. He wanted to keep them alive. It took me a while to realize why. I never asked him about

> that, but after a while, I realized he did it because he loved that music. I think he had a sense of being a custodian of sorts. I thought that was impressive and it was one of the things that got to be on a pretty long list of things that I appreciated about him.

As a musician, this was postgraduate school. Always fascinated by his father's classic orchestrations, written by Nelson Riddle, Billy May, Don Costa, and Gordon Jenkins, among others, he was now even closer to the charts and just what made them timeless classics. In time, he would push to include iconic charts that hadn't been played in years and to restore many of these arrangements to their original form. But he still wanted to work on his own, and to do that, there was a delicate balancing act to perform.

Assessing the situation at the time, Kauffman noted that "the more he worked, the more that people enjoyed him and would go to see him next time in the same venue. The fan base was expanding. But Frank still wanted to conduct for his father and at the same time didn't want to lose me. We would have discussions, and he would just say, 'Stick with me.' He didn't want to lose his career for the sake of his father, but he wanted to be his father's hero. This was really important to him, so I didn't pressure him."

Kauffman's balancing act worked like this: She called the elder Sinatra's manager, Eliot Weisman, for a list of Sinatra dates and then sent Frank Jr.'s pending schedule to Dorothy Uhlemann. In turn, Uhlemann would talk to Sinatra. Kauffman was only asked by Weisman to stay away from certain important dates, mainly in venues that Sinatra liked working, including the McCallum Theater in Palm Springs, the casinos in Las Vegas and Atlantic City, Royal Albert Hall, and a couple of other venues on small tours.

When the elder Sinatra looked at his dates and his son's dates, his only comment was, "Don't worry about anything." Fortunately, said Kauffman, "It never came down to a big conflict."

Then there was Ireland, a date facilitated for Frank Sr. by Kauffman. "After I put him into Ireland for the first time, Eliot, the little darling, went right behind my back and went to the same promoter and put him back in two years later. I wouldn't have known if Frank Jr. didn't call me and say, 'My father's going back to Ireland. Why didn't you tell me you booked him?' I said I didn't. That was really bullshit."

Because of the Ultimate Event tour that featured Sinatra, Sammy Davis, Jr., and Liza Minnelli (Minnelli replaced Dean Martin, who sadly lasted for only a couple of dates on the tour), the elder Sinatra was busier than ever in the year that his son joined as conductor. In 1988, there were about 103 dates in the Sinatra date book, meaning that there were around 260 or so open dates that could be booked for Frank Jr. The elder Sinatra's concert schedule eased up as time went on. He performed only 76 dates in 1989, 71 in 1990, 81 in 1991, a high of 92 for the years 1992 and 1993, and in his final year on the road, 57 in 1994. That left a lot of open dates to fill, and Andrea Kauffman set out to fill them.

One of the more notable shows was an early 1992 event spearheaded by Eliot Weisman, who called the event *A Total Eclipse*. The previous year, Frank Jr. brought his show, with the full orchestra, to the lounge of the Desert Inn in Las Vegas. This was said to be the first time a big band was booked in the DI's lounge. In early 1992, Frank Sr. was booked in the DI's main room, and Frank Jr. was booked in the DI lounge at the same time. The result was the *Total Eclipse*.

This was exciting stuff, and Frank Jr. insisted that Andrea Kauffman fly to Vegas for the event, which turned out to be unforgettable.

> I flew out, pregnant, and I went to his father's show. It was a midnight show. We were at ringside, and at the table were Vinnie Carbone, Frank Jr., and I, along with Don and Barbara Rickles, Steve Lawrence and Eydie Gormé, and Henry Silva. Sinatra got to "Soliloquy," and he said, "Every time I sing this song, I think of my two beautiful daughters. My sweet, sweet Tina, and my sweetheart, Nancy."
>
> Frank Jr. and I never had anything romantic going on, but I can tell you that we had very intimate moments as far as a relationship is concerned. Things that a brother and sister might share. He was holding my hand, and his fingernails were going into my palms. He was embarrassed. He didn't know what to do. His father was introducing Nancy and Tina, and his son was sitting right there in front of his face. Vinnie was kicking me under the table, and I'm sitting there, and I'm steaming. Sinatra finished "Soliloquy" then walked off to bows. He had two more songs to do. Frank Jr. wanted to get up and leave. I wouldn't let him. The old man came out again, and Frank, Jr. was squeezing my hand like mad. He introduced Steve and Eydie, Don Rickles, and everyone else

> in the whole damn room. Then he said, "There's one man I didn't introduce. This is a man who taught me everything I know about music. My son, Frank Sinatra, Jr." I'm crying; Vinnie's crying; Don Rickles is crying. Frank Jr. got up and took a bow.
>
> Frank, Jr. said to me, "I don't know what he means."
>
> Later, I asked Sinatra what he meant. He said, "As a conductor, Frankie has a sense of timing that's far beyond anything I've seen or have had on stage with me. He's a great musician."

Frank and his father may not have been great pals in the conventional sense, but the respect that Frank had for his son was becoming more and more evident. The love that they had for each other was another matter. However deep that love might have been was on public view by way of a CBS television special, *Sinatra 75: The Best Is Yet to Come*, broadcast nationally on December 16, 1990, four days after Frank Sinatra's seventy-fifth birthday. Produced by George Schlatter, who would go on to produce several other all-star Sinatra-tribute television specials, the program starred Roger Moore, Robert Wagner, Tony Bennett, Ella Fitzgerald, and a host of others. All paid on-air homage to Frank Sinatra on his birthday. One guest was not advertised in advance, and that was Frank Sinatra, Jr. Frank sang one chorus of "Love Is Here to Stay" to his father, seated with wife, Barbara, at a table in the audience. By the time Frank Jr. got to the final third of the song, his father was in tears, on camera. Barbara Sinatra sat there stoically next to her husband, looking like she didn't give a damn, which she probably didn't.

A few times during Frank's tenure as conductor for his father, he was pressed into service as last-minute star of the show. One of those times was November 24, 1991, and the place was the Sands Hotel and Casino in Atlantic City. Andrea Kauffman was there, and it was the second night of a two-nightweekend stand.

> It may have been the old man's throat; I'm not sure. I know there was a lot of drinking the night before. We all had dinner at the China Moon, the Asian restaurant at the Sands, and I remember stumbling out of there around 4:00 a.m. The next day, Frankie called and asked if I was going to see the show. I asked him if he had a ticket for me, and he said to just come back to the dressing room. That was like 6:00 p.m., and

> I had a feeling he already knew what was going on. I never sat in the audience. I watched the show from the wings. What happened was, the old man said to Frankie, "They're looking for me, but they're gonna get you." Frank, Jr. looked like a deer caught in the headlights, but it wasn't like he didn't think he could do it.
>
> The entertainment director at the Sands, Jay Venetianer, was so pissed off and made so many disparaging remarks about Frankie doing the show. He told the head waiter to sell a lot of liquor because, he said, "The drunker the people are, the better he'll sound." All I know is, Frankie did a great job and he got great applause. He sang his father's set list. And that wasn't the first time it happened. One time, Senior made Junior sing "One for My Baby (and One More for the Road)." And that also got great applause. But Sinatra made a disparaging remark after Frankie sang the song.

Hank Cattaneo remembered that incident well. "There was an embarrassing moment, when his father was doing a show," he recalled. "Frank Jr. was conducting, but during the show, his father asked him to sing. After he was finished, the old man said, 'Okay, let me show you how it should be done.' It broke my heart. He loved his son, but there was this competitiveness there. It wasn't his son up there. It was just another singer. He would never hurt his son in that fashion."

Actor/producer Tony Lo Bianco was a close friend of Frank Sr., and eventually became a very close friend of Frank Jr. He remembered a long talk he had with the father about the son. Lo Bianco recalled,

> I told him how wonderful I thought Junior was. He said to me, "He's very good with the books and very good with the conducting. He sings very well, but he's got a lot to learn." I don't want to say that his father was non-supportive, but that's what it felt like. I think that Junior really felt that. I told Junior many a time that his father loved him and really thought he was great, but I don't think he was that willing to accept that from me. He would have loved for that to have come from Frank. I think the name *Sinatra* belonged to Frank Sr., and I'm not sure he was too eager to give it up.

Not everyone involved in the making of this music was serious 100 percent of the time, especially on the road. Lisa Coffey remembered one hilarious instance that happened at a celebration of then-manager Vinnie Carbone's birthday.

> Vinnie was known as "Der Fuhrer," so I wrote a song with that title for his birthday. It was hysterical, and I bring it up in my own mind from time to time because it was so funny. It was in Atlantic City, and Andrea was there, and so was the old man. I write songs, and one of the things Frank Jr. liked about me was that I would write these parodies. "Der Fuhrer" was a parody of that German drinking song, the "Schnitzelbank." I passed out song sheets. Frank Jr. loved the song. He was prancing around the room. The old man was laughing his ass off, too. It was the most fun I've ever had. It was a splendid moment.
>
> I got to know him pretty well personally, and it was never a romantic relationship, much to the speculation of most of the guys in the band. He still would occasionally come up to me and say things like, "You know, I realize that you're married. But if that should ever change, I'd like to be the first to know about it."
>
> I said, "Really? So I could get in line behind the other 400 women?"
>
> He said, "It's only 350." But anyone who got close enough to know him authentically was likely to love him. He cared about us. He would say things like, "Be patient with yourself." He gave us time.

Still Spreading the News

Andrea Kauffman was seeing the restoration of the relationship between father and son, but she was also witnessing the physical deterioration of the father. During the time he was conducting, Kauffman believed Frank

> made the same mistake he was making with his own music. He was putting music into the show that was unimportant to the audience. Frank mistakenly assumed that by making his father remember all these lyrics to songs he hadn't sung in years, he would stay frosty on the music. His words. "Frosty on the music." But that wasn't working. With dementia, that's not what you do, and no matter what I said, he wouldn't listen. I called Frank Jr's doctor. I asked him if I was right. He agreed that routine is best for a dementia patient. He said he'd call Frankie, and would he explain.
>
> The on-stage teleprompters were first used about a year or two after Frank started conducting. We were in Charlotte, South Carolina, and the old man was in a terrible mood. He was very angry and very angry at his wife, Barbara. The next day, when we talked, was the first time I saw some early symptoms of dementia. "I can see the letters *L-O-V-E*, but I can't make my mind sing the word love," is what the old man said. That was an absolute, positive, symptom of his early dementia. We knew something wasn't right, but we didn't know what it was. Frank saw it, and while the old man didn't hide it at home, he could no longer hide it on stage.

> Eventually, the old man wanted the type font larger on the teleprompters. Joey Pavone, who handled the monitors, did what he could and tried to reprogram the the size of the words. That's when Frank, Jr. realized that things had to change.

Around the middle of 1992, the quality of Frank Sinatra's live performances varied widely. One night, he would be great. The next, painful to witness. He was blowing lyrics, even though the words on the teleprompter were a foot high; his memory and his hearing were going; and on any given night, his energy level would be low. Frank did everything possible to prop up his father, whether it was by challenging him to sing songs he hadn't performed in years or whispering to him onstage, "Fight, fight, fight!"

Tina wanted him off the road. "He's lost track of when to quit," she wrote in her book. "I went to him and said, 'Pop, you can stop now. You don't have to stay out on the road. You can ease up and relax.'" His reply was, "I can't stop. I've got to earn even more money, got to earn more money. I have to make sure that everyone's taken care of." Andrea Kauffman believed that Barbara Sinatra wanted her husband out on the road as long as possible, to continue the income stream.

Frank was, for the first time in his life, close to his father, and he was even closer to what had always consumed him: the music. But even he knew when enough was enough and that it was time for his father to call it quits. Andrea Kauffman remembered that "one of the arguments that occurred between Eliot and Junior was about that very thing. Eliot was screaming at him that his father couldn't stop working because he needed to make that money. Keep in mind that Frank Sinatra's Anheuser-Busch deal, which included ownership of a lucrative Budweiser Beer distributorship, all his endorsements, all his records, all the companies he owned, all these things made money. "Sinatra" was very marketable as a brand in those days. The Anheuser-Busch thing alone was enough to make him very comfortable. I'll give you an example of why he had to keep doing live performances. Barbara went to Roger Moore's home in Greece, and while shopping, she saw a pearl necklace, and she bought it. Of course, if you're a Sinatra, you don't write a check. You take the item out of the store, and you walk out with it. You're billed, and Sonny Golden would write a check. The pearls cost around a million and half dollars. He didn't want to say no to her. So he had to work, and she had to spend.

> He finally found something out that stopped him, and Tony Oppedisano, Sinatra's valet, was involved. Barbara would go to these haute couture houses and have these gowns made for events they had to go to and for the times when she had to stand up for three minutes when he sang "Barbara," a song that made my stomach turn. She would spend anywhere from $12,000 to $20,000 a gown. She would wear them once. Then she got Tony to take them to her girlfriend Linda's dress shop in Malibu and sell them for around half their value. She would give her girlfriend a commission, and Barbara would pocket the difference. With that money, she would play the horses. Dorothy Uhlemann told me that story, and Dorothy never said anything derogatory about Barbara, but she'd drop these little tidbits here and there.
>
> Sinatra was coming back from somewhere when he saw Tony O. getting in the car, leaving with seven or eight zippered garment bags. Sinatra recognized them because they were hanging in Barbara's closet. Tony put them in the trunk of the car and took off before Mr. S. could question him. When he did question Tony O., Tony admitted what he was doing but said it was the first time and that he planned on telling Mr. S. what his wife was doing. Sinatra finally got somebody—a woman—to go into this dress shop, and this woman saw on the tags "Barbara Sinatra . . . worn at, etcetera, etcetera." That ended that.

The success of the "duets" recordings in 1993, where singing partners, mainly from the world of pop music, were electronically spliced into "sing duets" with Frank Sinatra on his hits, kept him on the road that year. One of those duets was with Frank Sinatra, Jr., electronically cut in to make it sound like he was singing "My Kind of Town" with his father. It would have been better if they recorded it live. "Frank Sr. and Frank Jr. sang well together when you could get them together," said Hank Cattaneo, one of the "duets" producers, "and if you could get them to agree on how they were going to do something or address a track. There was competition always. His father was very competitive."

On March 2, 1994, Frank Sinatra was to receive a Legend Award during the nationally telecast Grammy Awards ceremony. Rock star Bono introduced Sinatra to wild applause. The honoree, clearly not

100 percent that night, began to ramble about not being asked to sing, about Dean Martin, and so on, and someone—various individuals have been cited for making the fateful decision—cut him off, on live television. The network went quickly to a commercial. Four days later, Frank Sinatra collapsed during a concert in Richmond, Virginia, while singing "My Way." He refused to go to the hospital and was back on the road several days later. He collapsed again in Atlantic City in August, though he did manage to complete the show. Tina was appalled, and, she said, even Eliot Weisman was "shaken." He told Tina that after the remaining 1994 dates were played out, that would be it. His last, final, full show, with Natalie Cole on board as opening act, was on December 20 at the Fukuoka Dome in Fukuoka, Japan. The show exists in its entirety on video and has been made widely available on various internet platforms. It's painful to watch, but for the moments that he pulled together, he was, somehow, still swinging.

Frank Sinatra would sing five songs at a gala for the Frank Sinatra Celebrity Invitational Gala in Palm Desert, held on February 25, 1995. Gregg Field, Sinatra's drummer since 1991, played that night and said, "It was the Frank of old. He didn't miss a word or note." But the end had finally come.

As I Remember It

The idea had likely been brewing within him for years, and now that his father was officially retired, and now that he had dedicated representation, maybe it could be done the way he wanted it to be done. *As I Remember It* would be a meticulously researched, recorded document of Frank Sinatra's musical history. Frank's concept was to take the listener on a musical journey, ranging from his father's earliest days with Tommy Dorsey and Harry James, through the solo Columbia Records era, the Capital and Reprise years, and culminating in "My Way." Frank would narrate this journey on record, sing all the songs, and conduct the orchestra. *As I Remember It* would be thoroughly detailed, even down to replicating the sounds of old radio and scratchy 78 rpm recordings. Given his attention to detail, penchant for minutiae, and encyclopedic knowledge of his father's musical history, something like this could be the ultimate Frank Sinatra tribute. And with Frank Jr. involved in every facet of the production, it could take years to complete.

Frank was fortunate in having a team of realistic professionals at his side who would have an eye on budgeting and recording-studio efficiency and would rein him in from whatever expensive whims he might have throughout the production process.

A deal was struck with the prestigious Angel Records label, an outfit that normally specialized in high-end classical recordings. With Angel connected with the project, it would no doubt be first class all the way. Andrea Kauffman, ever the voice of reason, was on the team, as were

Hank Cattaneo and veteran conductor Terry Woodson, who eventually would conduct Frank's shows.

Cattaneo was with Frank every step of the way. He said,

> So much work went into it and so much love. Anything that Junior did, he did with love. He was that kind of a guy. Everything he did was done with so much heart and so much desire. He had a love affair with music and the things he created. And on the recording, he did a bunch of takes, so he had alternatives to choose from. I used to tell him that I wish he was more like his old man, in that his father did one take, and that was it. He said he had to have alternatives. The love he put into everything that had his signature on it had to be perfect.

When the rehearsals began in October 1995 at New York City's Clinton Studios (recording logs say October 5 through October 10), Frank conducted the forty-four-piece orchestra, in addition to recording and writing the narration, coproducing, singing, and penning a lengthy essay for the CD booklet. It proved to be too much for him. Fortunately, Terry Woodson was on hand.

> I conducted and produced *As I Remember It*. I had to cut a lot of the talking, which he didn't like, and I programmed it so disc jockeys could go from one tune to the next tune. That was Frank's idea. He called me up to the house and said, "This is what I want to do." Originally, he was going to conduct and put his voice on later. The first session didn't go so well. Hank Cattaneo said, "Why don't you let Terry conduct it?" I knew all those charts, and I had gotten ready to conduct, just in case. He was happy with it. He stood in front of the band and sang, just like his father did.

Even an industry veteran like Rob Heller believed that the result was exceptional, describing it as "honorable, sincere, and as close to showing the genuine respect he had for his father and for his father's contributions. He does such a wonderful job on some of the songs that I'd swear it was his father singing. This was the most genuine that I ever heard him, in any circumstances." The critics loved it, but it didn't sell. "Jay Landers of Angel Records let it die on the vine," said Andrea Kauffman.

Frank wanted to do retakes, another take and another take. It started to go into overtime. He wanted this and this and that. He wanted to use his guys on it. I knew things weren't good. Jay Landers put the deal together, and he wasn't happy because it was going over budget. He ultimately decided that he'd rather take a loss than allow it to be successful, because Frank was so difficult. Jay just said, "Fuck the project." Critically, it was acclaimed, so we decided to buy the rights to the master. We took that album out on the road, and I have to tell you, we were selling so many, I had to hire people to sell it. Actually, we bought back everything he ever recorded, like *Spice*, *That Face*, and *It's Alright*. The estate owns it.

None of us were thrilled when we played the whole album. There wasn't a lot that could be on the radio. There was too much talking, and some of the songs weren't complete. There was so much psychological undertone to everything Frank did. Once again, it was the psychological hang-ups that prevented him from doing what was necessary because if it was successful, he couldn't be the victim.

Though the *As I Remember It* project took up a good deal of his time and attention, there was always time in the life of Frank Sinatra, Jr., for women. Aside from his relationship with Melissa Sue Anderson, and it's clear that he really did care for her, Frank shunned relationships with celebrities or other high-profile women. Sharing the spotlight, on or off stage, just wasn't his thing. Psychologists would likely have a field day in trying to figure out his attraction to the infamous "Hollywood Madam," Heidi Fleiss, but they did have a relationship of sorts from 1994 to 1999.

Fleiss came to enjoy her thirty minutes or so of fame by way of running a prostitution ring that catered to the stars. After serving twenty months in the federal penetentiary for tax evasion, she became a media sensation, at least briefly. Fleiss was the subject of two films, appeared frequently on television, and even wrote an advice column. Fleiss's claims about Frank should be taken with a grain of salt. When speaking with her, one gets the sense that she would do anything to be in the limelight again. However, judging by the existing letters that Frank sent her, he was madly in love with her wanted her to have his child. However, Andrea Kauffman has noted that Frank sent the same type of letter to plenty of other women.

Here's Fleiss's take on the relationship:

I was looking through this box and found all these letters from Frank Jr. It was like a whole other world and a whole other person from where I am today. As for his career, whatever happened was his own fault. Why would you follow in those footsteps? He asked me to marry him, but he had such a peculiar take on things. I really liked him. I confided in him, and he came to visit me in the penitentiary. But he wasn't quite reality based, to put it lightly. One time, we went to the Dodger game, and he took his kid. Of course, he had the best seats. But the kid was yelling the worst things at the visiting team, then he would duck, and it looked like I was yelling because he had a girl's voice. And Frank said nothing and stuffed him with every kind of junk food he could. He wasn't quite reality based.

It started when he called me. At the time, I lived around the corner from his house on Florian, which was like a dungeon. It was full of boxes. It was dark, with boxes everywhere. I liked him. I felt stable with him. But I'll tell you why I couldn't marry him: He thought O. J. Simpson was innocent. To me, that was a sign of only problems to come. Frank was so antidrugs, but the girls he went out with were the biggest drug addicts. He would say, "Oh, no. Never." He was just not reality based.

It was hard for me. My future was so uncertain. Having a boyfriend didn't seem the right thing to do. I was pregnant by him, and I had an abortion. I thought, "Hell no." I couldn't get it out quick enough. I wouldn't have been a good mother, whether it was Frank's child or anyone's child. Did he know? Of course. But it was my decision.

We were together from around 1994 to 1997. His father was still alive at that time, and he would have been horrified if he knew what was going on. Being a flesh peddler and a skin trader, I don't think Frank Sr. would have been into that. Tina was alive, too, which was probably scarier than the father. All I've ever heard is that Tina is a tough broad. If she's trying to protect the legacy, she hasn't done a good job, and her reputation, which is like a bulldog, is not very good.

He definitely was an old-fashioned, romantic guy, and he would say things to me that were really intense for me. I did like him. We had dinner with Don Rickles, and we had a lot of fun, but it just wouldn't have been a good match. He was a very intense man. I think he came twice to visit me in prison. That takes balls. I refused all visits after that. It was too painful to see the outside world. To see someone from the outside world was too painful, that I just pretended that no one else existed.

Frank was so strait laced. If I would drive, he would say, "Slow down, lead foot," or, "You're not on those drugs, are you?" Then I would hear people say that he was just like his father, and I'd say there was no way he was like Frank Sr. Let me tell you, the most traumatic thing in his life was that boarding school that he was sent away to as a child. He talked to me about that all the time. I don't know if he was molested or what happened there. That was more traumatic than the kidnapping. Maybe he was a momma's boy or something, but that was the turning point in his life.

But I do think that the guy who orchestrated the kidnapping (Barry Keenan) should be doing a life sentence. Anytime they glorify him or talk about him in a charming way is so inappropriate. It's disgusting the way they write about him and talk about him.

In the earthquake of 1994, he showed up at my house with a flashlight and an emergency kit. He knocked on my door, and I didn't know who it was. I slept right through it. Then he said, "Now I have to go check on my mother." He was such a good guy. I loved him, but I wasn't going to marry him. It wasn't the right thing.

This photo was taken on the first night of the first gig Andrea Kauffman ever booked for Frank and his quintet in the casino lounge at the then Trump Castle. From Andrea Kauffman's collection.

Andrea, Frank, and President Bill Clinton. From Andrea Kauffman's collection.

Bill Miller making Frank laugh. Photo by Andrea Kauffman.

Birthday celebration at Hard Rock Cafe in Florida. Photo by Paul Malin.

Frank mugging for the camera. Photo by John Loreaux.

Conducting at rehearsal and singing the show that night. From Andrea Kauffman's collection.

Credits for the Sinatra *Centennial Celebration* production. Photo by Andrea Kauffman.

Cynthia, Andrea, and Frank at dinner in Japan. Photo by Mike Smith.

A pensive shot from the wings. Photo by Andrea Kauffman.

Frank speaking at the dedication of the plaque in Ava Gardner's honor. Photo by Isaac Tamburino.

Governor's New Year's Eve Ball celebration, 1999. Photo by Andrea Kauffman.

Hank Cattaneo, Sinatra's production and road manager, with Isaac Tamburino, Frank Jr.'s coproduction and road manager. Photo by Andrea Kauffman.

The "High Hopes" segment from the Sinatra *Centennial Celebration* show. Photo by Andrea Kauffman.

Isaac Tamburino at four years old with Frank and Monica Tribuiani Giampa. Photo by Andrea Kauffman.

Joey Picuri, Frank, and Isaac Tamburino, New Year's Eve, after-show party, Palm Springs, 2014. Photo by Andrea Kauffman.

Dinner with the Sopranos after a show at Borgata in Atlantic City. Seated, left to right, are Tasha Van Horn, Frank, and Maureen Curatola. Standing, from left to right, are Vince Curatola, Tony Sirico, and Andrea Kauffman. Photo by Isaac Tamburino.

Michael Sinatra with his dad at a Dodgers game. Courtesy of Michael Sinatra.

NASA's Fiftieth Anniversary Celebration tour. From Andrea Kauffman's collection.

A shot from Pauli Walnuts (Tony Sirico) and Frank's poker scene in *The Sopranos*. Photo by Andrea Kauffman, taken from a TV monitor while rehearsing.

On stage at Ronnie Scott's with the octet, left to right, Jeff Morrison, Jim Fox, Paul Rostock, Frank, Bob Chmel, Mike Smith, Walt Johnson, Terry Anthony, and Tom Garling. Photo by Paul Malin.

Sinatra Sings Sinatra billboard. Photo by Andrea Kauffman.

Sinatra, unidentified guest, and Andrea Kauffman at a party in Dublin, May 1989. From Andrea Kauffman's collection.

A stage shot. Photo by Isaac Tamburino.

Showtime! Photo by Bob Barry/Jazzography.

Frank on stage. Photo by Bob Barry/ Jazzography.

Frank on stage. Photo by Bob Barry/ Jazzography.

Frank with the band. Photo by Bob Barry/Jazzography.

The many faces of Frank. Photos by John Loreaux.

The core band and original production staff. Top row, left to right, are Paul Rostock, Walt Johnson, Jim Fox, Jeff Morrison, Isaac Tamburino, Paul Malin. Bottom row, left to right, are Bob Chmel, Mike Smith, Terry Anthony, Joey Picuri, Ron Farino, and Frank. Photo by Andrea Kauffman.

Andrea Kauffman, Frank Jr.'s manager, and Eliot Weisman, Sinatra's manager, at Eliot's fiftieth birthday party in Dublin, May 1989. From Andrea Kauffman's collection.

Vince Carbone's wife, Smitty, Andrea Kauffman, and the incomparable Billy May. From Andrea Kauffman's collection.

March 17, 2016, the day after Frank's death, in Daytona Beach, Florida. Top from left to right, Julian Smith, who subbed for Paul Rostock that day; Karen Anthony; Meg Fox; Tasha Van Horn; Bob Chmel; Jeff Morrison; Randy O'Conner; Frank's financial manager, Walt Johnson; and Terry Woodson. Bottom from left to right, Terry Anthony, Isaac Tamburino, Joey Picuri, Mike Smith, and Tom Garling.

Gershwin's America

On July 4, 1997, Frank began a twelve-city, six-week Gershwin's America tour at New York's Battery Park near the Statue of Liberty. In addition to singing, the fifty-five-piece orchestra would be conducted by Frank and would include Gershwin compositions such as "I've Got a Crush on You," "Fascinating Rhythm," and "'S Wonderful." The finale of the shows, which were being presented under the auspices of the Recording Industries Music Performance Trust Fund, would be "Over the Land," first played publicly at a gala for the George Bush family in 1984. The fifteen-minute-long piece, which includes a spoken monologue, focuses on our nation's experiences with the US flags since the War of 1812. The piece is now housed in the National Archives. Kauffman remembered,

> We were only going to perform "Over the Land" one time, at Battery Park in New York, so we called in Terry Woodson to conduct. Frankie brought out almost all the flags that the United States ever had. There were several veterans in the house, and at the end of "Over the Land," Frank got a standing ovation. One veteran, sitting in front, stood up from his wheelchair. He was missing his left leg and right arm, but he pushed himself up and saluted. We all had tears in our eyes. Nancy Jr. was with us that day, and she was very emotional. We had six weeks to go on the tour, but after that show, Frank decided to perform it in every show. He also decided he wanted Terry Woodson to conduct for the rest of the tour. Frank said to Terry, "Send for your clothes; you're

staying." And Terry Woodson never left. He became Frank's permanent conductor.

Visiting backstage after the show played Los Angeles was Tina Sinatra. Kauffman recalled,

> The first time I met her, I didn't know who she was. I was sitting in the dressing room, talking to Sonny Golden, and a woman walked in. She said, "Uncle Sonny, when is this over? I can't stand it anymore."
>
> He said, "Why? It sounds great."
>
> I asked her, "How did you get here?"
>
> She said, "In a minivan that the family rented."
>
> I said, "I'll give you a couple of dollars. Catch the next bus home." With that, she turned on her heels and walked out. Sonny was roaring. He was hysterical. I asked him what was so funny.
>
> He said, "Do you know who that was?"
>
> I said, "I don't have a clue, and I don't care!"
>
> He said, "That was Tina Sinatra." Sonny used to say that I was the only one who could give her a run for her money.
>
> The tour was amazing. But Frank had a way of inflating things. If it was two inches long, he'd make it into seven feet. Now we have Terry coming out on the road, so we need another room, more airline tickets, and more salary. Two nights before the tour began, we were called to Frank's suite in New York. We couldn't walk through the halls. There were cardboard boxes stacked from floor to ceiling. There were two adorable young girls sitting in his living room. Frank turned to me and said, "Andrea, this is Shelly and Kelly. They'll be on the road with us." It was Merrill Kelem's sister and a friend of hers. Now there's more transportation, more rooms, and more money needed. He continued, "They'll be selling these." He opened one of the boxes and pulled out a T-shirt that had "100th Anniversary Gershwin Tour." They were all marked by size. And he had jackets made, too. There was a company in LA that printed them, the Flussberg Brothers. They had a clothing printing company in LA. He had five thousand T-shirts made. If he had had five hundred, and we sold out, we would have been ahead of ourselves. But five thousand? Now we had to take these two girls and transport five thousand T-shirts wherever we went. They had to get set up, and I had to advance the set-up details to make sure the shirts

would be displayed for sale. Towards the end of the run of concerts, we gave a lot away.

Fast forward to about six months later. Eddie Morgan, our lead trombonist, was a sweet, wonderful man. He, Terry, and I were called the Splinter Group. We were inseparable. One night in Chicago, Frank came down to the bar to meet us for dinner. Frank was a freak for jackets. He loved them, especially short leather bomber jackets. He wore them all the time. This particular night, he was wearing a magnificent jacket made of lamb skin. It was so soft. He must have spent thousands for it. Eddie had already had a couple of drinks, and he went over to Frank, felt the lushness of the lamb-skin sleeve, and asked, "Flussberg?"

The Final Curtain

The death of Frank Sinatra, Sr., on May 14, 1998, some three years after he last performed in public, was headline news all over the word. His influence and his legacy cannot be measured, and in terms of fame and the continued popularity of his work, only Elvis comes close. In life, he was a legend. Since his death, he has become mythical. His music was, and in many cases still is, the soundtrack of many lives.

Despite his stoic nature, Frank Jr. was a mess when his father died. Andrea Kauffman strongly believed that he was not prepared for the way he felt. She said,

> When his father died, I couldn't reach him on the phone. Barbara got valet Tony Oppedisano and Sinatra publicist Susan Reynolds to the hospital, but she did not call the children. I was a part of this phone loop. Nancy called me and said, "I've got to find my brother."
>
> I asked her, "What's the matter?"
>
> She said, "You've got to find my brother." Then she broke down. I knew how to reach Frank because I had a separate line for him that nobody had. I got a hold of him and told him he had to call his sister right away. He asked me what the matter was, and I told him I had no idea. He assumed it was about his dad, but he wasn't sure. He finally called his sister, and she told him. Then he called me and said, "Andrea, it's over."
>
> My mother and Frank's father were very sick at the same time. We were in Canada on the road for six weeks. Frank Jr. knew how sick my mother was and allowed me to fly home every Sunday and return on

> Tuesday. Sunday and Monday were dark days. We often talked about whose parent would pass on first.
>
> May 14, I got a call from Frank. He said, "It's over."
>
> I asked, "What's over?"
>
> He said, "I won!" He won our bet as to who would die first. Then he said, "Tell me something, darling. How did Barbara have to chance to call Tony O. and Susan Reynolds, his valet and his publicist, and not his children, to say, 'Dad's been rushed to the hospital?'"
>
> I said, "Frank, unless you get me in front of that woman, we'll never know."
>
> He said, "I wouldn't let you do that because I'm not visiting you in jail." She never allowed them to say goodbye. Oh what she did to those kids!

The funeral took place on Wednesday, May 20, at the Good Shepherd Church in Beverly Hills. In addition to family members Tina, Nancy, Frank Jr., and Mrs. Sinatra, there were around seven hundred mourners at the church, all there by special invitation. The guest list included Joey Bishop, Nancy Reagan, ex-wives Mia Farrow and Nancy Sinatra, Paul Anka, Tony Bennett, Vic Damone, Don Rickles, Kirk Douglas, Sidney Poitier, Jack Nicholson, Gregory Peck, Sophia Loren, Debbie Reynolds, Dionne Warwick, Liza Minnelli, Bob Dylan, and Quincy Jones. The eulogists were Robert Wagner, Kirk Douglas, Gregory Peck, stepson Robert Marx, and Frank Sinatra, Jr.

Tina Sinatra, never prone to complimenting her brother, was moved by Frank's words. "The warmest response went to Frankie, who spoke without notes, and with the ease and command of his father's son," she wrote. Not long after the eulogy, one of the mourners was overheard saying, "Now he has a career."

A week and a half later, Frank Sinatra, Jr., resumed his career. Andrea never forgot the first performance after his father died.

> It was a date in Chicago. I'll remember that night for the rest of my life because he asked me to sit on the stage. He wanted me to be there to give him support. I sat behind the harpist, and I didn't take my eyes off of him because I knew he wasn't okay. He told me he needed to sing. I wanted to cancel the date, but ticket sales were through the roof. He walked out on stage to thunderous applause. It was not easy for him. He chose to close with "Put Your Dreams Away," his father's old theme song.

> From a totally selfish point of view, I've never been more embarrassed in my life. I was sitting there, sobbing. And he's standing with tears coming down his cheeks. And he unabashedly let the audience see he was crying. It was such an emotional and personal moment. And even then, on that night, he was basically still doing his own show, where only a handful out of seventeen songs meant something to the fans in the audience mourning Sinatra.
>
> The first real celebration of Sinatra was *As I Remember It*, based on the recording. He was still fighting not to pay homage to his dad. He knew what the audiences wanted to hear, but he thought, "What am I, the cheap version? You'll pay $150 a ticket for Sinatra and $37.50 for me?"

Those who thought Frank's repertoire would immediately undergo a radical change after his father's death were disappointed. There were some changes and additions to the set lists in favor of Sinatra songs, but the changes were small. Musically, Frank pretty much remained his own man, and his shows were not all that much different from the way they were before his father passed.

Though Frank Sinatra, Jr., was now the "Sinatra heir apparent," he was not singing what audiences wanted to hear or what Kauffman needed to sell the show.

Co-road manager and sound engineer Joe Picuri joined the Sinatra fold in 2002 and became quite close to Frank. Picuri remembered that Frank used to say, "I've got to wear the old man's shoes; I've got to wear his coat; I've got to sing his songs." Picuri went on to say,

> It took me a while to understand that Frank was a solid singer unto himself. The songs he tended to gravitate toward weren't in the vein of his father. He liked the ballads, the more melancholy and introspective tunes, but that doesn't really sell, especially when you're Frank Sinatra's kid. I don't think Frank really reconciled himself with his father's music. I just thought, "Just do it. Like an act." He could impersonate anyone. I think he could imitate his dad much better than he did. He was really talented, but he couldn't let go. Somehow it was too much, like he was surrendering. Everyone was like, "Come on Frank. It's just a fucking gig." He loved his father. He wanted to be just like his father. But then it all turned on him and left a scar that stayed with him way too much. He could never let it go.

Jim Fox explained the challenging process of choosing what "Sinatra songs" were added and why.

> After his father died, we started adding, not hits, but songs like "I Guess I'll Hang My Tears Out to Dry." He did have a Sinatra medley in the book that he could pull out when needed. It had like a half a dozen Sinatra tunes that he could live with in this medley. At one point in the 1990s, we were on a little tour that took us from Staten Island to Pennsylvania and down to Florida. In Pennsylvania, we were working in a hall, and I said to Frank, "Would you think about doing 'Come Rain or Come Shine' with just guitar?"
>
> And he said, "We have a chart for that."
>
> And I said, "Yes, but we've never done it."
>
> He said, "It's too big a hit." That is a quote. He didn't want to do it because it was a hit. But he had a special respect and affection for the arrangers. He knew Nelson—Nelson taught him stuff, and he knew Nelson really well—and Don Costa, and he knew Neal Hefti and others. So I said to him, "That arrangement might be Don Costa's vocal masterpiece, and maybe the most influential vocal arrangement that he's ever written." And I sang him the string part, that bluesy stuff on the strings. Anyway, he heard me, and a month later, that chart was in the book, and we did it a lot after that.

Terry Woodson said that "Frank did not want to be another Sinatra wanna-be. He wanted to be his own man. The unfortunate part of it was that he picked a music style that was his father's music style. He was competing with him, though he would say, 'I don't want to compete with my father.' A lot of times, he'd do his own thing, but the audience would say, 'Hey, when are you going to do your father's songs?'"

Terry Anthony observed the changes, however subtle they may have been:

> In 1993, he still wasn't doing a lot of his father's material. When his father died, that's when it changed. I remember talking to him about it, and I said, well, here it is. You knew the day was going to come. You know what they want. It's up to you now. He wanted to take it on, but he knew he couldn't sing like his father. Who the hell is going to sing like his father? He made it clear to the audience. He'd say, "I'm here. I'm

> going to try to give you the best rendition of what I remember." When we first started out, he wouldn't do "My Way." He said it was too personal and too much "my father." He was really hesitant to do it. We had a six-week job in Canada, a very nice gig. We did three nights, and the promoter, a nice guy, came up to Frank and said, "You have to do 'My Way.' Otherwise, the people that backed us are going to let you go. You have to do it." We had the music shipped overnight, we did "My Way" the next night, and the people went nuts.

Andrea Kauffman explained,

> Frank's shows incrementally increased in interest and salability. We increased its value with *As I Remember It*. That was the first show when he did a little more Sinatra. In *As I Remember It*, after a big tune, he would walk off the stage, wipe his brow, and immediately walk back out, sit in the crux of the piano, back lit in blue. The resemblance to his father was shocking. The audience would gasp. After he sang either "One for My Baby" or "Angel Eyes," the screams and shouts, the applause that lasted for minutes prompted him to throw his hands up in the air. It was like him saying, "Okay, I'm my father's son. I look like him, and I sound like him. Okay, okay, okay, I hear you." Or it was, "I've got to embrace this. They'll think I hated him if I don't. And I didn't hate him. I just hated the way he brought me up."
>
> That show morphed into the *Sinatra Sings Sinatra* show. I think the title said it all. About 75 percent of the show was what the audience bought tickets to hear. The third and final production was the *Centennial Celebration Starring Frank Sinatra, Jr.* That was the pinnacle of all shows.
>
> It never occurred to me that that the passing of Sinatra was going to be his freedom artistically. Never did I think that the death of his father would be the door that would open to allow him to embrace his father's music. It was almost shocking that that's what it took.

Of that transitional time, bassist Paul Rostock could only say, "When he started singing his father's songs, the whole thing went up a level for us."

At the Nineteenth Hole with Barbara Sinatra

The Frank Sinatra Celebrity Invitational Golf Tournament, an annual event that benefitted the Barbara Sinatra Children's Center at Eisenhower Medical Center in Palm Desert, California, was first held in 1989. Frank Sinatra's last appearance there was in 1995. The 1999 invitational would be the first held after Sinatra's death.

Several months before the scheduled tournament, Frank Jr. received a call from Barbara Sinatra, asking him to perform. Frank called Andrea to get her take on it, and after finding out that some names from the "old crew" would be there, including Tony Danza, she said, "Who better to do this than you? Who better to honor him than you?" But she warned that he would have to do Sinatra songs from *As I Remember It* as that would be the night's theme. His feelings were mixed, but at Kauffman's urging, he decided to do it.

Barbara Sinatra, acknowledging that Frank Jr. agreed to perform, called Kauffman to thank her for her support. Kauffman replied,

> "I'm not supporting you. I'm supporting Mr. Sinatra and Frank Jr., and I want to make that clear."
>
> She said, "I get it. Everybody has to take a side. But I'm pleased. What can I give Frankie to represent my heartfelt thank you?"
>
> I told her I'd think about it and that I would call her back. Then I called Frank and told him what Barbara Sinatra asked. Frank said, "I want my grandfather's watch." This was a beautiful watch that Sinatra gave to his dad and got back when Marty Sinatra passed. The watch was

> promised to Frank Jr., and I told Barbara that Frank wanted that watch as his "thank you."
>
> Barbara said, "Brilliant," adding that she had the watch and that it was a wonderful idea for a gift for Frank. She said she would have it refurbished and sent to the house.
>
> Frank was a hit at the event, which was not easy for him. "It was kind of a painful evening for me," he said later, "doing his music with his orchestrations in that environment. A lot of us had tears in our eyes."

After the show, Kauffman couldn't wait to tell Frank about the gift he was going to get from Barbara. "The weeks came and went," said Kauffman. "Finally, Frank called me, telling me he just got a package from Barbara. I asked, 'Yeah, what was it, Frank?' He says, 'A book on airplanes.' I said, 'Are you kidding me?' That's Barbara. She put 'The Best Is Yet to Come' on Sinatra's headstone. Everybody had the same question: For who? Everyone had the same answer: For Barbara."*

---

* Some time in 2020, three years after Barbara Sinatra's death, Nancy Jr. and Tina had "The Best Is Yet to Come" removed from the headstone and replaced it with "Sleep Warm, Poppa."

The Vampire

Nancy Franklin penned a short piece about Frank's Gershwin tour, the status of his father's health, and the details about his future wife, Cynthia McMurrey, which appeared in the August 4, 1997, issue of *The New Yorker* magazine. It follows:

The Musical Life

By Nancy Franklin

Seated at Sinatra's right was his companion, a Texas-born attorney named Cynthia McMurrey, whom he met in Las Vegas, at the Desert Inn, five years ago. He said, "I saw her coming down the hall, and I went like this—" He shielded his face with his hands. "I said, 'Don't aim those weapons at me, they might be loaded.' She's got these blue eyes, and she uses them like weapons." McMurrey's current gig is at the United Nations tribunal at The Hague, where she is engaged in the defense of one of the Bosnian Muslims charged with war crimes. (Her client faces a forty-nine-count indictment.) "Frank came when the trial started, in March," she said. "He helped me punch holes and file papers." Sinatra said, "She was practicing law, and I was practicing Gershwin." While helping out McMurrey, he became something of a law student himself. "She sends me to a law bookstore; I end up buying more books for me than for her." He said he had just ordered a book on astral law, which will help lawyers sort out the jurisdictional difficulties that are bound to occur when, say, a Russian satellite is hit by an American satellite, falls out of its geosynchronous orbit, and lands on someone's head in Peru.

On October 18, 1998, about two months after *The New Yorker* piece and some five months after the death of his father, Frank Sinatra, Jr., married McMurrey. He may have had several reasons for marrying for the first time at the age of fifty-five. Maybe it was time for him to give his life some legitimacy, or perhaps he was doing it to make his mother proud. One of the problems with the marriage was that, almost without exception, everyone despised Cynthia. In some cases, "despised" is an understatement.

Frank met her the same way he met all the other groupies and hangers on. She was in the audience. Andrea Kauffman was there that night.

> She was in his audience, and she was looking at him. He said, from the stage, that "you could kill somebody with those weapons of yours," meaning her eyes. He called her "Weapons" from that day on. He always had a penchant for a certain look, a certain kind of woman. Long blonde hair, that Barbie Doll, Valley Girl look. The attraction, other than the eyes? She had credentials. She was an attorney. That impressed him. That's how he introduced her to people. He would say, "She's an attorney."
>
> While we were all in New York, Cynthia included, I got a call from Nancy Sr. She wanted me to take Cynthia to lunch. Nancy said, "I want you to tell that gold digger that if she marries him, Frankie is cut off. She won't get a penny. She won't get one red dime." Nancy was right. Cynthia was the wrong woman for Frank. We could see right through her. She didn't even bother to hide her motives for wanting to marry Frank. The way Nancy Sr. wanted to deal with it, through me, was not the way to handle this situation. The Sinatra family should have met with Frank and discussed their concerns with him. Cynthia told Frank what his mother threatened. Frank didn't talk to his mother for two years after that lunch. I believe Cynthia slowly killed Frank. She brought crisis after crisis to his life. His blood pressure was sky high, and she didn't care that she was the reason![*]

---

* Shortly after Frank Jr.'s passing, this book's coauthor, Bruce Klauber, called Andrea Kauffman, just to see how she was holding up. Klauber said, "I remember how emotional Andrea was that day and that one of the first things she told me was that she believed Cynthia was responsible for Frank's death."

They got married in Wharton, Texas, and Kauffman was a witness to the event via cell phone. "Did I advise against him marrying her?" Kauffman asked rhetorically. She said, "I didn't advise. I demanded that he not marry her. His mother, his sisters, his dearest friends, all of us were against the marriage. In his mind, she was a respectable, professional, attractive woman. She had a profession all right, but she sure wasn't successful at it. She was one of the worst attorneys I'd ever come across. Clients wouldn't pay her because she didn't do the job. She was fired by the lead council in The Hague. She was an awful human being who cared about no one but herself."

Joe Picuri pulled no punches, either. "To me she was a fucking vampire. This was one of Frank's tragic flaws. Frank loved women, and he loved the fucking freaks, too. Cynthia was a freak. She was smart, but she was just, want, want, want. I don't think she did anything for Frank. Cynthia was mean. When I heard she died, I thought, 'That's destiny. That's some kind of cosmic shit.'"

When the relationship was deteriorating, he confided in Ronna Brodsley:

> When I saw him, he was at some big hotel in LA. They hadn't married yet, but Cynthia was there with him. I couldn't take my eyes off her. Out of all the kinds of women I wanted to see him with, she wasn't it. She was awful. She wouldn't let him talk to anybody. She hovered over him. She was predatory. When he saw me, he gave me a big hug, but he didn't say that we should get together afterward. I realized later that Cynthia would never let him do that. She had to have him all to herself. She had to have control. Her eyes followed him everywhere. He called me when they split up, and he told me the whole story. From what he told me, she just did horrendous things to him, just horrible. She tried to strip him of everything. She wanted every shekel he had.

Sarah Jane Karloff is the daughter of horror film star Boris Karloff. Boris, as Frank Jr. told the story, used to coach Frank Sr. on matters of diction as well as the quality and potential of movie scripts he was considering. Sarah Jane showed up at one of Frank Jr.'s shows, and the two became fast friends. She spent time talking to Frank about Cynthia and to Cynthia about Frank. Karloff concluded, "Cynthia fell in love with the name Sinatra, and she was Mrs. Sinatra. She had Frank so bamboozled and wrapped around her little finger. It was disgusting.

She was so phony. She was nothing but a call girl. But I'd never say that to Frank. He was absolutely blind about Cynthia." Karloff described Frank as "a broken toy." Cynthia came with a lot of baggage as well. She was married four times and had three young daughters. Frank was no walk in the park, either. "I loved the fact that he would run around on Cynthia," said Kauffman, "but she was getting what she wanted from him, which was to be introduced as his wife and to get what she wanted financially. He bought her a house in Wharton. Her girls needed cars. He bought them. She got what she wanted. He got the bills. He might not hear from her for a while, and then he would fly down there for a week or two. They weren't living together. What a marriage."

Shortly after Frank and Cynthia were married, while on the road, Frank brought a "lady friend" to join all of us for dinner. Saxophonist Mike Smith, who says he "was always the wise guy in the band," had a funny plan in mind. Given that the new Mrs. Sinatra was a Texan, Smith had everyone at the table slowly join in to hum "The Yellow Rose of Texas." Frank, no doubt, got the hint.

Cynthia wanted them to go to counseling, but he wouldn't go. Kauffman believes that "he would have benefitted from therapy, but he would never allow anybody to get in that deep." She said, "I think that Frank's doctor always felt that he was bi-polar. His ups were so up, and downs were so down. He suffered from depression. He was given medication for it that he never took. Cynthia drove his blood pressure sky high. He took medication for that, but it wasn't enough."

Kauffman was with Frank on the road when the first symptoms of a prostate problem appeared. She explained,

> He was having problems urinating. When he got home, he saw a urologist, and after testing, he was told he had prostate cancer. It was the early stages and very curable with surgery. After the operation, he had to stay at home, in bed with a catheter. Cynthia had to change his bag in the middle of the first night. She found the job disgusting and complained to me the minute I walked in the next morning. I never heard the end of it. In her mind, there had to be some sort of payment for this. I never once heard her say, "I'm so glad he's going to be alright," or "I was so worried about him."
>
> He was very concerned about sex. He explained to me in detail what the issues were going to be after the surgery. He could become aroused,

but that was it. I believe Cynthia was secretly glad after his surgery because she thought she wouldn't have to have sex with him. She may have even been repulsed by him. She referred to him as the "Pillsbury Dough Boy" many times.

Cynthia wanted to be Mrs. Sinatra, to have money, the prestige, and to dig herself out of Wharton, Texas. She flaunted the name at every hotel we stayed in while on the road. I had several phone calls from hotel GMs and food and beverage directors who voiced their concerns about the way she spoke to staff and her demands. Fire after fire had to be put out in her wake. When I tried to tell Frank what was going on and how this could hurt us and the show, in the end, his response was, "Just keep doing what you're doing. You can smooth it out."

For many years, Barbara and Frank Sinatra hosted a golf outing and concert benefiting the Children's Center in Palm Springs. Cynthia and I were invited to the golf outing luncheon that was given for the women. It was hosted by Barbara Sinatra on the day before the concert. It was the very first concert and tournament after Sinatra's death. Cynthia asked, "How do I look?" I never saw a woman who could put on designer clothes and look like white trash. Who wears velvet pumps and a bag to match for a lunch in Palm Springs? That's how she looked! We sat down; Cynthia leaned into Barbara and asked, "What should I call you?"

Barbara looked at her and said, "Mrs. Sinatra."

I said to Cynthia, "What did you think she was going to say? Call me mom?" She just didn't get it. She wanted to be treated like Barbara was treated, but everyone recognized her for the classless woman that she was.

Jim Fox was diplomatic about the whole Cynthia situation, saying, "She was always nice to me and very nice to my wife, Meg. I know that people had stuff to say about her. But look, this was Frank's wife, and he loved her, and I didn't really make any judgments about her. Honestly. I'm not holding anything back. I just felt, there she is, and she's nice to us, and that's cool."

To this day, Lisa Coffey insists that Cynthia loved Frank.

I know that. He knew it, too. I remember that I was amazed when she was in the audience, and he was on stage. She was just enraptured by him. We were going to the airport in a limousine at one time. It was really early in the morning. She had her head on Frank's shoulder, and she was going back to sleep. I was sitting across from him, and he looked at me and pointed at her. He mouthed the words, "She loves me." At that moment, it occurred to me that that was a really rare thing for him. That a woman loved him, not to just be around him because he was Frank Sinatra, Jr. I know that she loved him. He told me that he had gone to a party to celebrate Cynthia's daughter's graduation from law school. At that party, he told her that that marked the end of his financial input. I sensed that the battle lines were drawn and that she was trying to get money from him. That struck me as a great tragedy of what I thought was going to be a wonderful thing in his life.

I do know that she thought it appropriate that men give her money. I think that was in her repertoire. I remember when he bought her a Buick. She ain't driving no Buick. No way! She sold it and bought a more appropriate car. Something hot and snazzy.

The breakup was long, sloppy, messy, ugly, and costly.

Kauffman said that Frank asked for a divorce.

I think he realized she was just too high maintenance and too little love. But they were together often. One of the problems the court cited when she sued him for common-law wife status and he fought was that he would introduce her as his wife long after the divorce. That worked against him when it came time for the court to decide. I'd tell him to stop introducing her as his wife because she wasn't. He said, "Am I supposed to say I'd like to introduce you to my ex-wife? The woman I used to be married to?"

I said, "Why don't you say, 'This is Cynthia?' Why does she have to be your wife?" She was hanging on for dear life. Her big issue was the money. She wanted more.

They had a prenuptial agreement, so she was only going to get so much money for every year they were happily married. That was two years, and none of it was happy. Cynthia was aware of several criteria that their relationship had to meet for Texas common-law ruling. If you met most of those criteria, the marriage would have been considered common law. She thought she had it in the bag. I was able to show that he never lived in the Wharton, Texas, house with her for more than a week. Six weeks is what they needed to prove one of the criteria. I documented all the details of his travels

> with credit card charges, airline records and phone calls. He didn't live with her. He visited!
>
> One of the other big surprises was when Cynthia accused him of cheating on her. She told the court that she saw him in a restaurant having an intimate dinner with a woman. On cross-examination, Frank's attorney asked Cynthia if saw Frank eating food. She said, "Yes of course." Frank's attorney called him to the stand. Frank said he hadn't been in a restaurant on that date or for months prior to that date. The attorney asked Frank to show the court why he didn't go out to eat. He stood up, unbuttoned his shirt and showed the court the feeding tube. He didn't eat solid foods. The ruling was still in her favor, and she won the case, granting her common-law wife status. It was one of the most crooked, tainted rulings I've ever read. Frank's attorneys couldn't understand the final ruling in Cynthia's favor after the evidence they presented. The judge and Cynthia's father were old family friends from Wharton. The ruling was aggressively appealed.
>
> She just wanted to be a Sinatra, which she assumed would entitle her to all the trappings being a Sinatra could bring. She got millions in gifts out of him for a while after their divorce. Eventually, he didn't have any more to give her. Three weeks after he died, his lawyers won the appeal. Frank won. Just a little too damn late.
>
> She killed him, and I'll say it over and over again. Everyone who knows him will say it. I'm not the only one.

When it was over, Kauffman asked Frank if he loved her. "In my way, as much as I could love anybody," was his answer.

Indicative of the monetary demands Cynthia made of Frank, even after the formal marriage was over, concerned John Brink. Cynthia was married to Texan John Patrick Brink from 1985 to 1989 and had two children with him. Sometime after they divorced, Brink devised a scam to sell phony securities—to the tune of $200,000—mainly to the elderly. By the summer of 2000, the law caught up with him. In July, he pled guilty to one count of securities fraud and one count of misapplication of fiduciary property and was sentenced to sixty years for each offense. Cynthia wanted to help her ex with the appeal. She went to Frank and asked him for $10,000 for Brink's lawyers' fees. Frank gave it to her, but in December 2001, the appeal was denied. In the end, the verdict was overturned. Brinks claimed, said court records, "that he was denied the right to counsel of his choice, as well as the right to effective assistance of counsel." The court agreed.

Karen Anthony, wife of Frank's second alto saxophonist, Terry Anthony, frequently joined her husband on the road. She became quite close with Frank, with Andrea Kauffman, and with the other "road family" members. She was particularly eloquent when writing about the often dysfunctional Frank/Cynthia relationship:

> Each was exactly what the other deserved. They were beautiful liars who adored each other while they were lying. There was no stardust in this woman eyes, and I truly believed she loved the real guy. Sure, she loved who he was, but that *is* who he was. Frank, for all his peccadilloes, never married anyone but Cynthia. And he had children with women he didn't marry.
>
> He divorced Cynthia after a short time but continued their relationship, and we all thought of her as his wife. In those days, she was allowed to keep the Sinatra name, and that drove Andrea crazy. Andrea was aware of the inner workings of the relationship. Cynthia and Andrea were stepping on each other's shadows. Cynthia was not working in Frank's best interests, but in her own. Frank called me one night to ask how could it be that the two most important women in his life didn't like each other?
>
> Time moved on, and the love affair with Cynthia had become tarnished. Frank was close to finished with her, yet they were often together, and she called herself his wife. We were all gentle and respectful, as it was their choice until one night in Connecticut.
>
> Cynthia was coming in from an interview with Court TV in New York City and asked me to save her a seat at Frank's show. She hoped to be there before the overture. I walked into the showroom a little early. All the tables were empty except one near the front of the stage. There were two people seated who I didn't know, plus an orchestra wife. I headed to that table. Frank always liked to sing the slow songs to Cynthia, and they had a few private "I love you" hand signals, like lovers do. Perfect! She would be right under his gaze.
>
> While I sat with my orchestra friend, the other couple, a pretty woman and a gay escort who loved Sinatra music, introduced themselves. Nice folks. It somehow came up that she was a newspaper writer who focused on local business. She had been speaking with Frank a lot

about ways to increase the house. This morphed into my explanation that Terry, who taught high school music, brought his class to a Sinatra rehearsal for a clinic, and pizza, at Franks urging.

Frank loved to teach, encourage, and support young musicians of his genre. She wanted to write about it. It would make for great public relations. So, we became chatty and friendly, and then she asked me to keep a confidence. I thought, "Sure!"

Frank was going to announce their engagement tonight from the stage.

Did I mention I was saving a seat for my friend/his wife, Cynthia? Or that I have a poker face?

The showroom was starting to fill up. I stand up to see where security people Merrill Kelem and Johnny Pizza—and Andrea—are because I'm thinking we're going to need our security here soon. I see them, and they're watching the crowd. One hand signal, and one of the guys will be there. Both are very smooth guys. They will handle the bloody, messy, screaming, and unavoidable cat fight that will break out when Frank's "wife" sits next to his "fiancé."

One nanosecond before curtain, Cynthia took her seat next to me.

I know, beyond a doubt, that somehow this will be my fault.

Curtain opened. Our table in front of the stage is the first one he sees. He misses his cue. Cynthia is oblivious and sweetly buys a round for the table. Frank gets his cue this time but sings like . . . like his wife is sitting next to his fiancé! I make Cynthia change seats with me, putting her a little farther back and behind me from the fiancé, looking toward the stage door. Andrea is there staring right at me. She knows, and we're good.

Thank God! We may survive this! But poor Frank delivered the very worst and shortest show he has ever sung.

Remember my accolades about his empathy and sensitivity? No. Not that night.

Cynthia McMurrey died on April 20, 2017, in Sugar Land, Texas. She was sixty-four and was survived by her three daughters: Brittney and Victoria Brink and Jessica McMurrey.

The Sopranos

In early 2000, Frank guest starred in an episode of HBO's ultrapopular crime drama with a Mafia focus, *The Sopranos*. The episode, titled "The Happy Wanderer," focused on an all-night, high-stakes poker game taken over by lead character Tony Soprano (James Gandolfini) as Junior Soprano (Dominic Chianese) was under house arrest and couldn't participate. Frank played himself.

The idea for a guest shot originated with Terence (Terry) Winter, who joined *The Sopranos* in season 2 as executive producer and writer. Andrea Kauffman was all for it, though Frank was a bit hesitant about it at first because the show was all about the Mafia. "He would never say the words *Mafia* or *Cosa Nostra*," she said. "But he decided to do it, and I really wanted to see how this would play out. The experience was fabulous. It was one of the best experiences of our lives. I never saw him laugh the way he laughed during *The Sopranos*' taping. The guys were loose, they were fun, and they were sweet."

The cast members were impressed with Frank, personally and professionally, and some fast friendships were formed, particularly with Tony Sirico and Vincent Curatola. "He was a very, very humble man and a respectful guy, with not an ounce of ego," Curatola recalled. "He was so interested in where the cameras were, how the lines were read. You know, the guy just had something in his blood. He was for real. He definitely would have had a future as an actor."

Bonds were forged with the cast, and several members came to see Frank's performance in Atlantic City. One night was particularly memorable. As Kauffman tells it,

> Most of the guys were coming to the Golden Nugget to see him. They came in after the lights went down, and of course, they sat right in front. For this occasion, he used the word *Mafia*. On the stage, Frank said something about his father, like, "Everybody thought my father was in the Mafia." Then he said, "There's no such thing as the Mafia. These guys don't exist. And if they did, I'd give them what for." And he was creating this dialogue about how he'd stand up to the Mafia. I had Tony Sirico, who played Paulie Walnuts in *The Sopranos*, waiting in the wings, and while Frank was specifically misdirecting the audience and telling them how "these tough guys can't tell me what to do. They can't tell me what to sing!," Paulie Walnuts walked out on stage. The audience went berserk. They were all screaming.
>
> Paulie said, "Sing Summer Wind." Frank immediately turned to the orchestra and counted off "The Summer Wind." Everybody applauded.
>
> Tony Lo Bianco, who, at this juncture, had become the national spokesperson for the Sons of Italy, was disappointed about the way Frank's guest shot was handled. "I wasn't happy about him doing the show," Lo Bianco said. "What I wasn't happy about is the scene where he was playing cards and then left the room. When he left the room, the guys started talking disparagingly about him. I thought, 'No, no, no. You don't let that happen.' That's what I didn't like."

Still, the importance of Frank's appearance on *The Sopranos* cannot be overestimated. The program was a ratings bonanza for HBO, and millions of viewers tuned in weekly. Though his part was small, and he only had to play himself, it was clear that Frank was at ease on camera, comfortable in his role, and perhaps even more at ease before the cameras than he was on stage. Kauffman took note of this and the fact that he had an uncanny ability to reproduce dialects and foreign accents with startling authenticity. Two years later, he appeared on the FX network's sitcom *Son of a Beach*, playing over-the-top character Stinkfinger. He was hilarious.

As a result of his out-of-character, comedic turn on *Son of a Beach*, Frank ended up in another comedic role, this time as a cartoon version of himself, on the animated sitcom *Family Guy*. The program, which began airing on the Fox Network in 1999, was created by actor, writer, singer and Sinatra fan Seth MacFarlane. "Seth went to lunch with us in Palm Springs at Frankie's request," Kauffman remembers.

> Frank wasn't familiar with the show, and a lot of people were also unaware that Seth was a singer. Frank started to tell stories. He entertained at the table for hours.
>
> Seth asked me, "Does he do any acting?"
>
> I said, "What do you think he's doing now?" Then I got a call from Seth asking if Frank would do the show. I didn't love the contract that was first presented to us in the beginning, but I did get some changes made. I took it to Frank, and I told him I got what we wanted and thought he should do it. It was a crossover audience.

Andrea's son, Isaac, sealed the deal by saying, "Mom, he's got to do it. It's one of the most popular shows on television."

Frank made nine appearances on *Family Guy*, with the first one airing in 2006, and the last in 2015. Given the popularity of his turns on *The Sopranos*, *Son of a Beach*, and *Family Guy*, his proven acting ability and drawing power via the Sinatra name, Kauffman thought there was potential for him as an actor. She thought seriously about steering his career in that direction when and if Frank decided to call it quits as a singer or limit his performances to special events. Sadly, it never happened.

This Is a Musician Singing

Frank was most comfortable on the road, with his road family. The set list was slowly changing, and more "Sinatra songs" were creeping in, though not nearly enough for Andrea Kauffman when the audiences were clamoring for "The Summer Wind" and "My Way."

In the summer of 2001, Frank embarked on an ambitious, two-month tour of Europe with another ghost band, but this ghost band wasn't selling nostalgia, ala Tommy Dorsey. This was the Woody Herman band, and throughout his life as one of the most forward-thinking band leaders in jazz history, Woody Herman's concept of a "nostalgic anything" was, quite simply, distasteful to him. Though Woody passed in 1987, the band was kept alive, at least when good gigs came along, by long-time reedman Frank Tiberi, a progressive player when with Woody, who was even more modern by 2001.

To augment the Herman band for the tour, which began in July in Istanbul, Frank took his rhythm section (drummer Bob Chmel, pianist Jeff Morrison, bassist Paul Rostock, and guitarist Jim Fox), alto saxophonists Mike Smith and Terry Anthony, trombonist Eddie Morgan, and trumpeter Walt Johnson, all conducted by Terry Woodson.

One of the shows, which emanated from San Sebastian, Spain, was broadcast almost in its entirety. After a swinging set by the Herman Herd, a relaxed and loose Frank Jr. hit the stage, clad in an oversized "Woody Herman Tour" T-shirt. This set demonstrated everything that was right, wrong, and otherwise about the performing talents of Frank Sinatra, Jr., some forty years after his first professional job at Disneyland. Vocally and stylistically, he had evolved. His range had expanded, his breath control was impressive, his phrasing was relaxed and more focused, and his stage presence and mannerisms were pretty much set in stone. Indeed, Andrea Kauffman once commented that nothing the audience *saw* on stage was ever spontaneous, such as when singing the word "heart," he pointed to his heart. Still, he seemed comfortable and sincere, even with the mannerisms. The voice was not unattractive and was actually quite appealing in the lower register, where he sounded most like his father. But a vibrato had manifested itself, which would widen with the years, and there were some intonation problems here and there, which could be chalked up to fatigue, a variable sound system, and the fact that this was a hot and humid outdoor event.

The issue, pointed out continuously through the years by management, bookers, buyers, road crew, and musicians, was the choice of songs and the pacing of the show. Sure, this was a jazz show with the Woody Herman band, presumably performed before an audience of jazz lovers, but programming three long and drawn-out ballads in a row violates one of the primary rules of showbiz: Do not bore the audience. In his set, he performed, one after another, the minor-keyed lament "A Cold Wind"; followed by Victor Herbert's "Indian Summer," long a favorite of Frank Jr. that his father had recorded with Ellington; and Barry Manilow's "I Was a Fool (To Let You Go)." Only two songs, "Come Back to Me" and "I've Got the World on a String," were associated with his father, with "Come Back" being something of an obscurity.

Problems aside, there is a segment in this show that demonstrates, definitively, that Frank's musical capabilities went way beyond that of a good nightclub singer whose last name happened to be Sinatra. Well worth detailing in this show was Frank's rendition of "A Cold Wind," which he identified, on-camera, as a Duke Ellington composition. It was not Duke's tune, nor was it composed by Duke's alter-ego, Billy Strayhorn. According to Mike Smith, this lyrically and harmonically striking composition was penned by the iconic arranger Pete Rugolo, who, said Smith, "based it on a television or music cue." The orchestration, which Frank requested be done in the Ellington style, was by Las Vegas veteran Bill Rogers. Frank wrote the lyric to Pete Rugolo's melody.

After a lengthy, very Duke-ish, instrumental interlude, Frank's moody and atmospheric vocal begins, and it's clear from the start that "A Cold Wind" is not going to be easy to sing. Frank sings the minor-keyed melody, played at a bluesy lope of a tempo as if he were another horn negotiating the difficult intervals with ease, bending several long tones ala a trombone or alto saxophone. Frank is clearly emotionally invested in the lyric about the sad end of a love affair. As a whole, "A Cold Wind" would be tough for even a classically trained singer to perform, but Frank proves that his ears, like those of his father, were phenomenal. This is not showbiz. On "A Cold Wind," we hear a trained musician singing.

Had he not been burdened by the Sinatra albatross, perhaps, in his later years, he would have been moved to explore challenging tone poems like this, rather than something like the wholly inappropriate "The Curly Shuffle," which the band hated.

But in another year or two, the pressures to include more "Sinatra material" increased, and at long last, Frank had added "Luck Be a Lady," "New York, New York," "Don't Worry 'bout Me," "Where or When," and "Moonlight in Vermont" to the show, though it was still heavy with obscurities like "Pete Kelly's Blues." Kauffman remembered,

> When he changed the ratio of his song choices versus Sinatra songs, he was getting accolades and standing ovations. I said, "Didn't you see the difference? Didn't you feel it?"
>
> He'd say, "So?" He was difficult. He did not know how to read an audience, and he didn't give a damn. He did it for himself. He got off. The audience sometimes didn't. Unless you were there for the music, the horns, the arrangements, and to hear Frank, who was a wonderful singer, it was a nice musical treat. If you were there for what most people spent their money for, the first half of his show with no Sinatra material was a major disappointment. We had argument after argument. I'd hang up so frustrated. It was like talking to a wall.
>
> I'd say, "How can you be so stubborn?" But you couldn't get him riled. He'd yell when something happened that he couldn't control, but I couldn't get him to yell back at me. He might get angry and might not talk to me, but that was it.
>
> He once said, "I'm not here to make you happy."

I said, "No, you're not, but if I'm not happy, and the buyers aren't happy, you wouldn't be here at all." He was tough, and it wasn't easy.

I said to him once that the fact that he could do his father's music, that he knew the people, that he knew the players, that he knew the arrangers, that he knew how his father felt about "Strangers in the Night" . . . that gave him credibility. He said the only thing that gave him credibility was that he was Frank Sinatra, Jr., and that he was Frank Sinatra's son.

No matter where I booked him, they liked him and enjoyed the show. But I couldn't get him booked a second time. I'd have to constantly find new places to book him because he wasn't doing what people wanted to hear, especially after his father retired in 1995. They wanted to hear Sinatra music. "Help us." "Give us what we want," is what they said. There were times when I'd feel sorry for him.

I thought of getting out so many times because it was so frustrating. I hated watching him bleed. I knew he was hurting. Maybe it was time to stop. If I argued with him, he'd say, "You're just like the rest of them." If I didn't argue with him, he'd say, "What am I doing wrong?" I tried to explain what I needed from him, and he'd say, "I'm not my father. Just let me be Frank." I'd try to explain what the audiences wanted, and he'd say, "I'm not giving in to their demands." He asked, "What does the audience want me for? They can listen to records." It was a constant, constant battle. But it was one that he wanted to fight. He wanted to be told he was good. And he was. He was a brilliant musician. He wanted to be told that he was good in his own right. He didn't want to be told that he was only wanted for his father's music. It's not who he wanted to be. We tweaked it and tweaked it, and finally, when we got the standing ovations, and we got the gasps from the audience, and he finally sang songs where people applauded after hearing the first four bars, I noticed that he felt the success, but he wasn't happy with it because of why he was successful. It was such a sad story, and yet there's no doubt in my mind that he loved his father and that he needed his father. It was the same thing onstage.

Charles Granata is a record and radio producer, author, music historian, and archivist. He has written four books on music and sound recording, including *Sessions with Sinatra: Frank Sinatra and the Art of Recording*, which has become something of a reference work among

Sinatraphiles. He was also the producer of Nancy Sinatra's weekly *Nancy for Frank* program on the Sirius radio network. He was a youngster when he first heard Frank Jr.'s *Spice*, and from that moment, he became a fan. Granata got to know Frank quite well, personally and professionally, in the years following, and when asked to describe the man and his music in one sentence, Granata could only say, "You can't hide your brilliance for very long."

It all started for Granata with the Sinatra Capitol albums.

> My mom had a fairly large record collection with all kinds of music: classical, pop, Broadway, world music, and of course, she had a lot of the Frank Sinatra Columbia albums. That was my first exposure to records and to Sinatra. When I was about twelve or thirteen, when I was delivering newspapers, I came upon a garage sale a few blocks from my house. I had been a record lover since I was two years old, so I stopped my bike, went over to a box of records, and I saw all those great Sinatra Capitol albums. I fell in love with the covers. I biked home, got some cash, pedaled back to the garage sale, and filled the basket on my bike with those albums. I put on *Sinatra's Swingin' Session* first, and it was just a whole new sound for me. When I heard that big band with those killer Nelson Riddle charts, I became a Sinatra fan. I tore through those sixteen or seventeen albums, and I learned how to play jazz drums by playing along with those records. I thought, "Man, this is propulsive."
>
> Fast forward to my high school years. I was listening carefully to Frank Sinatra and getting to know a little more about him. Remember, there was no internet then, and it wasn't quite that easy to access information. At another record store or a garage sale, I ended up finding a copy of *Spice*. I thought, "Oh, Frank Sinatra, Jr., and Nelson Riddle." I knew the name *Nelson Riddle* from all of Sinatra's great albums, so I took it home, and I put it on. To me, it was like hearing a young Sinatra sing in that "middle Sinatra" period. It blew me away because it featured the same kind of big-band, high-intensity, swinging charts. When I learned later that Frank Jr. had written *Spice*, that really endeared me to him as a musician and as a composer. *Spice*, to me, [is] indicative of his sense of humor. It's fun, but with a little bit of depth to it. It has a nice angle, though it may be politically incorrect today.
>
> The first time I saw him in person was probably in 1994 at one of his Tavern on the Green performances in New York City. I was curious

about his eclectic repertoire, but I believe that I had read a review in one of the New York papers where he talked about doing something very different than what Frank Sr. was doing. I was prepared for the performance to be a little out of the ordinary, though I'd hoped he would do some of the things on *Spice*. I had already grown to like his voice, and I eventually found the country album *It's Alright*, and then later, *His Way* and *Young Love for Sale*. But I really liked the *Spice* album.

What I really loved, and still do, is his cover of "We've Only Just Begun." It's my favorite version of the song. His intonation and the way he approached *it is just* perfect. I'm sure that he had a lot of input, as his dad did, into the arrangement. But that Nelson Riddle chart and Frank Jr.'s *approach is just* perfect to me.

Around 1997, I had been involved with Nancy Jr. and the family, and I had started doing work on Frank Sr.'s recordings. Nancy and I went to Frank Jr.'s Battery Park concert on July 4, and I got to meet Andrea. We all hung out on the bus all day, and I could already see—right until the end and until the last show I saw—Andrea was there. She was with him. I think that her loyalty was incredible, and I think she played a big part in his career. And on that day, I got a whole different view of Frank Jr. I realized that he was so much deeper than I thought, and so much deeper musically than other people really knew.

I was just amazed, not only by his knowledge of music—and not just his dad's music—but his knowledge of film and his knowledge of airplanes. It was just incredible. I found that he was just not a talented and creative and inquisitive person, but a very bright person. You can't hide your brilliance for very long. I could see that he was quite cerebral. I enjoyed just listening to him talk. As time went on, I got to be more a part of the inner circle, and I spent more time backstage, in the dressing room, at rehearsal, going to dinner, sharing food in the hotel room with the band and with Frank Jr. after the show. That's when I got to ask him more about music.

I loved watching him interact with the musicians. I learned so much about his depth of knowledge from listening to his conversations with the musicians, either at the rehearsal or after the show when they were just hanging out.

After I met Nancy in 1993, she would come into New York City quite often and stay for a couple of weeks, either to perform or to visit friends. I believe that Nancy was her brother's greatest fan in music and in life.

I admire her so much for being that person. I saw nothing but a really warm and wonderful relationship. She just adored him. If you listen to the interviews we did with him on Nancy's Sirius radio show, and there were a number of them, you can tell. I don't think a week went by that we didn't program Frank Jr. in on Nancy's program. People who listened would say, "Oh, Frank Sinatra, Jr., right?"

I would say, "Yeah, but hold on a second. You don't understand how truly deep he is musically. He's the best kept secret, who's hiding in plain sight."

People didn't realize that this gentleman had an amazing well of talent. Certainly, he admired his dad like most kids do, and he wanted to do what his dad did. I give him a lot of credit for following in those footsteps. But he had the talent. It wasn't like some progeny who don't really have the talent or the creative sense that a parent does. Junior had it. I think he had a wonderful voice. He would have made it on his own had there not been a Frank Sinatra, Sr.

It was a wonderful thing when Frank Jr. was asked to conduct for his father. That's when I started to gravitate more towards Junior and learn more about him. I thought, "Wow." It was so neat to see a father and son like that. You could tell that Junior had a great sense of humor, even with his dad. Onstage, when he was conducting, he would turn around to the audience and give that "mock fright" look. That wasn't lost on me.

I saw that this was an individual who had great respect for what his father did musically. I started to listen to Frank Jr.'s interviews, and he would always be deferential to the Nelson Riddles, the Billy Mays and the musicians. That was another endearing quality of his that I loved. I think that if Frank Sr. was loyal, then Junior was loyal to the nth degree. I don't think I ever saw anyone who was so concerned about the people who worked for him. And they gave him that respect back. They played so beautifully for him. He was so intuitive. It was just so great to see. It didn't matter if Frank hadn't performed in months. The same core group would be there. You could see that there was a lot of respect there.

After his father's death in 1998, in his own shows, he always tried to keep his dad's music separate from his own in his own. Maybe my expectation was that he was going to sing a lot of his father's songs, but he didn't. It was a different sound than his father's, and I thought that was fascinating. Then there was *As I Remember It* recording, and then he started doing the Sinatra shows, which I thought was an interesting transition.

I can't imagine that it was easy for him because of the inevitable comparison to his father. When he started doing the all-Sinatra shows, I thought it was a real kick. Number 1, I started understanding who he was. He started pulling out songs that Frank Sr. hadn't sung in thirty years. All of a sudden, Frank Jr. was doing what I wished his dad had done for the last fifteen years of his career, that being to pull out a couple of songs that were unusual. I was impressed with that, but the moment that really overwhelmed me emotionally was when Junior was at Town Hall in New York City. I met them early at rehearsal, and Andrea kindly got me great seats that were raised up a little bit. I was watching, and it hit me that he looked just like his dad. He walked out of the wings, and I thought, "Holy shit!" It was at that moment when it really struck me. Frank strode out on stage, and I got a chill. It was truly like watching his dad.

I respected the *Sinatra Sings Sinatra* angle. He didn't want to be thought of as a copyist, so the way the performance was constructed was unique: He was singing different songs. He pulled things out of the book that people remembered but hadn't heard Frank Sr. perform in years. Still, I wish he would have sung more of his own material. And he eventually did that. There were other concerts in Atlantic City, where he would do some of the songs from the *That Face!* recording. It was always a treat to hear him sing his music.

When he passed, if I never knew him, I would think that an extension of Frank Sr. went away and disappeared. He carried the music on legitimately with the name, with the talent, with the charts, and that was the end of an era. But from the point of view of someone who had a little idea about who he was, and how musically astute he was in his thinking, I thought, "Oh my gosh, the opportunity for him to make his own kind of music is gone." That saddened me. My first concern, when I heard of Frank's passing, was Nancy. I know how deeply she cared for him and loved him and supported his work. I thought that we had lost someone who was vital, and still young enough to go in the studio and do more work. I wish that he had done that. I wish there were more albums and that he would have embarked on some things that his dad had wanted to do and didn't get the chance. That was a big part of my feeling of loss. I thought there were very few people left with that deep of a connection to the music.

His passing was a loss for everyone because, in my view, he didn't record more when he could have and should have and because we didn't get the opportunity to see where he could have taken it in his later career.

Yes, there were legendary stories of Frank Jr. being a bit odd and a bit standoffish, and so forth. But I remember the first time I had called on him was when I was doing my book. I think he was appearing in Atlantic City. I wanted to talk to him, and I left my number. I came home from work, and there was a message on my answering machine that said, "Chuck Granata, this is Frank Sinatra, Jr. It is 15:30 hours."

I stopped, and I had to get my wife and say, "Listen to this!" I said, "I'm a cop, and I don't talk like this." I thought that was great, and I laughed. He was so precise, and he used military time. Fast forward. I got to know him. What I loved was that he was brutally honest. He was direct. What I saw was a very different person.

I cannot imagine enduring what he endured in being kidnapped and not be profoundly affected by it for the rest of your life. What I saw, as someone who was trained to study people and to observe people and their reactions to situations, I saw someone who was guarded, and for very good reason. I can only imagine that he suffered greatly from anxiety from that experience. And that was part of the reason he found it a little difficult to let people in, and that's totally understandable.

What I wish everyone could have seen was the Frank Jr. who was totally relaxed, comfortable in the environment and with the people he was with, who could laugh and tell funny stories and talk about the old days when he started performing. That's when he could just be himself, and in those moments, he let us in. It was just remarkable because he was a great storyteller. He could laugh with the best of them and had a great sense of humor. I wish everyone could have seen that. And I wish that he had more confidence. When I would give him words of praise when we were talking on the air and playing his music, he was genuine.

I wanted another Frank Jr. album. There were so many great characteristics of his artistry and his singing that was very different than his father's. I wasn't looking for a substitute for his dad. I liked what he did, and I like what he did on the *Spice* album. I play it all the time because it's a great album. Remember that he wrote "Black Night." It was totally different than what you would expect because he proclaimed to hate rock and roll, but that really is a rock and roll song. I saw these dichotomies in him. But I saw a person who, when he was comfortable, could be the most engaging and charismatic and interesting person around.

That term *interesting* means that he just wasn't interested in music. He would ask me questions about the police department. I once gave him a book by Joseph Wambaugh, who created the movement in policing called "street survival." He said, "I am going to read this." He was interesting and erudite, and more musically astute than anyone really realized. I only wish that he had recognized that and that he didn't always downplay it. He would say things like, "Who wants to hear me? No one wants to hear me."

I said, "I do."

There are no bones about it. I respected Frank Jr. and I loved his music. It will always be a part of my life. The fact that I got to observe how he worked—and the fact that I got to know him—are things that I'll just carry with me forever.

Radiance

Frank's brilliance extended to areas other than that of performing. Sometime in 2005, he had an idea for a radio program that he called *Radiance.* Andrea Kauffman was given thirteen episodes of the program to sell. The concept is difficult to explain on paper and really needs to be heard to be understood and appreciated. *Radiance* was a brilliant and innovative combination of storytelling and music, with the music designed specifically to enhance and heighten the emotion of the story. Through the combination of narrative and music, an actual picture was created in the mind's eye, even though these were purely audio episodes. "Frank got some great people to narrate the programs," Kauffman recalled. "One was narrated by Adam West of television's *Batman* fame, and another was done by voice characterization legend June Foray, best known as the voice of Rocky the Flying Squirrel in the *Rocky and Bullwinkle* cartoon series. The shows were calming and thought provoking."

But not a lot of things were easy with Frank, and again, roadblocks were put in Kauffman's path. For whatever reason, Frank refused to let *Radiance* be pitched to the Sirius radio network, which may have been an easy sell. And there was one more stipulation that would make a sale nearly impossible. That stipulation was that *Radiance* would not be broadcast before midnight. Kauffman said,

> I don't remember saying much, but I thought that was crazy. When we met a week later, I told him that most people are in bed by eleven and

that even television news comes on earlier. "Who's up at midnight?" I asked him. You, me, and musicians. I felt that he had literally handcuffed me with a condition that made it impossible to sell this radio show. He wouldn't relent. Rob Heller and I worked on it together, and the only bite I got was a podcast, which would have been great. But he wouldn't do that.

He knew the program had tons of potential but sabotaged any possibilities. I believe he was afraid of success. If he was a success, no one would feel sorry for him anymore.

He wouldn't relent. And here I was stuck with this radio show that was brilliant. Rob Heller and I worked on it together, and the only bite I got was a podcast.

That Face!

Some ten years after the 1996 recording of *As I Remember It*, Frank decided it was time to record again. Though the arrangements are by Nelson Riddle and Don Costa, there is no "Frank Sinatra" material among the fourteen songs on the CD. There's a good remake of Frank Jr.'s original "Spice"; and a couple of songs that he had been performing for several years, including Manilow's "I Was a Fool to Let You Go"; and a few numbers, including "Cry Me a River," that were earmarked to be recorded by Frank Sr. but were never recorded. On one of the cuts, Frank does a light-hearted duet with the popular Steve Tyrell on Bobby Troup's now politically incorrect "Girl Talk." It's generally a pleasant, often swinging effort that showcases members of Frank's regular road band to great effect. Frank admitted publicly to several interviewers that he wasn't really satisfied with how he sounded on *That Face!*, as the recording was made when he was undergoing treatment for prostate cancer. However, his voice is strong throughout.

Tyrell, for one, was thrilled to be a part of the project. "He was one of the kindest and most soulful guys I've ever known," said Tyrell, adding that "he personally encouraged, inspired, and influenced my own musical journey in countless ways."

As for the session itself, Kauffman and Hank Catteneo were the voices of reason and tried to rein Frank in from recording, as Kauffman said, "songs that no one would give a damn about." His mother and sister came to the recording sessions. "They were both very critical," according to Kauffman.

If she didn't like a song he wanted to record, his mother would say, "Frank, nobody wants to hear that." Nancy Jr. was trying to get him to roll his Rs a little bit, but he wasn't listening to that. It was an uphill battle. But Terry Woodson, who conducted, had a brilliant way of handling Frank. He never fought with him. Never. Frank never saw him as the opposition or as the enemy. Terry would say his piece and let it go. No matter what Frank said to that, Terry wouldn't try to express his own point of view. He wouldn't try to change Frank's mind. He said his piece. That was something Frank responded to more positively than when his manager, me, would say, "Are you out of your fucking mind?" I became the adversary and the enemy. He was fighting me, not the idea. I learned a lot from Terry and from Hank.

High Hopes

The Kennedys Revisited

Frank Jr. didn't voice his opinions about politics publicly very often, as opposed to his father, who was an outspoken Democratic liberal from the FDR days through the early 1970s, when he shocked his friends and family—mostly daughter Tina—by turning Republican. Of all the presidents and politicians he knew and supported, he was closest to John Fitzgerald Kennedy.

The two became close when Kennedy was a senator, and he often visited Sinatra and his pals in Vegas and Hollywood, or, it's been said, wherever there was a party and wherever Hollywood celebrities congregated. When Kennedy ran for president, Sinatra campaigned tirelessly for him, enlisting cronies like Dean Martin and Sammy Davis, Jr., to perform at fundraisers, benefits, and all else. Peter Lawford, married to Kennedy's younger sister, Pat, was also brought into what became known as the Rat Pack, or the Summit, the name Sinatra preferred. Kennedy's father, Joseph P. Kennedy, Sr., wanted more. Old Joe wanted Sinatra to use his "connections," questionable and otherwise, to bring out the Democratic vote in the wards, on the street, with the unions, and any other place identified as possibly Democratic. Sinatra went as far as recording a single, based on the melody of "High Hopes," that literally sang the praises of Jack.

Kennedy won by the narrowest of margins, and Sinatra produced a memorable star-studded Inaugural Gala. Shortly after that, the trouble began, and the trouble began when the president's brother Robert (Bobby) was appointed attorney general and began a public investigation into organized crime. One of the first orders of business for Robert was to have the president cut ties with anyone he believed to be connected to organized crime, including Frank Sinatra.

On Easter weekend, 1962, the president was scheduled to visit Sinatra at the Sinatra compound in Palm Springs. Sinatra went to enormous lengths to make the residence secure, including building a new guest house and installing a heliport. At the eleventh hour, Bobby and/or other powers that be at the White House convinced the president that such a visit would look bad, given Sinatra's alleged connections to organized crime. The visit to the Sinatra compound was canceled. Instead, the president visited the Palm Springs digs of Bing Crosby, a staunch Republican.

Frank Sinatra was infuriated and among other things, severed ties forever with Peter Lawford, who was the one unfortunately chosen to deliver the bad news. Bobby Kennedy did call Frank Sinatra and offered help and support when Frank Jr. was kidnapped, and Sinatra did support Democrats and Democratic causes for almost a decade following the Palm Springs incident. But Frank Sinatra was not one to forget, and the split with the Kennedys was permanent. Some maintain that his eventual switch to the Republican Party was due, in part, to his feelings about the Kennedys.

In retrospect, it looked like it was. Kauffman summed it up, saying, "Kennedy becomes president and brings his brother Bobby Kennedy in as attorney general. And what does this self-righteous ass want to do? Bobby wants to arrest the very same guys that helped get JFK elected. Basically, Sinatra was told, 'That's politics.'"

Sometime in 2007, Ambassador Joseph Paolino, who had been the mayor of Providence, Rhode Island and served as ambassador to Malta under Bill Clinton, called Andrea Kauffman's office. Frank Jr. had already played a couple of events for Paolino, who told Kauffman that he thought the Kennedys were going to do a fundraiser in Hyannis Port and he was going to recommend to the Kennedys' that they get Frank to perform. Given the Kennedy/Sinatra bad blood of long standing, Kauffman was dumbfounded. She asked,

> "You're going to get my Frank? Good luck with that."
>
> He said, "Should I talk to Frank?"

I said, "No, you should talk to the Kennedys because this is a pipe dream, but if the Kennedys agree to it, I will talk to Frank."

In a limo from Rhode Island returning to Atlantic City after an event for the ambassador, my cell phone rang. A representative of the Kennedys called, and said, "I'm calling for Senator Kennedy for Ms. Kauffman."

I said, "Okay, please put Mr. Kennedy on." Right away, Frank's head just snapped toward me. It was Patrick Kennedy, Ted's son.

He got on the phone and said, "Andrea, maybe we can bury the hatchet. Maybe we can smooth things over, and maybe we can form new friendships with the Sinatras and the Kennedys." At this point, Frank is waving his arms frantically. I asked him specifically what he had in mind. Patrick Kennedy said, "We do a fundraiser every year. It's not very big, and the public isn't invited. It's for our guests, diplomats, major contributors and the like, and we would like to have Frank as our guest entertainer."

I said that this was a very sensitive situation and that I was having a hard time going to Mr. Sinatra about it. He asked, "Can you hold on a moment? My dad wants to speak with you."

I said, "I'm in the car with Frank. Is this a conversation we should have when I'm in the car with Frank?"

He says, "Maybe my father and Mr. Sinatra could have a word." He says, "I think this is going to work. We'd like to do it in August of next year."

I said, "I'll let Frank talk for himself," so I said, "Senator Kennedy . . . Frank Sinatra." I never said "Junior." And in that car, I heard Frank and Senator Kennedy bury the Sinatra/Kennedy hatchet.

I'll go on record by saying that Frank wasn't happy about it. He couldn't completely forgive the Kennedys for hurting his father so deeply. That was ugly. But he felt it was time to forget. The next call I got was to go through the details, negotiate a price, and advance the date. In May of 2008, Senator Kennedy was diagnosed with a brain tumor, and the date never happened. But when he passed in August of the following year, Frank sent a magnificent flower arrangement on behalf of the family. The most important result was that the senator and Frank came to a truce, on my cell phone, in the car on a ride home from Rhode Island to Atlantic City. If Sinatra were alive, this never would have happened.

On Broadway

Frank Sinatra, Jr.
AS I REMEMBER IT

A Tribute to Frank Sinatra: The Music, the Times, the Man
36-piece orchestra under the direction of Terry Woodson

Bringing the story of Frank Sinatra, starring Frank Sinatra, Jr., to the Broadway stage, came very close to happening. Even the formal title and billing were worked out. Charlie Pignone works for Frank Sinatra Enterprises and has long served as the Sinatra family archivist. He was also a dear friend of Frank Jr. Pignone was contacted by Las Vegas producer Nick Howey, who had the idea of producing a Sinatra touring stage show that would hopefully end up on Broadway. Howey was no small-timer. As the head of New House Entertainment, Howey, among his many other accomplishments, went on to produce many of Andrew Lloyd Webber's projects in North America. Frank was interested, but as always, there were sticking points. The general concept was that it would present the musical journey of Frank Sinatra's life. The main issue, not surprisingly, was content, an issue that Andrea Kauffman believed she could handle. Nick and Charlie knew exactly what songs were important and submitted a forty-song list of, as Kauffman described it, "allowable songs." Out of that list, Frank was asked to pick twenty tunes. He picked seventeen or eighteen and used that as a bargaining chip to use three of the more obscure songs he wanted. Kauffman said,

Every conference call was some kind of bargaining session. Charlie got to the point where he felt it wasn't worth it anymore. Nick knew he had something good and believed the Centennial, celebrating the one hundredth birthday of Frank Sinatra, was coming up, and this show would be important. The one drawback, and I never said this to Frank, was that if we saturated all the major venues, in all the major cities with the show, how hard would it be to go back into those venues without all the elements of the show? I had many conversations with Nick about how fragile Frank was when it came to telling him what to do. His resistance was at a point where there was just no give and take. It was "my voice," "my music," and "I'll do it my way." He agreed to as much as he agreed on because he knew he needed the money. We figured he could make around $15,000 a week for five shows per week. Nick needed a Sunday matinee. I tried to convince him how important a Sunday afternoon show would be, especially because his audiences were older. He wouldn't do it. Nick acquiesced.There was one paragraph in the contract from Nick with a hiccup in it. I knew it was going to be a sticking point with Frank. I had gotten him to agree and believe the show would work. We were right there. We were on a four-way conference call—Charlie, Nick, Frank, and me—and we were a pen stroke away from signing the contract. Then Frank asked the question, "Can't I choose a couple of the songs of the twenty I need to sing?"

Nick was about to answer, when Charlie jumped in and said, "Fuck it. If I have to twist your arm, then fuck you." Charlie hung up.

I called Nick, and I asked, "What happened here?" We all worked so hard, including Frank, who made as many concessions as I've ever known him to make. Charlie understood that this was like stripping himself bare, but something happened to make Charlie blow his stack. I do know that Frank needed the money, and this would have been a wonderful solution for a couple of years. Charlie blew it, and Nick would never do it without Charlie. Everyone knew the potential. Then it was over.

On the other hand, Frank was enthusiastic about writing comprehensive linear notes to CD reissues of his father's most notable projects, including the "duets" recordings such as "Ring-a-Ding Ding!" and "Only the Lonely," and he even wrote the copy for Keely Smith's Sinatra tribute CD, *Keely Sings Sinatra*. He got involved with his father's recordings in a much bigger way in 2012 with the reissue of 1963's *The Concert Sinatra*, where he not only wrote the notes, but served as producer, coengineer, and comixer. It was a project close to his heart, and the mechanics of the original recording of it fascinated him for years.

The master tracks to *The Concert Sinatra* were actually recorded on a type of thirty-five-millimeter film. Frank found the original film and helped restore it and remix it to a quality never before heard. Frank's goal, as he explained in the notes, was to allow the listener "to notice the amount of music, originally recorded on the master film that was never present before on any of the previous CD issues." Frank was also insistent on removing almost all the reverb on his father's vocal track. "The singer, unvarnished, is up front in the mix, though not at the expense of that stunningly full orchestra." The finished product was a landmark work that received rave reviews for both the music and the technology.

The Worst Nightmare

Throat cancer is a singer's worst nightmare. He broke the news to Andrea Kauffman in his usual stoic way. "I have very bad news for both of us," he told her. "I have throat cancer." No one knows what caused it. It could have been the exposure to second-hand nightclub and casino smoke for more than forty years or the fact that he simply didn't take care of himself. He never exercised, and his diet was appalling. One of his favorite breakfast treats, said Ronna Brodsley, was barely warmed bacon. He hadn't looked healthy in years.

Kauffman remembers the situation vividly.

> He was having problems swallowing. He had a couple of polyps in his throat and went to have them looked at. The result was cancer. He was sure he was done singing. He had surgery, then radiation. The radiation caused swelling, irritation, and horrible sores on his face and neck. It was a very rough road for him. After the radiation, he had to have chemo, which made him so sick. He couldn't eat and lost forty pounds. The doctors had to put a feeding tube in him. He wouldn't see anybody. He had all the curtains closed throughout his house, and he wouldn't let his housekeeper open them. He wasn't afraid of dying. He was afraid of never singing again. That took a lot for him to admit to me. We talked two or three times a day, literally for hours.
>
> After regaining some of his strength back, he played the dates he had to cancel. He was doing concerts while he had the feeding tube in him.

> One day, his housekeeper, Gwendolyn, took him to the doctor, and the doctor said that they couldn't take the feeding tube out yet. His depression got even worse. He wouldn't answer the phone, and he made Gwendolyn swear not to tell anyone that he'd been to the doctor. His sister Nancy called me and said she couldn't get her brother on the phone. This is the second or third time that had happened. I had a couple of private numbers for him. I called one and told him that his sister was looking for him. I called her back and told her that he saw the doctor and that the feeding tube couldn't come out yet. I said that Frank was processing that, and he'd be in touch soon. Nancy said, "You're aware of how I lost my father! I never want to be in the dark again. You tell my brother he may not keep me in the dark or avoid my phone calls. EVER!" I said I'd tell him but that she would have to tell him as well. I told Gwendolyn that as long as his mother was alive, "when a family member calls, you must tell Frank to call back, or you answer that damn phone. You don't take it upon yourself not to answer the phone to a family member."

Frank's last serious relationship was with Tasha Van Horne, a college professor at a small West Coast college. Though Frank's friends and colleagues had very mixed feelings about her, she was instrumental in helping nurse Frank back to health. Tasha was there for the diagnosis of his throat cancer and, at least initially, was on feeding tube duty. It was Isaac Tamburino, who ended up handling the feeding-tube duty. He was feeding Frank three times daily, especially on the road.

> Tasha was a sweet, quiet, and very shy woman in the beginning. But when Frank got better, she wanted to walk in like a queen and have everyone bow to her. It was like she was saying, "I nursed him back to health. I am the one who's been here for him in the hardest part of his life." But she turned into a nightmare.
>
> When I was first starting out on the road with Frank, the motto was, "Let the kid do it." That's how I ended up helping with the feeding tube. It was the job nobody else wanted. Tasha had been handling the feeding, and after she taught me how the whole thing worked, I was drafted into doing it because he wanted to go on the road. He was still on the tube, but he was just dying to sing. He said that we had to get the guys back on the road because they needed to eat. He wouldn't walk away

from them. He was willing himself back to health. Then the shows got booked, and I had to learn how to use the tube because it had to be done three times a day, every day.

The Last Dance

Tasha was a professor, an academic. Such things impressed Frank. Kauffman believed she really cared about him at first but that "women that he was attracted to would never be attracted to him if his last name wasn't Sinatra. Maybe back in the day, when he still had the pompadour, the pinkie ring, and smoked the cigarette, maybe then. Cynthia called him 'the dough boy.' His shoulders in his jackets were padded. He had a bit of a paunch. He was not strong. He was flabby and unhealthy looking. Was there something attractive about this?"

Ronna Brodsley described Tasha as

> just a lunatic. She would have tantrums. She hung on him and would eat off his plate. She just wanted to sit in his lap and have him all to herself. He had to go to Arizona. He had an evening flight. She wanted to go, but at that time, money was a real problem for him. Tasha just wanted, wanted, wanted and he couldn't comfortably do some of the things she wanted him to do. First, she said she didn't want to go to Arizona, so he bought one ticket. Then, she said she wanted to go, but he left. She called him, hysterically crying, and said, "How can you do this to me?" Logic didn't come into that relationship. He did send her a ticket, but it was getting close to the end of his patience. More importantly, he was losing his freedom. She never left him alone. She would have little girl tantrums—stomping her feet and everything—in front of everyone. He hated confrontations, just like his father. He said to me, "I don't know what to do."

At one point, Tasha had gone to Frank's mother's house, and Nancy Sr. gave Tasha some of her old clothes. One of the pieces was a very fancy sequined jacket. The jacket caused a problem on the road. Kauffman remembered,

> We were at the McCallum Theatre in Palm Desert, and it was a wonderful show. Frank was taking his bows before the encore. Tasha finagled her way up to the front row during "My Way." She was standing and waving at him with the sequined jacket on, and the spotlight caught the sequins. It was very, very distracting. It looked like a disco ball flashing throughout the theater during "My Way." I saw this on the monitor backstage. After the show, while Frank was in the dressing room getting changed, we heard pounding on the door, accompanied by Tasha saying, "Let me in! Let me in!" I said to Frank that if I let her in, I'll rearrange her new face lift. It's your choice.
>
> He said, "Let her in." I stopped her at the front of the dressing room. I told her that if she ever waved her arms and was a distraction like she was this night again, I'd ban her from all of Frank's shows. That was one of the most unprofessional, arrogant stunts I've ever seen. I wanted her to apologize to the GM of the McCallum Theater as well as to Frank.
>
> She said, "I won't do any such thing."
>
> Frank said, "If you want to stick around, you will."
>
> When Frank passed away, Isaac was telling me how she was lying in bed with his body. She was acting like a lunatic. We all knew it was an act. After they read the will, she called me and said, "He was supposed to leave me money. There's no money. He gave me the Lexus!" I told her she was lucky to get that.

At the death scene, Isaac Tamburino said Tasha "was just an emotional wreck. Why she came out to Daytona to cry and to involve herself in a situation where there was nothing but chaos and sorrow, was beyond me." Still, Tamburino believed that Tasha "did absolute right by Frank, and it did seem like she had his best interests at heart. She was a little crazy, and I didn't think she was Frank's type, but I think she had good intentions. She got thrown some crazy loops." Jim Fox agreed, saying, "I think that Tasha deserves credit. Because that's not the kind of thing that people are going to be saying, but I'm going to tell you that, because I know it to be true."

The Victim

Frank was getting good write-ups, working first-rate places—even pure jazz venues like Ronnie Scott's in London—was getting good money, and had a first-class band whose members were his devoted friends.

Wil Haygood, then writing for *The Washington Post*, spent some time on the road with Frank and company, penned a piece on July of 2006 that had the heading "Frank Jr., the Unsung Sinatra: He's Got a Big Heart and His Pop's Voice, but Just a Shadow of His Success."

Haygood was a first-class journalist. Two years after this was published, the award-winning author wrote "A Butler Well Served by This Election" for *The Post*, which was the basis for the film *The Butler*. Frank should have been thrilled at notoriety like this and comments within the piece—"legions will tell you he's gifted in his own right" was just one—but he was not. Instead, he denigrated himself and moaned and groaned about what he perceived as the sorry state of his career. Talking about the then-recent release of *That Face!*, Frank said, "There is no demand for Frank Sinatra, Jr., records. There never has been. Rod Stewart is now doing the Great American Songbook. So is Harry Connick Jr. and Michael Bublé. Well, Frank Sinatra, Jr., has been doing it for forty-four years."

He wasn't finished with the sad story he told Haygood. "I was never a success," he continued. "Never had a hit movie or hit TV show or hit record. I just had visions of doing the best quality of music. Now there is a place for me because Frank Sinatra is dead. They want me to play the music. If it wasn't for that, I wouldn't be noticed. The only satisfaction is that I do what I do well."

"I do what I do well." That's as positive as it got with Frank.

Three years later, he was the subject of a lengthy and positive profile, written by the eminent jazz critic Nat Hentoff and published in *The Wall Street Journal*. Of the *That Face* CD, Hentoff wrote, "Backed by an invigoratingly swinging big band, his singing made me feel good with his personal, signature sound, infectious jazz time and conversational phrasing," and later added, "If I were still producing jazz records, I'd ask him to come into the studio." Note the mention of the word *jazz*.

But Frank, as was his wont, had to step on the praise and saw fit to tell Hentoff, "There's very little demand for my recordings."

At the end of the piece, Hentoff asked, "Is there anything you haven't accomplished yet that you want to do, and expect to do?"

Frank replied, "Success would be nice," he said. "Even a little, you know."

That's just the way he was, and there wasn't a lot that could be done about it. Andrea Kauffman tried, telling him to stop being self-effacing, to stop being a victim, and to finally show some confidence in his work. Kauffman said,

> He said he was a victim. He got the accolades by saying he never got it. That was him. He was a brilliant musician. He wanted to be told that he was good in his own right. He didn't want to be told that he was only wanted for his father's music. It's not who he wanted to be. We tweaked it and tweaked it, and finally, when we got the standing ovations, and we got the gasps from the audience, and he finally sang songs where people applauded after hearing the first four bars, I noticed that he felt the success, but he wasn't happy with it because of why he was successful. It was such a sad story, and yet there's no doubt in my mind that he loved his father, and that he needed his father. It was the same thing onstage.

He might make himself the victim in some of these newspaper stories, but in two *Today* show appearances, he became the victim. There was another side to him, and that was the side that demanded honesty and respect. After forty years on the road, he believed he was entitled to at least that much. When he didn't get the respect he felt he deserved, anger and chaos would ensue. This happened in a public forum. Twice. On NBC television's *Today* program.

On May 13, 2008, Frank appeared on *Today* with his sister Nancy to promote the issue of the Frank Sinatra postage stamp. That's what he was there to discuss, and that's what the producers told him they would discuss. It didn't turn out that way, and what aired was disastrous. Terry Anthony remembered situations similar to what happened on the *Today* show.

> They would put him on television shows, and he would say, "They can ask me anything, but if they want to ask personal things about my father, I'm not going to do it." If they did to it, he would stand up, take the mic off his lapel, and he'd walk out. They promised him the world, but it always came back to the same shit. "What kind of relationship did you have with your father?" "What was your father's favorite song?" Those were some of the questions he would get.
>
> He'd say, "Why didn't you ask my father when he was alive?"

Andrea Kauffman had to handle the backlash. She said,

> The *Today* interview was so bad that I got a call from Brazil, from Raphael Reisman, the impresario of the upcoming Brazilian tour. He said, "If that's how he's going to handle the press, then I'm canceling the tour."
>
> When it was over, I was just shaking my head, and I was thinking that I've got to get a hold of Johnny Pizza, his majordomo at the time, and get him to get Frank out of New York. Then my phone rang, and it was Tina. She said, "Just know that when I see your client, I'm going to kill him. I'm going to kill him!"
>
> Then Bob Finkelstein came on the line and said that she's not going to kill him. "Let's not get that on record. She didn't mean that," he said.
>
> And I heard Tina in the background saying, "Yes, I fuckin' did mean it! What a moron! What an asshole! I'm going to kill him," over and over.
>
> Then his mother called and said, "What in the world is wrong with Frankie?" I just told her I didn't know. How could I explain it to them? They'd never understand.

Perhaps at the request of the Sinatra family, the clip of the May 13, 2008, debacle has been made unavailable by those in charge of the NBC archives, and the posting of it has been removed by YouTube.

The *Today* producers must have had short memories. On October 14, 2015, Frank was again booked on the show, this time to hype the publication of *Sinatra 100*, a book that celebrated Frank Sinatra's one hundredth birthday. The coauthor, Charles Pignone, was also on hand to promote the book, which was sanctioned by the family. Frank was in a foul mood from the outset. When *Today* co-host Hoda Kotb asked Frank, "What made you decide that this was the right time . . .?"

Kotb couldn't finish her question, as Frank chimed in, saying, "I didn't decide. It was done by a committee."

From there, his answers were matter of fact and straightforward, without one ounce of warmth or humor. Smiling was out of the question. When asked to describe a photo that came up on screen, a picture of his two sisters receiving gifts from their father, Frank simply answered, "I don't know anything about that one because I was not present."

The booking was a mistake. Frank and Pignone were no longer close because of the fallout from the failed Broadway show project. And Pignone, who also slipped in a plug for Sinatra granddaughter Amanda's $1,000 picture book, was there, on television, hyping books that contained the same pictures that he went through hell to obtain. The fact that Frank was also touring, with tremendous success, with a centennial salute to his father, was not mentioned.

The next day, Hoda Kotb proclaimed, on-air, that her interview with Frank was the worst that she had ever done. Hoda and Kathy Lee had a big laugh over that one, but at that point, no one really cared. Frank Sinatra, Jr., in 2015, was doing better than ever and was making more money per night than ever.

All Things Must Change

A Question of Repertoire

The Evolution

Very early on in his career, Frank did sing his father's songs. And then he just stopped. Kauffman believes, "There was some shutdown, some disconnect, some problem that occurred that caused a severe emotional aversion to singing his father's music. Even Vince Carbone, Frank's previous manager, couldn't get him to sing the songs audiences wanted to hear: his father's songs. He loved his father fiercely, defended his father fiercely, respected him and respected the music his father sang, but there was some break." When it came to singing his father's songs, despite pleas from his agents, his own musicians and friends, and Andrea Kauffman, his consistent answer was "no." She said, "There was a very slow evolution that began with his father's passing. Although heartbroken, it freed some psychological barrier. The result can be heard on the critically acclaimed recording *As I Remember It*, Frank's first recording in decades."

The situation was in dire need of change. Kauffman explained,

> In the beginning of my relationship with him, it was assumed by the buyers that he would be singing many of his father's songs, though at no point in the very beginning did a buyer say that they needed it contractually. Word was out that the show was disappointing. The potential

buyers disappeared. The buyers that did buy the show were not bringing him back. The harder I worked, the less he worked. I was fighting for my financial life. What audience wants to hear "A Horse with No Name" with a twenty-piece band? And the songs of this father's that he was singing were the "B" sides of his father's records. He sang his father's obscurities. He'd say, "That was my father's song."

I'd say, "Frank, no one knows that other than you and your father." I think the tipping point was his guys telling him, "Andrea can't work any harder for you." And me telling him that I left my business partner and a successful agency to become his personal manager.' He was sabotaging both our careers.

Sinatra Sings Sinatra

When Frank Sinatra died in 1998, Kauffman suspected that Frank Jr. didn't know how to deal with the loss, nor did he know how that loss would affect him, given that his emotions were so conflicted. He dealt with it in the best way he knew how: through music. "The only way that he was able to honor his father's memory was to do at least a little bit of this father's music," Kauffman remembered. "We talked about doing a segment of *As I Remember It*, and that we could use *Sinatra Sings Sinatra* as the title of the show. He still wanted to maintain his identity so he could continue to just be Frank. His compromise was to five or six songs of his liking up front. When he finished with the songs from his own book, and the closer was often "'S Wonderful," he walked off stage.

This first presentation of *Sinatra Sings Sinatra* at the Sands in Atlantic City was attended by Sonny Golden, his surrogate father and business manager, his sister Nancy, and his father's manager, Eliot Weisman. After the show, they all went to dinner. Kauffman recalled,

> While we were sitting there, Eliot decided to say something like, "You know, Junior, I like this *Sinatra Sings Sinatra*." Then he went on to talk about various ways that Frank could *be more like his father* in the show. "Let your hair grow a little bit," he said. You could see Frank choking down every bite of food.
>
> After dinner, he said to me, "I bet he'd like me to wear blue contact lenses, too. I'm done. I'm not doing that." The resistance was right back where it started because of what Eliot said. It was not the time to say

those things. Eliot wanted in. He saw the reaction from the audience, and he saw the dollar signs.

What I said to Frank was, "Don't do anything we'll both regret. Don't cut off your nose to spite your face." Frank saw the credibility in the show. He saw money. He saw success. Don't you dare do this because Eliot, in essence, said the right thing at the wrong time.

We kept doing that show, and the more we did it, the Sinatra segment came earlier and earlier in the show. The show was working, and we were working like crazy.

Now that we were working so much, and he was experiencing a level of success he hadn't achieved before, he wanted to go back to Vegas. He hadn't been there since the mid-1980s, when he performed at the Four Queens, off the strip. He wanted, almost demanded, a gig on Las Vegas' main strip. He was right. It was time. Little did I know what his intensions were.

I booked him in Las Vegas for two, one-week engagements in August and October of 2002. We were working for Bob Kane of the Global Entertainment Group, at the MGM Grand. It was the first week of the two one-week dates that I reached my breaking point.

Vegas was very, very important to Frank. Frank was aware of what Kane needed for this show to be successful and agreed. Kane wanted the show he was hearing raves about. The show was billed as *Sinatra Sings Sinatra, Starring Frank Sinatra, Jr.* All the billboard ads and light boxes had photos of Frank Jr. on top, holding a microphone, singing with a hazier photo of Sinatra, below, holding a microphone, and singing. The title of the show and the ads said it all. The audience knew exactly what to expect.

Frank called me to tell me he wanted Hank Cattaneo to go on the dates with us. To me, this was a good omen. He wanted his father's production/road manager with him for positive reinforcement.

Hank was aware of some of the problems with Frank's repertoire in the past. He was aware and understood my concerns. I was confident that we wouldn't have those problems for this show because this was Las Vegas. Frank wouldn't jeopardize these dates! We'd been doing such successful shows recently. Maybe the show had too many ballads, or maybe he wasn't singing his father's biggest hits, but we were getting there. Hank's gentle nature and calming manner would help me maneuver around the issue of repertoire if that issue came up. What a relief.

On the first day of rehearsal, Frank passed out the song lineup for the musicians and put one in front of me at our table. The lineup was not what Bob Kane contractually asked for. I was in shock. In structure, it was the show we had been doing, but the song choices were all wrong: "Get Me to the Church on Time," "But Beautiful," "Don'cha Go 'Way Mad," and "Can I Steal a Little Love?" were some of the choices.

This was not what he promised. I called him over to discuss the song choices. He was arrogant and nasty. He claimed that if he can't be who he is in Vegas, he'll hang it up. Wow. That blew me away. Why in Las Vegas, his father's stronghold, would he choose to sabotage his first opportunity in the city he was hounding me to get him? He made it clear that was going to sing this line up and if I didn't like it, tough! He wouldn't budge. I yelled at him, "You're ruining your life, my career, and the band's livelihood. You will always remain the victim because you make yourself one. How much more can you destroy before you see that you're fucking *everything* up?" With that, I left the stage. I had never done anything that was so unprofessional. Later on, it was Hank who calmed things down. He explained to Frank exactly what Frank needed to do to meet the contract's obligations and get me back. Then, he added a couple more important songs, though it was never the show it should have been. The second week in October was a little better, but not the slam dunk of prior shows

My ex-partner, Dan Mulhern, flew out for moral support. We decided he should interview the audience on video camera, as they came out of the showroom, asking what they thought of the show. We didn't know if we'd use the tapes for advertising purposes, or if I was going to use it, unedited, just to let Frank know what people thought. "I never want to see that show again"; "That was the best show I ever saw"; "Boy, he could really sing"; "Why didn't he sing more of his father's songs?" were just some of the comments. I let Frank watch the tape of those unedited comments. When he saw the people's faces when they were talking about the songs that were his father's, he could see such love and happiness. You could see they were reminiscing in the best way possible. They were thinking about how good it felt to hear those songs. I think he started to see it.

Cen Cel

The One Hundredth Birthday

"We were coming up to Sinatra's one hundredth birthday," Kauffman remembered. "We were maybe eighteen months away from December 12, 2015. We needed to prepare something very special for the audiences." She viewed this as cause for celebration and suggested to Frank that "something be planned for the centennial. The "something special" she spoke of had to do, in part, with using video.

"No, I'm never going to use video," Frank said. "I never want to use video." Kauffman's argument was that multimedia would mean so much to the audience because they would get to see someone they love. "I'm not ready yet," was his reply. Kauffman knew when she had to shut down an argument.

The seed, however, was planted. Kauffman recalled,

> We were on the road, and my son, Isaac, who was so important in Frank's career, said to him, "You know what song you never do, Frank? You never sing 'It Was a Very Good Year.' Well, you should sing it."
>
> He looked at Isaac and said, "You're a little young to know that song."
>
> Isaac said, "I'm working with you, Frank. I have to know everything there is to know." Frank was really taken aback and told Isaac that he thought it was a good idea, but that's as far as it went. Isaac told me and a couple of other people about the conversation he had with Frank.

About a month or so before we were due at Borgata, in Atlantic City, Frank said, "I've been thinking. We're going to do 'It Was a Very Good Year.' I want you to find me six or seven pictures of my father that represent his age progression—when I was seventeen, when I was twenty-one, thirty-five, etcetera—in the song." I found some good photos, and we sent them to Hank, who put them together in visual sequence to match the timing in the song. Now we had, as Frank put it, "videx." But it was just for that song. We had two monitors on each side of the stage with these fabulous pictures of this father. We got standing ovations, and Frank felt the love. At first, he was moving himself out of the way of the monitors because he didn't want to compete with the video. But gradually, he was moving further downstage, and eventually, he was right in the middle and surrounded by the video.

Frank knew that the video worked well, and that's what audiences needed—and wanted—to understand and enjoy the true premise of the show. In January of 2015, preparations for the multimedia element of the one hundredth birthday celebration show began. Frank, Isaac, Joe Picuri, Hank Cattaneo, and I worked in the video office of the Borgata because we were going to give the show to the Borgata first. We worked on the collection of Sinatra photos for four weeks. Frank paid Hank and Joey and the Borgata tech crew out of his own pocket to put the video together. Frank picked the photos and incorporated them into the video portion of the show before we had the proper permissions to use them. I needed almost five months to work on clearances, permissions, and licensing in order to clear the photos.

The photo-selection/permissions process was difficult because Kauffman encountered an unexpected obstacle: the Sinatra family. Many of the photographs were needed for the multimedia/video element of the show, and the rights to many of those photos belonged to a Sinatra-owned company. Amanda, Nancy's daughter, was putting out a coffee-table book of Sinatra photos, and they didn't want photos that were earmarked for the book to be in the show first. Kauffman recalled that she had to go to the family to get pictures. Nancy wanted to know, "What's he doing with them? What's it going to make us look like? What songs is he going to sing? Why does he need so many?"

"The family just kept putting up roadblocks," Kauffman explained.

Frank was like a mouse in a maze, and whatever the prize was, they kept changing the way he could get to it. It was clear they had no love for what he was trying to accomplish. They had no respect for him. He was unusual. He was hard. He was weird. But he would give you the shirt off his back if he thought you were cold. Couldn't you do this for him once? What would it cost you for a picture that the company his father created owns? Why does Amanda get it and not Frank? Why does Tina have the say and not Frank? Eventually, it worked out. Amanda withheld the photos she wanted for her $1,000 book, and we got what was left to choose from gratis. The cost for permissions from other estates was about $15,000. We opened before all the permissions were granted. When you add in the cost for staff, the use of Borgata offices, and equipment and Hank and Joey, the show's cost was mounting up very significantly.

In that Frank had to have a code name for almost everything, he took to calling the birthday tribute shows *Cen Cel*, short for *Centennial Celebration*. No matter what it was called, it was an epic success. Kauffman explained,

There was no script, per se. It was more like an outline. It started out with sound clips of scratchy, 78-rpm records; followed by Rudy Vallee and Bing Crosby—Vallee and Crosby were two of Frank Sinatra's vocal heroes—and on through the timeline of Sinatra's career and success. Frank was quite emotional while creating the Sinatra *Centennial Celebration* show. This show was totally and completely built around Sinatra. It was hard for him to go back, especially looking at all the pictures, but now he was finally and completely celebrating his father. When his father was alive, he had no excuse, no good reason, for singing his father's music. But the birthday celebration gave him an excuse. This was absolutely, without any doubt, one of the best things that happened to Frank. He finally got out of his father's shadow and felt the warmth of his own sunlight.

He was on top of the world. He was at the top of his game. He made the best money he ever made. There was always some pushback because he didn't want the reason for the monumental success to be because he was dedicating his shows entirely to his father's music, life, and career. It was the only reason, and I know that disappointed him. But he was the

> *only* person that could do it with the authenticity of the charts, photos, his voice and his looks. His audience felt like they got Sinatra back.
>
> I said to him, "The fact that you can do your father's music, that you knew the people, that you knew the players, that you knew the arrangers, that you knew how he felt about 'Strangers in the Night'; that gives you credibility." He said the only thing that gave him credibility was that he was Frank Sinatra, Jr., and that he was Frank Sinatra's son. He was doing what he really loved, but it wasn't necessarily on his terms.

Mike Smith's perspective was that the Sinatra tribute show could have gone on for years. "That show was extremely popular," he remembered. "And Frank was finally getting comfortable with that, and it was on his terms. A lot of people said, 'We can make it better if you do this and do that,' but he stuck to his guns, did it the way he wanted, and the people enjoyed it."

In an interview with Craig Byrd, in the April 29, 2015, issue of *Los Angeles Magazine*, Frank talked about some of the reasons behind the show's success. "I was an on-the-site witness, and I believe that to be very significant," he told Byrd. "There is the legend, and there is the person. The legend they know. The music they know, which is the backbone of our program. Frank Sinatra was a very red-blooded heart-beating human. This is what has been lost."

The reviews came in from all over the world, and they were all raves. In the June 28, 2015, issue of the *Manchester Evening News*, Teresa McMahon reviewed Frank's concert at Bridgewater Hall in Manchester, England, and said, "Frank Sinatra, Jr., had the audience in his palm with an impressive set list of 'Ol' Blue Eyes' classics in this modernized, multimedia performance. Frank Jr. pulls off the show with charm and confidence. This was a night to celebrate and pay tribute to a magical man."

Rachel Ward, who reviewed Frank's Royal Albert Hall performance in the July 3, 2015, issue of *The Telegraph*, said, "Frank Sinatra, Jr., oozes the same velveteen bass baritone as his late father."

Andrea Kauffman summed up the *Cen Cel* experience, saying, "Finally, after almost fifty years in this business, it took the death of his father and his own confidence for him to be totally honest and true to the music. He now believed he was the only person who had the right to sing that music. The imitators keep it alive and keep it in front of audiences, but he extended the life of Sinatra and didn't even realize what he was doing at the time." Or as Hank Cattaneo said, "Frank Jr. finally realized that that's what people came to see and hear: his father's songs. He was the only legitimate person out there to do them."

Frank may or may not have found inner peace in his last years, but musically, he came to grips with his father's legacy and as a vocal artist, developed a maturity and an interpretive sense that only the years could bring. Through the decades, Frank was always able to get "inside" of the orchestrations. And in his later years, he was finally able to get "inside" of the songs lyrically, rhythmically, and harmonically. There's ample evidence to believe that audiences finally appreciated him for who *he* was and for the legacy *he* represented. The critics took note as well. The reviews were now overwhelmingly positive, to an extent where he could no longer play the victim and bemoan his "lack of successes." British music journalist Clive Davis's September 18, 2012, review for *The London Times* is just one example of just where a mature Frank Sinatra, Jr., stood with the music writers.

FRANK SINATRA, JR., AT RONNIE SCOTT'S

By Clive Davis

It might easily have turned into an episode of *Stars in Their Eyes*, but to see the son pay homage to the father was, in the end, genuinely moving. It helped too that Frank Sinatra, Jr.—now pushing seventy himself—is endowed with a twinkling sense of humor, not to mention an immaculate backing group.

He knows all about the dynamics of an orchestra, having served as the grand old man's conductor in his final years. I have vivid memories of a night at a megacasino in Connecticut where Sinatra Sr. in one of the last shows of his career, suffered memory lapses and began to snap at his son. Not a pretty sight, to say the least.

This evening, of course, was all about remembering the great man in his pomp. Sinatra, Jr., possesses a polished baritone that generates a remarkable facsimile of the slightly heavier but still honeyed voice of the Reprise era. His knack of conducting with his free arm was mildly distracting, but in place of that famous Hoboken swagger, there was amiability and a willingness to make fun of his own modest recording career.

He even supplied his own support set of sorts, rifling through the odd novelty tune and even indulging in a gaudy impersonation of that other pillar of the Rat Pack, Dean Martin. But with the Sinatra material, we arrived at the real business of the evening. "I Get a Kick out of You," "A Foggy Day," and "I've Got You under My Skin" were all dispatched with authority, a four-man horn section led by the reeds player Mike Smith creating a miraculous wall of sound adorned with the occasional Harry Edison-style arabesque.

As for the joyful explosion of brass on "Luck Be a Lady," Sinatra's old friend Billy May would surely have approved.

Because I'm Not Done Yet

Given the success of the *Centennial Celebration*, there seemed to be no reason why Nancy couldn't be a part of what seemed to be a windfall. "There was a follow-up to the *Cen Sel* show," Kauffman wrote.

> I knew that Nancy was having trouble walking. She had bad knees. I created a show where she was sitting, almost like a fireside chat. She would talk about her father's life and how it affected the family. We would bring in other acts to sing the songs, and Nancy wouldn't really leave the stage. If she did, she would be on a kind of truck that could be pushed on and pushed off. I just didn't want to leave her out. I wanted her daughter, AJ Lambert, to be a part of it.
>
> Charlie Pignone, Terry Woodson, Isaac, and I met at the Musso and Frank's restaurant in Hollywood. I pitched it, and I think Charlie said, "You're never going to get that to fly with Frankie." But they liked it. Frank said that if I got this concept to fly with Nancy, I could go to work for Nancy. I asked him why. He said, "Because I'm not done yet."
>
> I said, "Here's the big question: What do we do two years post *Cen Cel*, when we can't do *Cen Sel* anymore?"
>
> He said, "You leave it to me. I'll make sure you're happy." I took that to mean that he would leave the show intact but take out all the multimedia elements and go back to *Sinatra Sings Sinatra*.
>
> Honestly, if it did happen, I think Nancy would have fucked it up. She wasn't directable anymore. And if you really look at that, Frankie was the only one that was really willing to bend over backwards, in his

own way, to break his own spine that he kept so stiff over the years, to celebrate his father. I think Nancy just wanted to see pictures up there of her looking adoringly into her father's eyes—while wearing her white boots—and that wouldn't have been enough for everybody.

Put Your Dreams Away

In March 2016, *Cen Cell* made its way through Florida. By the fifteenth of March, Frank, the musicians, and the road crew were in Daytona Beach, enjoying a day off before the next day's show.

Frank had a special female visitor while he was ensconced at the Hilton Garden Inn in Daytona Beach. Catherine Denise was a blues singer and guitarist from San Antonio, Texas. Though blues wasn't Frank's particular cup of musical tea, he did have one thing in common with her: Both were consumed by music.

She first saw the elder Sinatra in person, in 1981, when she was still a youngster. She was fascinated with the music, and when a magazine article about Sinatra Sr. mentioned that he had a son who sang, she just had to see him in person. "I was just drawn to him," she said, "I don't know why."

Almost twenty years later, she finally saw Frank Jr. in person. "I was so amazed when I saw his show," she said. "I was overwhelmed. I was floored. It was heaven for me." After becoming a frequent visitor to his performances, they finally met when he performed in Omaha. She told Frank she would be in touch with him when she visited California. "I called him when I was out there, and he invited me to his house," she said. A relationship developed.

He was kind of a difficult person to know," she explained, "but the relationship was very nice. I didn't want to push it. I never really expected anything, and I never really wanted to push anything.

Whatever he wanted was okay. I was doing my own thing at the time. If he wanted to see me, I'd go see him." The arrangement lasted for years.

Frank invited Denise, her mother, and her sister to Daytona, around March 14, 2016. Denise remembered,

> He said he had a couple of days off and that he'd be able to spend some time with us. We spent a lot of time with him in Daytona. My sister left, and it was the night before his show, March 16. I went to hang out with him. I went to his room, and we were watching a movie. He said, "I don't feel very well."
>
> I said, "What do you mean?" He said he felt like he had a chill up his back. I said, "Just relax." He just didn't feel well. I was going to go back to my room, but I was afraid to leave him there. I didn't know if he wanted to go to the hospital or what. I didn't want to push him. You couldn't push him. He would have to be the one to decide.
>
> I went to my room, I fell asleep, and when I woke up, I was really scared. He called me about 2:30 in the afternoon, which was something he hardly ever did. He wanted to hang out before the show. I went to his room. The hall was empty. It felt like a weird dream. I went into his room, and we started talking. He told me that he had been sick in December. I told him he really needed to see somebody. I was sitting on the bed, and he was coming over to me, and he collapsed. I freaked out. I didn't know what to do.
>
> Part of me already knew that he was on his way to dying. I was confused. The first people I thought of were his sister and his mother. I tried to wake him up, and he wouldn't wake up. He started to make these weird noises. He had a bruise that started to get bigger over his eye. I called downstairs and told them to call 911 because I thought Frank had a heart attack. The hotel manager came up; then Jim Fox came up.
>
> I went to the hospital. They said he still had a slight pulse. They were working on him. Part of me had hope, but part of me said, "This is the end." I just knew something bad was going to happen on that trip. Part of me didn't want to believe it. Part of me already knew.

Jim Fox

Both my wife and I were traumatized, deeply traumatized, I would say, for two years, following his passing. My wife and I were both in the room with him when he passed. And we were the only people on the staff that were. We carried that with us for a long time, and I do, still, think about him and mourn his passing every day. But the trauma part of it was two years, and it still hits my gut. I just felt terrible about this loss, and I just felt terrible for him.

I wanted to speak with Andrea before I went on the record for the book because Frank was a very private person, and I generally don't speak about him to people. That's maybe one of the reasons we got along well because I really respected that. I never pried into his private life. I was at his house a lot of times because we both lived in the Los Angeles area. But I never, you know, wanted to know about his private life. I didn't think it was appropriate. I was his employee. I was there to serve his needs. That's what a service business is: when you provide a service, as opposed to goods, as in goods and services. But, yeah, I was there, and it was a day, every moment of which I'll never forget.

We were in Daytona. We had played Florida and had a day, maybe two, in Daytona. We were in a smallish hotel, the Hilton Garden Inn. They had a small desk. Terry Anthony had flown home because he had, I think, something at home, maybe a funeral or something like that. So, he flew to Boston, and he was coming back with his wife, Karen. And I was going to pick them up at the airport, which was close to the hotel, so I went to front desk to get his room key because I was going to give Karen the room key and then take Terry to the sound check.

So I knew what was going to happen. I was going to pick the two of them up, I was going to drop them off at the hotel, Karen was going to go to the room, and we would go to sound check and then come back to the hotel after that. Well, when I got to the front desk, the manager looked out of the door, and he said, and he knew us because we had the day off, and he knew us all by sight because it was a small hotel, he said, "Mr. Fox, Mr. Sinatra has fainted in his room." And I was with my wife, we were going to go to the airport together, and I said that we had to go up. The manager said, "I know CPR."

I said, "Let's go!" So I took the manager, and we went up to Frank's room, and he was unconscious. Breathing, but unconscious on his bed. And I held his shoulders and his neck up to open his breathing area. I held from underneath while he gave CPR until the paramedics arrived, for about ten minutes. My wife was there with me in the room, and the paramedics came into the room. When the paramedics came into the room, I hadn't called anybody yet because we were right in the throes of trying to save his life or revive him.

The paramedics came in, and I stayed in the room because I thought that somebody close to Frank had to be there. So we stayed in the room. Then when they decided to get the electric paddles out to try to revive him, they asked me to step out for safety. So I stepped out, and the first thing I did was call, and I'm not sure of the order, I called Terry Woodson, who was in the hotel and who was the most in charge of anybody that was there.

I called Andrea in Atlantic City and told her what was going on. Then she gave me instructions, and she said to me, "I want you to take care of things. I want you to run point on this. You have to call Joey and tell him the show is canceled tonight. They have to handle the theater, and he has to handle the buyers over at the theater and promoters or anyone else over there, and we have to cancel everything. We have to pack everything up and tell Merrill to go to the theater and make sure that all the stuff is okay over there." Isaac, Andrea's son, was over there at the theater as well. Joey Pircuri, our sound man, was over there. So, I stayed. When they were transporting Frank, my wife and I just followed the ambulance over to the hospital. We were met with the chief of police and the head of security for the hospital, the chief executive officer, or whatever he was called, of the hospital. And they were saying, "You can't go through." I told them I had to. I was with Frank.

They took us to a waiting room of the ICU where they were working on him. As soon as it was established that he was no longer alive, the family legally took over what was going to happen with the body. That's my understanding. I'm not a lawyer, and I never saw a document, so I can't say. But that was my understanding because I was on the phone with Andrea from the hospital. I believe I was talking to a family attorney from the hospital once, because they called me, I believe.

What little publicity it was given, they said that he had a heart attack, but I knew he had a massive stroke. Because I could see that the area around the eyes was completely bruised. I could see it. So I knew that he had had a stroke. So when it was in the news, the news reported that he had a heart attack, I didn't think it really mattered. They said he died of a coronary-related incident, but it really didn't matter. But I knew. You don't have to be a doctor to know that.

Andrea Kauffman

Over the last few years, *Sinatra Sings Sinatra* was a huge success. Andrea Kauffman had good reason to be happy. After thirty-one years of stress, strain, conniving, convincing, cajoling, deal making, and constant hard work—often at the expense of her personal life—she could sit back and be proud of what she had created and facilitated.

By mid-2015, the new show, *Sinatra Sings Sinatra: The Centennial Celebration*, filled with video celebrating Sinatra's life, was an even bigger success. Frank had finally learned to deal with singing the songs made famous by his father, audiences all over the world loved the show, sellouts became the norm, reviews were unanimous in their praise, locations were more and more prestigious, and the money was better than it ever had been. The road crew, spearheaded by Isaac Tamburino and Joe Picuri, ran like a well-oiled machine. "There was nothing left to chance with the two of them," Andrea Kauffman declared. "They had everything covered. And the show and Frank's performance couldn't have been better."

She was also grooming her son to step into her place eventually. "The less I went on the road, she said, "the more Isaac would have to handle issues that might come up. I wanted him to take over management. I think between Isaac and Joe Picuri, they could have handled the whole deal." If Frank's health held out, there was no reason the show couldn't continue touring the world successfully for another couple of years."

Late on December 10, 2015, Frank, musicians, and crew were traveling by bus after a show in Phoenix. They were heading for Los Angeles for a concert at the Saban Theater. It was a very special date, December 12. It was Frank Sr.'s one hundredth birthday.

> Mike Smith called me and told me that Frank had the bus stop at a roadside "eat here and get gas" type of place. He ate two cheeseburgers and a pile of fries and drank a milkshake. At some point, while on the bus, he got violently ill. He was sweating, he threw up, and he had chest pains. I said to Mike that I thought Frank had a heart attack, and he agreed. Mike was very concerned and wanted to call a doctor. Frank said, "Absolutely not." He said he was fine, that he ate too much of all the wrong foods. Mike was extremely concerned.

> Because of the significance of the date and the fact that Los Angeles was his father's hometown, I know he wouldn't have canceled, even if he suspected that what happened the night before was a heart-related incident. I was already in Los Angeles when he arrived. When I saw him, he looked fine. He was alert, and he wasn't even tired, but there was something in the back of my mind—and it was in the back of Mike Smith's mind—that he had had a heart attack. He certainly wasn't taking care of himself. I saw him eat a pound of lox with a fork. I can't tell you how many cups of black coffee with Sweet and Low he had during rehearsal.
>
> And Cynthia had not made life any easier. He was fighting her lawsuit that claimed they were common-law man and wife, which would have meant that she was entitled to more money. The argument went on for months. He was always on the phone with his lawyers. So, his blood pressure was totally out of control. The only time that it probably wasn't was when he was on stage.

But by and large, things were running smoothly, and Kauffman was finally able to reduce the amount of time she spent on the road. She said,

> I had been touring for over thirty years. I wanted to get off the road. I missed so much with my kids and didn't want to lose that time with my grandchildren. There were times when Frank would say, "You've got to come out here." I was also trying to save Frank money. The more he made, the more he spent, so the less he made. He was always chasing his tail when it came to money. Not that my going out would cost a fortune, but it was money that he could have saved. There were times when Frank would say, "I need you to come out here now." I had no choice but to go.
>
> The decision to go or not to go to a date was based on several factors. It really depended on the venue, the city, and the problems the venue or city posed. Every date was important, but if the venue was in a major city where I'd have to deal with a major press presence, I made sure I was there. Or, if it was the kind of venue that was in a small town that may not have the caliber of musicians that we needed—or if our rider was a challenge to the buyer—I'd be there.

Wednesday, March 16, 2016, began like any other day. The show that night was to take place at the twenty-five-hundred-seat Peabody Auditorium, Daytona Beach, just another stop on Frank's Florida run.

When I wasn't at a date, my day proceeded this way: I would talk to Isaac or Joey early in the day, asking if travel and load-in went okay. After rehearsal, Frank would call me. Then I'd talk to him before dinner, which was after the show. When he was on the road, Frank and I spoke three times a day, and I'd speak to Isaac or Joey at least twice a day, before the show and once after.

Because I had to order an airline ticket or arrange for an additional room, Frank always let me know if he had a special friend/guest on the road with him. But I did not know that Catherine Denise was with him at Daytona Beach until the day he died.

He had one day off before Daytona. The day he died, I was on the phone with him for thirty-five minutes thirty minutes before his death. The time was 2:25 p.m. He was talking about how great the previous Florida shows were. He wanted me to come down. I was an avid saltwater fisherman, so he said, "Don't work. Fish! I want you with us." He said that Karen Anthony was coming down, and he knew I adored Karen. I said okay, and while I was on the phone with him, I sent Dorian, our travel agent, an email, asking him to make the travel arrangements, as Frank wanted me to be in Daytona the next morning. The plan was for me to arrive on the seventeenth at around noon.

About an hour after my phone call with Frank, I got the first phone call. It was from Merrill Kelem, who was working security, though he was no longer on the payroll. He said Frank was taken to the hospital and was unresponsive. I asked him what happened, and he said he didn't know. Then Jim Fox cut into the phone call. Jim knew a little more. He said that he was in the room with Frank and that the hotel manager was trying to resuscitate Frank while they were waiting for the paramedics. When the paramedics came, they gave him oxygen and started an IV. Jim was on the phone all this time, giving me all the information. I wouldn't let him hang up. He kept saying, "I don't know. I don't think he's breathing." But they wouldn't declare Frank dead in the hotel. Even in the ambulance, they were still trying to revive him.

When they left for the hospital, I told Jim to call me the moment they got there. Merrill called me a second time from the hospital. I told Merrill that he was not to say a damn thing until we knew what was going on. Then I got a call from Isaac. He told me it was over. Isaac was sobbing. He got to the point where he just kept saying, "Oh, Mom. What do we do? What do we do now, Mom? He's gone."

His cry wasn't about work or what the next steps were to be taken. It was more like, what do we do without Frank? Then I heard somebody ask him something, and he answered in a perfectly calm voice. Somebody in the band told me that he couldn't believe that Isaac would sit in the corner, just crying, but when someone told him something needed to be done, he would deal with it, without any emotion. Then he would sit down and start crying again.

He was gone. I would have to make the appropriate calls. I called Nancy, but I couldn't get through, so I called Bob Finkelstein, who got a hold of Nancy. I also called his son, Michael.

I'll never understand in a million years why Bob—the lifelong family attorney and friend who was once engaged to Tina—didn't come to Florida. The family sent Randy O'Connor, the financial manager who took Sonny Golden's place, and Tasha. That's how hateful this family was when it came to Frank.

Tasha was lying in bed with the dead Frank. One by one, the guys were coming in to say goodbye. She wouldn't let them take the body away. By the time she chose to get out of the bed and the hospital staff needed to take Frank to the morgue, many of the guys were sitting in the room with him. They would not and did not leave him alone. That was an order I gave to Isaac and Joe Picuri. At no time, until they took his body to the morgue, did I want him alone. I talked to the hospital administration, explained how we needed to proceed and what they had to do in order to protect Frank's body.

I won't go into detail, but I can tell you that, after talking to Catherine Denise, I know what really happened. Much to my begging him not to talk to anyone about this, Merrill was giving out misinformation to whomever he spoke to, including some of his friends.

By the early evening, Randy had arrived. They couldn't fly the body home immediately. The hospital had to do an autopsy because he didn't die in the hospital; he actually died at the hotel. Then they cremated him, and then he finally came home in a box carried by

Tasha. My job was to change all the flights and call the venues. I was very busy in the office for the next few days. When I got it all done, it hit me.

Bob wanted to put out a press release, but Nancy stopped him and said *she* wanted to put out a press release. We had to agree on what we were saying. I heard that the doctor told Tasha that it was a stroke, but Nancy chose to say heart attack. Why? Because a heart attack is an easier explanation than a stroke. Because he had high blood pressure, did that show another deficiency in his character?

If I was in Daytona that day, what would have been different? For one, I would have been in Frank's suite, or we would have been having breakfast together. Maybe I could have asked Catherine to come around after the show. I know that he was told not to take the "little blue pill," but I believe he did. Isaac was sent into his room to pack up his personal belongings before Tasha got there. He saw them and made sure they were packed up in his stuff and taken out of the room. I think he died because he took it. I think that's what caused his stroke. And eating at him each day was the constant anger, disappointment, bitterness, and sorrow about how Cynthia ended up treating him. Those are the major factors that killed him.

The night before everyone left, Randy hosted a dinner at the hotel. They had their final dinner. Their last supper. Each person got up and said a little something about what Frank meant to them. Terry and Karen called me so I could be a part of it.

There was never a burial, there was never a memorial, and there will *never* be any closure for his real family: us, his road family. Our brother, mentor, father, and best friend never got to hear a farewell from us.

Isaac Tamburino

"Isaac was telling me how Tasha was lying in bed with his body," Andrea Kauffman recalled. "They were trying to get Frank out, and she was acting like a lunatic. We all knew it was an act."

At the death scene, Tamburino said Tasha "was just an emotional wreck. Why she came out to Daytona to cry and to involve herself in a situation where there was nothing but chaos and sorrow, was beyond me." Still, he believed that Tasha "did absolute right by Frank, and it did seem like she had his best interests at heart. She was a little crazy, and I didn't think she was Frank's type, but I think she had good intentions. She got thrown some crazy loops."

Joe Picuri

The morning when he passed, I took the van, and Frank called me and asked what I was doing. I told him I was taking a little ride just to go to the beach and put my feet in the water. Then he started going through guest lists and sound check times, and the normal type of exchange we had. I went to the beach, and Isaac and I went to the gig, and we were setting up. I was rigging up the monitors and trying to get some sound. Then Jim Fox called me and said Frank collapsed in the hotel room, and they couldn't revive him. I thought, "Holy fuck." I don't think he was declared dead just then, but we knew he wasn't playing the show. So we talked to everybody and said, "This ain't happening." Then a heavy cloud descended upon us at Daytona Beach, and the next thing we heard, he was pronounced dead.

It was like getting hit with a bat. He had his health struggles with cancer, but he was looking pretty good in general, but I guess he was more fragile than we knew. Isaac and I had to take Frank's luggage and gear, and we had to send it home. One thing Frank was very specific about was his luggage. He had covers for his suitcases and stuff. I remember Isaac and I at the loading dock of the warehouse where we were unloading his stuff, and we said to the guy, "Please be careful of Frank's luggage, man. He's really . . ." Then we realized that Frank was totally in our heads. He's dead, and we're telling the guy to take care of his luggage.

It ran deep. We said goodbye in person. He was in the hospital bed. I gave him a kiss and said thank you. That was a tough one. It was like a bunch of kids around their dad. He was ice cold. I remember it vividly.

Missed

Ronna Brodsley

Ronna said, "When I heard the news that he passed, I sat down on the floor and cried and cried. I realized how truly alone he was. It just made me so sad for him."

M. Michelle Martin

The day he died was just terrible. His daughter, Francine, called me and said, "Have you talked to my dad?"

I said, "I talked to him yesterday" and asked her why she was asking.

And she said, "He had a heart attack."

I said, "What?"

She said, "He died." That's how I heard. I sat on my couch for eight hours without moving. I was so upset and was in so much shock.

Isaac Tamburino

He and my mom designed this family, whether they did this on purpose or not. It was the right combination of the people at the right time, with Frank and my mom at the head of the table. You had to understand what this human being named Frank Sinatra, Jr., went through and had continued to go through internally and externally. It wasn't until you found that respect for him deep down that he would have real respect for you. We had to take him with his bullshit, and if you showed that you could take him with his shit, and you're not going to let his shit bother you too much, then he was as loyal to me as I was to him. You had to accept him. He was never accepted for who he was. He always had to be his father's son or something. "Let me be Frank" was all he ever wanted. We would hear him say something ridiculous and not take it at face value. We'd say, "That's just Frank." And there were not a lot of people who would do that and just move on.

With all the stories and the feelings I was privy to about how he felt about his father, the *Sinatra Sings Sinatra* shows had to be a bittersweet experience every day. I can't imagine what that was actually like to be him. He wanted to sing the worst songs, and he was privy to the greatest music catalog in history. But he wanted to do the worst stuff. It was just his taste. He would never speak ill of his father. And he would never speak ill of his siblings. It was always respect.

Nothing about his career ended up being "his music." He wanted to be a film composer. He had music to write, and he never wrote it. As an artist, he never showed any real part of what he was. I think he was executing what people wanted. His potential was never realized. In the music he did do, his attention to the detail and to all the parts of the score was almost like, "Hey Pop, I'm putting my mark on it, too."

Monica Tribuiani Giampa

Monica, the daughter of Andrea Kauffman, grew up surrounded by "all things show business" and recalled being about four or five when she got an idea of what her mother did for a living. "My mother had her office in Atlantic City, and I went to see her after school and hung out in the office," she remembered. "She included me in a lot. She took me to some wonderful dinners and took me to see some wonderful acts. It was like, 'Wow. This is very different.' My mother was definitely powerful, even at that stage of her career. It was very meaningful, as her daughter, to watch her work."

Being included, in Monica's case, meant attending Frank Jr.'s rehearsals while still in a baby carriage and being pressed into "hostess service" by Frank himself when she was around seven. She fondly recalled the memory.

> We were all in Frank's suite at the Atlantis Hotel and Casino in Atlantic City. He was hosting everyone for a closing night party. He said, "Monica, would you like to help me out here?" And there I was, passing out drinks and mingling with everyone. It was a blast just to be around these people. But after a while, I needed a break. My feet were tired. I said, "Frank, I have to stop. I have athlete's feets."
>
> After Frank stopped laughing, he said, "Exactly what does that mean?"

Then there was the issue of the mask and the cape Frank wore during the short time he was singing "The Music of the Night" from "Phantom of the Opera." The seven-year-old Monica, while backstage with Frank while he put the phantom's costume on, was very, very scared of the mask. "He showed me the mask," she remembered, "and he told me the whole story of what the mask was all about so I wouldn't be afraid of it. He was great with kids. Awkward at times, but very sweet."

Monica already knew, at a young age, that representing Frank

> was a very big deal. I remember those conversations in the family and realized that this was a huge break and a huge undertaking for my mother. As I got older, there were times when it was, like, "Oh my God, this is Frank Sinatra, Jr." Then there were other times when I saw him as just another close friend of the family. He was someone who we got know over many dinners, and many shows, and many events. I saw how close my mom was to him. She spoke to him several times every day. He became almost like a brother to my mom. Over the years, the relationship and how we looked at Frank changed.I saw my mom go through a lot with Frank over the years. There were lots of fights, lots of tears, lots of conversation, and lots of agony. There were times when I thought she was just going to say, "I can't do this for another minute." But at the end of the day, it wasn't just a job. She loved him, so the fights just weren't between a manager and a client. It was like a brother-and-sister relationship.
>
> It absolutely had an effect on the family. It was always the topic of conversation, and I can't tell you how many times she got called away because he was calling, and it was urgent because he was going through something. And all the stuff he went through with his divorce was brutal for her.

> We had many talks, and I sometimes saw her frustration with Frank. But at the end of the day, he kind of grew on all of us because we knew this other side to him. As difficult as he could be, there was never a doubt that he didn't love her—or me and my brother, for that matter. Overall, you had this sense that he was a damaged man, but you accepted him for who he was. So I never faulted her for sticking it out with him. I never said, "I don't understand," or "How could you be doing this to yourself?" I knew that she really cared and loved him and that they made a difference in each other's lives. We just all accepted it.

Through Andrea's thirty-one-year association with Frank and all that came with it, her daughter never felt that her mother was an absentee mom. Monica stressed that she

> never felt that way, even though my mom was on the road a lot. She was there for all the important stuff, and if anything, I think she shaped who I am, in the sense that I'm an entrepreneur, even though I went in a totally different direction. I think watching her run the business for all those years, was very inspiring to me in my own career and also as a mother, because I have two children of my own. I learned from my mom that I can do both.*

Monica will not forget the day she was told the news of Frank's passing.

> My mother was hysterical when she called me to tell me Frank had passed. It was a real shock, and the fact that my brother was there made it even tougher. But she took care of business. Always. And that was hard on her. She didn't have the same opportunity to mourn that she should have because she had to jump right in and take care of everything. It was a mess. Such a mess.
>
> There were so many layers to it. She lost one of her best friends. And she lost her career. Her career, as she knew it at that point, was all Frank. She had put everything else aside. That was a whole other layer

---

* After college, Monica spent three years as a talent agent with ICM and then decided that life was not for her. She moved back to New Jersey, started a family, and now owns and operates two preschools in Atlantic County.

to it that was deeply upsetting for her. Her whole career, and her whole identity that she had at that point, was taken from her. I was devastated for her for the personal loss, and I was devastated for her professional loss. She wasn't ready for that. I think that her not working at that stage of her life was not what she wanted. At that point, she wasn't ready to reinvent herself. She was just going to move on from it in the best way she knew how.

Joe Picuri

He touched a lot of souls. I think about it on so many levels. When we were hanging, it was really fun. We really connected, and all the guys had little subtopics that they connected with Frank about. He could talk about a lot of different things. Everyone loved jumping on the flight to do a "weekend warrior" type of thing. We'd go out to dinner, we'd laugh, we'd hang, and then we'd get to do a show, and even if it was a fucked-up show, it was still a show. A lot of energy swelled around Frank. It wasn't just a gig. It was an event for us.

I feel that we need to do some kind of celebration of his life, some kind of recognition for him in a public setting by us (meaning the band and road crew). It's absurd to me that we haven't gotten together. The family pushed that whole thing down, and I say fuck 'em at this point.

Mike Smith

Had he lived, I think we would have gone on with that Sinatra show, the multimedia thing, because that show was really popular. He was finally getting comfortable with that, and it was on his terms. I miss him terribly. We would talk all the time on the phone. He's the godfather to my kid. Was he happy? He was happy when he was hanging with us and playing music. Off stage, there was a lot of shit going on. He was going through a bad divorce. That was king of messy. And he still hung out with her, and then she sued him for common law. She was always around. I asked Frank what it was all about. He'd say, "Oh, I love her, and I love the kids." It was very messy.

Lisa Coffey

> He could have been a famous brain surgeon. He could have been anything he wanted to be, and the fact that what he wanted to be was a musician was doubly indicative of his motive. I think that being the son of Frank Sinatra made that difficult for him in many ways. And in many ways, it made it easy for him, too. Had he not been Frank Sinatra, Jr., there may have been a broader public awareness of his brilliance. But he was really driven by his passion. I miss him. And he gave me some of the most memorable musical moments I've ever had.

Tony Lo Bianco

Tony remembers, "He was the end of the Sinatra line. The mystique, the magic, the sound, the music, the comfort, all of that is gone now. I guess we all feel cheated. I miss him tremendously. Had he lived, I think our friendship would have gotten stronger and stronger."

Jobell Yonley

Jobell Yonley is a jazz singer and the former wife of Paul Malin, who was the road manager for Frank Sr. and Frank Jr. Yonley knew Frank Sinatra, Jr., well and remains a close friend of Andrea Kauffman. Upon hearing the news of this book's publication, Yonley was moved to write Andrea the following:

> The camaraderie, the music, laughs, dinners, rehearsals, and at the center of it was Frank. He loved you. He always spoke of you with so much trust and respect. I can hear his voice saying, "Andrea." He created a lifetime of amazing memories. You'll cry over him for the rest of your life. That's what happens when we love someone. But I'm proud of you for putting your thoughts down and writing. It's cathartic. I'm glad there will be a book about him. It will show who he was to people who never got to meet him. His whole life was in the public, but he was a private man and was probably misunderstood by the public. Being the son and caretaker of a national legacy was a huge responsibility, and Frank did it with class, and respect for his father, the composers, the arrangers, the

> musicians, the inner circle . . . everything. It's your love and caring that will cement his legacy. Be proud. He would be proud of you.

Frank Sinatra, Jr.

In an interview with Nick Duerden of *The Guardian*, Frank said, "Over all these years, I have never had a hit movie, never had a hit television program and never had a hit record. To my way of thinking, that means success has not been achieved. I have made no mark of my own creation. This is something to be considered. But if the audience comes, and likes what I do, then that's enough for me. I'll settle for that" (August 31, 2012).

The Funeral That Wasn't

Andrea Kauffman

Tasha took his ashes on the plane back to Los Angeles, and they were given to Nancy Sr. I called Nancy Jr., and I wrote Tina, asking what we were going to do about a memorial. Nancy said, "We're not going to do anything until my mother's gone." I asked why, and she said, "I don't want everybody coming out of the woodwork. I don't want them walking in with their kids saying, 'That was your father.' I don't want that. I'm not going to put my mother through that." And you know what, that could have easily happened. She was right. But Nancy Sr. has been gone since July 13, 2018. You would think that, in the last several years, there's been some opportunity to plan and have a memorial for Frank.

There are thirteen devoted *family* members that never got closure or had the opportunity to give Frank the proper, respectful memorial that he so deserved. Thirteen of us that spent more time with him than his sisters ever did. From what I've been told, Frank's ashes still sit in a dark closet. In my heart, I know that isn't our Frank. The remains mean nothing. I must believe that, without a formal funeral, he knows how much we loved him and miss him.

The estate was settled about three years after his death. I know Michael was very disappointed that Francine was being difficult. Leslie, Josie's mother, wanted everything she thought she was entitled to. It's a shame they didn't fight over his well-being the way they picked over his estate.

He thought of his road family in the most beautiful way. He left us the rights to the music to loan out or rent out to colleges, symphonies, pops orchestras, and other singers for a fee. He wanted us to have some sort of income generated by the music after he was gone. Money never meant much to Frank. The music meant everything. In essence, we, his road family, received, in theory and intention, the most meaningful of legacies.

Unfortunately, and he'd never know, it was a fruitless gesture. The lawyer who wrote the will made sure the wording was so convoluted no one could really get a handle on how this would be executed. The executor of his will, who was Frank's divorce lawyer and a very dear friend of mine, suggested I have the document reviewed by our own attorney. I paid to have it reviewed and interpreted. He asked if Frank's attorney got paid by the word because he never read so many words that said nothing.

We knew we didn't own the music; we only had the rights to loan it out. But the family sold the music out from under us. My dear friend, at the time, somehow got the family to agree to a small monetary gesture that was given to the musicians, staff, and me. Frank used to say the music was worth a fortune. Seth McFarlane bought the whole library for under $200,000. At least that's what Charles Pignone told me. Now, it's basically worthless.

A few months after Frank's death, I received four big boxes. They were filled with his tuxedos, shirts, and dress boots. I was given instructions to give them to the guys who I thought were about his same size. It didn't surprise me that Frank's $5,000 tuxedos, $2,500 boots, and $300 shirts meant nothing to our guys. Those items were worthless to all of us. It was the music we knew was most important to him, therefore to us. We knew that the provision in his will was the singular most important gesture he could have made to us.

At one point, for specific business reasons, Frank and I talked about forming a company. We were fooling around with different ways to combine our names. Combining our two names didn't work, so I asked Frank jokingly, "Why don't you just pick a name that describes you, like Crazy, Inc.?"

He said to me, "Anomaly." And that's what it was. *And that's what he was.*

Acknowledgments

Bruce Klauber gratefully acknowledges the following:

Joel Klauber: For introducing me to jazz and the music of Frank Sinatra.

Bruce Kaminsky: For your support and enthusiasm about this project and everything I've done through the years. And without your backing on the bass, I'd end up singing along with a tape in a parking lot.

Frank DiBussolo: For always being there for everything.

Linda Richardson Korman and Steve Korman: For your interest and encouragement throughout this project, your editorial insights, and most importantly, for welcoming me into your family.

Sid Mark: You were my friend since we first met when I was eight years old. Your dedication to the music of Frank Sinatra was remarkable, but equally remarkable was what you did throughout the years on behalf of Frank Jr. Your microphones were open to him whenever he was in the neighborhood, and you were one of the very few who really knew him. Sleep warm, Sidney.

Isabel Czech and Paul Hilger: For your friendship and support.

Elizabeth Rosenthal: My thanks to you for always being there with good advice and counsel.

Eddie Bruce: Your friendship and support of all my endeavors mean the world to me. The successes we have shared have made me happy beyond measure.

* * *

> It's not the candle in the window to remind us to remember him. It's not the light in the attic shining on dusty boxes as we unpack our memories. It's these people that will keep Frank alive.
>
> —*ANDREA KAUFFMAN*

Andrea Kauffman gratefully acknowledges the following:

Michael Sinatra: You are the best of him! You're a very special man. Thank you for your contribution to the book. I am grateful to you beyond measure.

Hank Cattaneo: Thank you for sharing your knowledge with me. You are the epitome of the word *gentleman*. I looked forward to every date you worked with us. You bolstered Frank in so many ways. Sergeant Major, you're a four-star general in my eyes.

Chuck Granata: As record and radio producer, music historian, archivist, and author of four books on music and sound recording, including *Sessions with Sinatra: Frank Sinatra and the Art of Recording*, your support and advice were deeply appreciated. The time you spent with all of the Sinatra family made you a dear and close friend to them. The time you've given Bruce and me and the hand of friendship you extended to me over the years will always be treasured. Thank you.

Terry Anthony: You were the other brother. You completed the family. What a package deal he got with you. You were his "go to" musician and dear friend for decades. You never complained no matter how unsettled things got. In all the years we worked together, I don't ever remember you being anything but supportive of me and the voice of reason. You wanted success for all of us, and you helped facilitate that. Thanks for making our road life easier.

Karen Anthony: Thank you, Karen. You were my best, nonstaff friend on the road. I'm sending you a hug right now! Nobody could corral the road wives and girlfriends like you did. You steered all the nonsense out of my way. I don't know where one person can get all the patience you had, but you are amazing. I loved how you handled any situation no matter how touchy it got. You're a beautiful, smart woman. You are certainly a hero of mine. Thanks for traveling with Terry. I couldn't have done all those years on the road without either of you.

Bob Chmel: Your other name, *Uncle Salty*, was a misnomer. Under the growl is the sweetest guy. Your bark had no bite in it. Thank you for being such a great road brother. You will be missed.

Walt Johnson: You are one of a kind. Thanks for all the high notes you brought to the show and the road.

Jim Fox: You were such a wonderful influence on both Frank and the band. The way you played seemed effortless. The "Swingin' on a Star" night will be one of my favorite memories. From my heart, thank you for not leaving him.

Jeff Morrison: Frank aptly called you "Moses." The Bible you carried with you on the road was so well worn and marked. Your devotion to God was admirable. I know you believed it was His gift that made you the wonderful musician you are. Thanks for finding every McDonalds in every city of every country we visited.

Joe Picuri: I can't thank you enough for your integrity and impeccable work ethics. Your ability to make Frank and the musicians sound their absolute best was magical. Every venue brought different problems, but you were never fazed by them. What the audience was listening to was the very essence of why they were there. You made it perfect. And your deep devotion to Frank never went unnoticed or unappreciated. He was always in the best care in your hands. I'm so glad we're more than business associates, we remained friends, and that our families got to know each other. Thank you, Joey.

Paul Rostock: Your calm and cool demeanor was so soothing. You never got ruffled or angry. You were with Frank the longest, so I suppose you were used to the craziness. Your bass was the heartbeat of the music. Thank you, my friend.

Mike Smith: You were his brother, confidant, and musical advisor. Aside from your brilliant playing, he depended on your musical knowledge. You were the sound of reason when he was veering off the rails. You didn't take any crap from him, and his respect for you was obvious. You were also my rock. You knew of the problems I had dealing with so many personalities. You were able to bridge the gap between staff and management. I couldn't have done so much of it without you. We're both still trying to heal from his passing. "Where Do You Start?"

Terry Woodson: To our conductor, who passed away before the book was complete, thank you for the laughs, shared breakfasts, martinis, and an extraordinary friendship. Also, thank you for keeping me safe when I fell into a couple of black holes with you and Eddie Morgan.

JoBelle Yonley: Thank you, dear friend, for the support you gave me every time I needed it. Your shoulder, ear, and hugs were appreciated more than you realized. See you in room 517.

Monica Tribuiani Giampa: In you, I got what every mother would want in a daughter. I know your childhood was very different than most. When you were younger, I had to bring you to auditions, dinners, and meetings because we couldn't always afford a babysitter. The entertainment buyers, musicians, and celebrities adored being around you. Frank adored you and treated you like one of his nieces. You saw me struggle between my time at home, the office, and the road, and you comforted me. You heard my apologies a hundred times for not being there for something that I knew was important to you, and you never once complained. When you became a teenager, you picked up my slack. Even while you were in college, you were my rock.

Today, you are a very successful businesswoman. I know you think you got much of your business knowledge from me, but it was a mutual exchange of insight. You're an old soul my sweet daughter, and what I learned from you made me one of the most successful women in the world, business aside. I love you, Coo.

Isaac Tamburino: From the first time Frank brought you on stage during a rehearsal, put ear plugs in your ears, and gave you the mallet for the gong, there was a unique connection. You were about four. From that day on, you became someone very special to him. Frank loved you so much. He got such a kick out of you. You brought something out in him that was a cross between father, mentor, and friend. Frank knew you played piano and drums and were interested in a career in music. When you became fifteen, he told me to bring you on the road on the weekends. He felt that the road was where your musical education should start, followed by your college education at Cal Arts. You worked for Frank until the day he died, running his show, sharing production duties with Picuri, calling lights, and transporting our road family from city to city, country to country. You were baby bear and completed our family. Thank you for taking such good care of him. I love you so, Sunny.

Dane Tamburino, a.k.a. Dane Anthony: You paid the biggest price of all as we began to build our life together some forty years ago in this crazy industry. We worked so hard to get the opportunities that made us successful. You became one of the best and most sought-after entertainers Atlantic City ever had in their lounges, and I went on to have Frank Sinatra Jr, as a client and dear friend.

While I was on the road, and you were working five nights a week and singing four sets a night, you got up with the kids, changed dirty diapers, made breakfasts, got them to and from school, chauffeured them to after-school activities and doctor's appointments, and helped with their homework while getting dinner together.

How many times did you carry my luggage up and down the stairs? How many times did you take me to the airport so we could spend another couple of hours together on the drive? How many times was a phone call our only hug or kiss goodnight? I remember it all, and I'm grateful for it all.

I couldn't have a better, more supportive life partner. Thank you, Dane. I love you.

Special Thanks

For their time and their insights, the authors wish to thank Michelle Martin, Mike Smith, Karen Anthony, Terry Anthony, Bob Chmel, Bill Boggs, Gloria Galante, Jim Fox, Dan McIntyre, Les DeMerle, Ronna Brodsley, Kent McCord, William Rinehart, Heidi Fleiss, Paula Jane D'Amato, Tom Dressen, Sara Jane Karloff, Hank Cattaneo, Chuck Granata, Rob Heller, Joe Picuri, Lorraine Hunt-Bono, Paul Rostock, Isaac Tamburino, Catherine Denise, Steve Tyrell, Paul Malin, Merrill Kellum, Tony Lo Bianco, Lisa Coffey, Michael Francis Sinatra, JoBelle Yonley, and Monica Tribuiani Giampa.

Special thanks to Craig Gill, Katie Turner, Jennifer Mixon, and everyone at University Press of Mississippi, as well as freelance copyeditor Camille Hale, who helped make this book a reality.

The following friends/colleagues passed away while this book was being written: Bobby Rydell, Terry Woodson, Bob Cheml, Tony Lo Bianco, Paul Malin, and Sid Mark. May they rest in peace.

Selected Bibliography

Kaplan, James. *Frank: The Voice*. Doubleday, 2010.

Kaplan, James. *Sinatra: The Chairman*. Anchor Books, 2016.

Levinson, Peter J. *September in the Rain: The Life of Nelson Riddle*. Billboard Books, 2001.

Levinson, Peter J. *Tommy Dorsey: Livin' in a Great Big Way*. DeCapo, 2005.

Levinson, Peter J. *Trumpet Blues: The Life of Harry James*. Oxford University Press, 1999.

Sinatra, Nancy. *Frank Sinatra: My Father*. Doubleday, 1985.

Sinatra, Tina. *My Father's Daughter: A Memoir*. Simon & Schuster revised edition, 2015.

Index

About the Authors

Photo credit: John Loreaux

Bruce Klauber grew up in Philadelphia in a musical home. His mother was a dancer and singer who performed in local vaudeville houses. He was eight years old when he saw Gene Krupa on television and was so mesmerized by what he saw that he decided he wanted to be a drummer. At the age of eight, after a few months of lessons, he was deemed good enough by an area bandleader to play his first professional job. Through the years, he's played with any number of jazz icons, including Charlie Ventura, Milt Buckner, Buster Cooper, Anita O'Day, Al Grey, Marty Napoleon, Joanie Sommers, Bernard Peiffer, and Peggy King. He was the cofounder of Philadelphia's popular All-Star Jazz Trio, and he still plays—and sometimes sings—today. He has recorded for several notable jazz record labels, including DBK Jazz and Concord Jazz, and has produced historic reissues and discoveries for England's Jasmine Records, Barcelona's Fresh Sound Records, and the US Dot Time label.

Following his parents' advice to "learn something else in addition to drumming, just in case," he became involved in journalism while a student at Temple University. Combining his love for jazz and his talent for writing, Bruce wrote and edited books on Krupa and Buddy Rich and produced more than a dozen videos for Warner Bros. and Hudson Music, focusing on drummers such as Elvin Jones, Roy Haynes, Max Roach, Louie Bellson; vibraharpist Lionel Hampton; and various others. Narrators for those award-winning videos included Mel Tormé, Ed Bradley, and Steve Allen. His film and jazz background led to his stints as technical advisor on the Oscar-winning film *Whiplash* and the Mickey Rourke movie *Tiger.*

He graduated Temple University with a bachelor's degree in communication and theater, was awarded an honorary doctorate by Combs College of Music for his "contributions to music journalism and jazz performance," and was recently honored by Drexel University for his "lifelong contributions to music education."

As a journalist, his articles have appeared in dozens of local, regional, national, and international publications, including *Down Beat, Jazz Times, Jazziz, Atlantic City Magazine, The Trentonian, Naples Daily News, National News Bureau, The Drummer, Icon, The Broad Street Review, Inside Magazine, Video Insider, Film Bulletin*, and *The Counselor.* He currently writes a weekly column for the Atlantic City–based *Shore Local Newsmagazine.*

Photo credit: John Loreaux

Andrea Kauffman, now retired, was a powerful, respected, and influential entertainment-industry concert producer, personal manager, and agent, responsible for bringing dozens of jazz legends—including Mel Tormé, Bobby Scott, George Shearing, Mongo Santamaria, and Morgana King, just to name a few—to Atlantic City hotel/casinos as well as produce, along with her partner, the only show to play three casinos in the Atlantic City market, *Shaboom*. She brought Frank Sinatra, Jr., to the mainstream casino showrooms and concert stages that had eluded him prior to his involvement with her.

Born in Philadelphia and raised in the suburbs of Philadelphia, Kauffman aspired to be a singer. Her mother, Dorothy, was a dancer and had a successful dance school. Her father, Herman, who was in the plumbing and heating wholesale supply business, played thirty-two instruments. It was her father's love for music that inspired Kauffman to stay in the business and eventually open her own agency.

Her first client, Dane Anthony, a singer, was a diamond in the rough. She polished, promoted, and finessed him into one of the most successful singers/lounge acts in Atlantic City, and he remains so today. Her agency flourished. She became partners with Dan Mulhern, and together they produced innovative and exciting lounge acts, special events, and production shows. But jazz and music were her true love. She became involved with the management of Frank Sinatra,

Jr., in 1985. Several years later, she became his personal manager and remained in that position until Frank's death in 2016.

Kauffman has a daughter, Monica, and a stepson, Alphonse, from a previous marriage. She married Dane Anthony, and the family grew with the addition of Dane's daughter, Tara. Dane and Andrea have a son, Isaac. Andrea found herself with the best job ever, mother of four and grandmother to six. Dane and Andrea have been together for forty years.

From the time she was able to walk, Andrea was an avid saltwater fisherman. When she moved to the Jersey shore in 1986, she resumed her old passion for fishing and became an accomplished surf fisherman as well.

The entertainment business was second nature to the Kauffman family. This has been a successful, enjoyable, and rewarding career for Andrea Kauffman.